#MIXERMAN

AND THE

BILLIONHEIR APPARENT

#MIXERMAN

AND THE

BILLIONHEIR APPARENT

MIXERMAN
PUBLISHES

Published in 2016 by Mixerman Publishes
Distributed by Backbeat Books
An Imprint of Hal Leonard Corporation
7777 West Bluemound Road
Milwaukee, WI 53213

Trade Book Division Editorial Offices
33 Plymouth St., Montclair, NJ 07042

Printed in the United States of America

Book design by Lynn Bergesen, UB Communications

Library of Congress Control Number: 2016904966

ISBN 978-1-4950-2670-6

www.mixerman.net
www.backbeatbooks.com

ACKNOWLEDGMENTS

My most sincere thanks to:

Tanya Rodriguez
John J Dooher
John Cerullo
Don Put
Slau Halatyn
Michael Selverne
Josh Blake
Marisa Blake
Tebbe Davis
Suzannah Tebbe Davis
Deanna Allen
Cliff Mott
Polly Watson
Aardvark
Mom and Dad
Swati Lele
Greg Sarafin
Maximilian Sarafin
All the fine people at Hal Leonard Inc.
Redondo Beach
California

and Paulie Buller, who is missed.

CHAPTER ONE

PANEER KANISH

There is a long-lost ancient Hindu proverb that states, "A great writer may seek a story, but a great story shall find its writer." Or maybe it's a Buddhist saying. It doesn't really matter. It's ancient and it's a proverb, and that would certainly be the case here—a great story found me. I'm just here to tell you about it.

While it's true that I'm a writer—what with this being my fifth published book thus far—I'm first and foremost a record Producer, and that means a lot of things to a lot of people, most of them wrong. Admittedly, the definition of Producer has expanded somewhat over the course of my two and a half decades making music, and much of that has to do with the plethora of neophyte wannabes distorting the term. I don't denounce this phenomenon. I accept it. Rank amateurs are exactly what the Music Business was built upon—now more than ever.

Much like my first story—*The Daily Adventures of Mixerman*—this one contains a serialized documentation of, and commentary on, what I can only classify as extraordinary events. I can assure you, were this the kind of story that required a live daily entry like my first, I'd have run for the hills. I decided long ago that I would never again put myself under that kind of pressure—the kind that comes from too many viewers crashing the servers in wait. This was back when bandwidth could be an issue, mind you. I mean, there were mornings that I couldn't even get on the site to post my own entry. Hey, the reaction I'm good with. The stress that comes with it? No fucking way.

Setting overall truthiness aside, this story in many ways is at least as stunning as my first, and I'm hoping you find it even half as riveting as I did going through it. And while this is not a diary per se, it was written like one, such that these entries were hatched at a time when events were freshest in my mind. Unlike a purely fictional work in which a good story is tightly and cleverly weaved into a yarn, this one is a bit more like life. Think of it like a reality show that you read.

Our story begins upon my receipt of a rather strange and somewhat forward email.

To: @mixerman
From: @paneerkanish

Dear Sirs,

I would very much like to speak to you about available internships with Mixerman.

Thank you,

Paneer Kanish

That note made me hungry. What with Paneer being an Indian cheese, and a Knish a tasty potato delicacy found in New Jersey sporting arenas, how could it not? And while I found that particular combination of food somewhat intriguing, this was surely a prank. So, I did what anyone would. I went to breakfast without giving it another thought.

The overt act of ignoring written Internship requests is standard procedure around here. I don't dare answer these sorts of inquiries, for I know that the moment I turn down the request, I'll be inundated with a whole slew of follow-up questions in regards to how one gets into this fucked-up business. The answer is, don't.

Really, I'm just not into the whole slave labor concept. In my experience you tend to get what you pay for, and as a wise friend once told me, when you pay peanuts you get Elephants. Or maybe that's monkeys. Whatever. The fact of the matter is that Interns tend to be a great big time sap, and there's really no guarantee that I'll get any return on my investment.

For starters, I don't own a multi-room commercial studio complex. I have a private mix room, and I'm the only one that uses it, hence the term *private*. Then, of course, sometimes I do other things—like write books, or record them as audiobooks, or make supplemental film clips. I've got quite a bit going on! Which is slightly problematic, because I could spend months training some kid to do things exactly the way I like, only to lose my perfect Super-Assistant to someone else the moment I find myself between records.

I can tell you exactly how it'll all go down, too. Somehow, I'll muster up the Herculean patience necessary to spend months teaching someone the art of assisting me as I endure countless fuck-ups on our journey to Assisting-Me Nirvana. And once we reach the promised land together? My slave will leave me and use all the knowledge I've bestowed upon him for someone else's benefit. Of course, I suppose that's the whole point of taking an Internship. To get ahead. But what of me? How does training someone expressly for the purpose of leaving help *me* to get ahead?

You have to understand, things aren't what they were in the Music Business, and were it not for my ability to hustle—a trait that was handed down by my father—and to do so with a calm demeanor, a trait passed on to me by my mother, I'd probably be working at a TV station right now. Kill me. Seriously. The energy sap of performing a mindless audio job would be a fate worse than death for someone like me. I need to create, and that's all there is to it.

Surely there's nothing wrong with taking a job running sound for a TV station. It's good work if you can get it. You're paid well because TV makes money. You can even have a life. So who am I to criticize? It's totally reasonable, particularly when you get into your mid- to late forties, only to realize you're competing *not* against other talented individuals with a track record of making great music, but rather against any kid with a computer and a pair of headphones. Oh, and the best part? The kid probably dispenses recording advice on the Internet. Because it's not bad enough that music is one of the top ten most competitive fields there is; writing also makes the list. I suppose that makes me a verifiable glutton for self-loathing.

It's kind of funny in a disturbing sort of way, because sometimes I'm asked to produce an album that someone else has already agreed to produce for free. Can you imagine that? A band accepts an offer from a Producer to work on their tracks for free and then they attempt to use that bid to leverage a deal with me. For the same price! Because somehow my free is better than that of my competitor. And guess what? My competitor isn't necessarily some schmo working out of his mother's basement. Sometimes the other Producer (this has happened more than once, can you tell?) is a professional with a bona fide track record of multiple Gold and Platinum albums who now finds himself working out of his garage.

Admittedly, this would also describe me, except I can't and won't compete with free. I really don't understand how others do.

As fucked up as the Music Business currently is, this is not the time for me to go into a sickeningly detailed rant about it. So, let me just put this in simple, concise terms for you. These days I'm paid about half as much for twice the work as I was before the crash of 2008. And as if that's not enough, for whatever reason, everything seems to take twice as long as before. You do the math.

Given this, I could use the help! And so I *do* occasionally consider accepting an Intern. In fact, I get requests for the position on a weekly basis. I even keep a spare bedroom available for that day that some obnoxious kid does come into my life and then refuses to leave. And while I'd prefer to use the room as a place for clients to crash after a late-night mix session, the reality is, I meet only a small percentage of the Artists and Producers who hire me to mix their records these days.

I certainly think I could justify accepting an Intern. Room and board have value as does the School of Mixerman. But anytime I consider teaching someone what it is that I actually need from them—frankly, I shudder. I find the thought somewhat overwhelming. What I really need is some kid so fucking aggressive that he or she somehow manages to teach *me* what it is I need. That's fucked up, I realize. It's also true.

Breakfast at the Cozy Cafe was delicious as always. There was the usual spirited debate between the patrons seated around the U-shaped counter. I typically stay out of the kibitz-fest, beyond the occasional fake smile, but I was feeling a bit feisty. I suppose the banter had distracted me, because as I paid my check, I noticed that I'd somehow missed four calls, all of them from the same international number. The country code was 91.

India.

The first three messages were identical in nature, delivered by an Indian woman whose exotic accent had a slight British lilt to it.

"Please hold for Mr. Kanish."

Of course, the voicemail ended abruptly because cellphones don't continue recording silence. You'd think they'd know that in India, since that's where all my tech support calls seem to go.

The fourth voicemail started the same way, "Please hold . . ." but this time around the woman was interrupted by an agitated man with an impossibly thick Indian accent. "Give me the motherfucker phone!" he said, followed by the usual static that comes from such a violent physical transfer.

Were it not for the many holidays I've spent talking to my nearly indecipherable Indian father-in-law—one sibling removed—I probably would have had no idea what the agitated man was saying. It seemed as though his tongue couldn't catch up with his brain, and as much as I'd like to relay it to you phonetically, we'd all be working far too hard for that. And so I've limited myself to altering just the "verys," if for no other reason than because he seemed quite fond of the word.

"Mixerman, my name is Paneer Kanish. I am leaving this message because I sent you an email the other day, and am vehdy, vehdy, disappointed to not have heard from you. In fact, I find it rude. It is urgent that I speak to you about an opportunity to mentor my son to become the world-famous Producer of Bollywood music."

Bollywood music? What the fuck do I know about Bollywood music? Other than the goal. Which as far as I can tell is to cram as many musical parts into the upper midrange as humanly possible so as to exert great auditory pain upon anyone within earshot. This was not a concept that interested me. And what the hell was he playing at calling it *my* opportunity? How was mentoring his son *my* opportunity?

"I shall pay you handsomely," he concluded.

As much as I find the concept of slave labor repulsive, indentured servitude was something I most certainly could get behind.

I'd barely gotten the name Paneer Kanish typed into my search engine when my phone began to squawk in an unfamiliar fashion. It was a Facebook call. Who knew someone could call me from Facebook? Oddly, it was Paneer Kanish. I didn't even know I'd accepted his "friendship," although admittedly, that's really not all that surprising. I'm pretty liberal with my friendships. Come to think of it, how the hell did he get my phone number?

Who was this Paneer fellow?

I decided to click "Feeling Lucky" on Google, which I haven't done for, I don't know, fifteen years? As it turns out, I *was* lucky! A slick webzine splashed my screen. Headline: "The Top Twenty Wealthiest Men in India."

Wouldn't you know it? One of them was Paneer Kanish!

My Facebook app, which was still buzzing the phone, was now also ringing my computer's Skype, which is somehow and most annoyingly linked to Facebook. Because I would want for total strangers from the other side of the world to reach me so easily. And while I'm clearly being sarcastic with that remark, in this particular case it's true. Billionaires can call me any time they like.

"Please hold for Mr. Kanish."

A scowling, perhaps even snarling Mr. Kanish appeared on my screen. It was the same man pictured in the article. Paneer was indeed a Billionaire. Happy days!

"Mixerman. I assume this is what you prefer to be called. I am Paneer Kanish. You are a difficult man to reach."

I'm not sure he was going to be denied reaching me, but okay. After a quick toss of my hair, I engaged my own camera.

For the most part, Paneer was intense, serious, and presented himself as devoid of joy. His confidence was supreme, as one would expect from a Billionaire, and while he wasn't by any stretch of the imagination beautiful, he had a certain charisma that popped so ferociously from the screen, I swear it was like he was in the room with me. He also wasn't one to chit-chat. He had a twenty-one-year-old son who—as he described it—was lost. Apparently, his poor child wanted to become a Music Producer.

"Thus far, my son has done what is expected of him, although just barely. He has somehow managed to graduate from Eton and then Oxford, but now he defies my wishes for him to go to Wharton. He insists to me that he is Producer material, whatever the motherfuck that means."

"It sounds familiar," I replied.

"What am I to do?" Paneer lamented. "I could cut him off from his Trust, but if music is in his heart, who am I to cremate his dreams before I give him the opportunity to fail of his own volition? Let me tell you, I have been against this from the moment Kanish came to me."

"You call your son by his last name?"

"I do not! My son's name is Kanish Kanish. His last name is also his first. Why is it you interrupt me with this stupidity?"

Although I did find it truly fascinating that the boy had the same first and last name, my true aim was to shake Paneer off his most awkward confession. This wasn't a therapy session, and I'm not his shrink. All I really wanted to determine was the level of pain I would have to endure were I to agree to mentor his son.

"Look, Paneer. Does Kanish Kanish have musical talent?" I asked.

"According to his uncle and his mother yes—both carry Bleating hearts, I might tell you—but they insist he has the gift. I am at my wits' end!"

Paneer paused the already dramatic moment to pull a red silk handkerchief with lace fringe from what, I swear to you, looked to be a solid-gold tissue box. He unabashedly discharged his nose one nostril at a time into the silk hanky and then immediately tossed it behind his shoulder before returning to his confessional.

"Kanish is the Heir to my fortune. But do not think for a moment that this is a given. I expect my son to be successful, and I will accept no less."

"And what does success look like?" I inquired.

"What do you mean by this? What does success look like? Success does not have a look."

"I mean, describe success. Does that mean riches? Fame? Power?"

"Yes. Of course!" Paneer replied.

I was hoping he'd pick one. I should have known he'd take them all. I suppose you don't get to be a Billionaire by leaving anything on the table.

Really, I'm not sure why the fuck I cared how he defined success. By the time anyone could make that kind of determination, I'd be long out of the picture and fully paid. It's not like Paneer could get a refund should his child prove talentless. All I could do was introduce the kid to the thinking behind good recording techniques. I can't turn someone who is ostensibly tone-deaf and with no musical talent whatsoever into a world-class record-maker. There are limits.

"Let me put it this way," I started. "How do you wish to describe your son a few years from now?"

Paneer rubbed his chin in thought, and then he began to wag his finger at the camera.

"That is a vehdy interesting question that you ask of me. It shows remarkable insight into your personhood. Quite simply, in three years from now, I would vehdy much like to say . . . that my son is the greatest Bollywood Producer the world has ever known!"

"You could say that right now," I retorted.

"What do you say? How could I make such a claim?"

"You're a Billionaire. Don't you just say it and it happens?"

"Yes, yes, vehdy good, you have done your research, just as I have researched you. Frankly, I find you a bit shady."

"Shady! What the fuck are you talking about?"

"Things happen on the Internet when you're around."

I laughed aloud, it was such a preposterously ambiguous claim. What the fuck does that mean, anyway? *Things* happen on the Internet when I'm around?

"So, if you believe that I'm shady, why do you want me to teach your son?"

"You are not without your redeeming qualities. Besides, Kanish reads your books and watches your videos, and he is big fandom. It vehdy much seems to me that you are in the ideal position to offer him success. And despite your flaws, I find you to be a safe bet."

There's no such thing as a safe bet in the Music Business. There never has been. But I certainly wasn't going to tell *him* that. He's a Billionaire. As far as he's concerned, money fixes everything. And in general, he's probably right.

"It vehdy much seems to me that you are in the ideal position to offer him success," Paneer repeated.

"And how much time do you think that's going to take?"

"How could I possibly answer that question? You are the expert in this matter! I would suggest that you take a year!"

Paneer went from "I can't answer that question," to answering it definitively without missing a beat. It was impressive. No wonder the guy was a Billionaire.

"A year!" I scoffed.

"I will pay you handsomely for your time, of course."

"And what does handsomely look like?" I inquired.

Paneer was once again unable to navigate his way through the idiomatic term of "look like," and so I asked him if he might just make me a fucking offer already. As it turns out, it was handsome indeed! In fact, the offer was so attractive that I admit, I probably should have accepted it outright. But I didn't. He was far too desperate for that.

Let's just evaluate this for a moment. Based on his proposal, not only do I get an Intern, but I also get paid what essentially amounts to half my yearly nut, and that's before I've even earned a dime producing projects. I admit, had I not been staring at Paneer's net worth in the multi-multi billions of dollars, I might have accepted the job without counter. But to do so would have been to ignore the cardinal rule of a negotiation: Understand your opponent's ratio of desperation to cash. In the case of Paneer, both seemed to be in endless supply. Sadly, my own desperation was also high and my cash almost depleted, but then, he didn't know that, and I certainly wasn't going to tip him off.

If there's anything I've learned about negotiating over the years, it's that you tend to have the upper hand so long as you're willing to walk away. Really, you need only give that impression, but this usually means you're *actually* willing to do it. Of course, overtly threatening to end the negotiation before determining all the terms of a potential deal is nothing short of foolish. The trick is to portray strength without using threats to do it. This is achieved through vocal tone and body language until such time as you fully nail down all expectations.

It was clear to me in under two minutes time that Paneer was determined to save family face—a concept that I find foreign. I mean, all I can do as a middle-class American parent is expose my child to as much opportunity as possible so that he may find his strengths and passions. This hopefully manifests as success, not as I define it, but as my son might. It's his life, not mine, and I won't try to dictate what he chooses to do with it.

It seems to me that Paneer viewed this somewhat differently than I do, and I'm not sure it's as much an Indian thing as it is an über-rich thing. You see, Paneer was clearly unwilling to leave his child's success to chance. Destiny is far too risky for the likes of Paneer to depend upon.

As for my situation, if I were to be brutally honest with you, and I suppose I should be, my coffers were low and my need for cash relatively high. The business has been tough in the last eight years, and the toll of operating in the red since the crash of 2008 has left me somewhat behind. The pathetic part is, I'm doing better than most. Still, with no immediate job prospects on the horizon, I had to take Paneer's offer seriously. At the moment, it was money I could ill afford to turn down.

Since Paneer was under the impression that I was the perfect person to act as a surrogate father to his son, and since he carried immense wealth in combination with a deep-seated need to purchase a father's pride, I felt as though I was in an exceptionally strong position to counter. Given this, I was willing to draw a line in the sand and accept the results.

You see, setting a price for a deal that you could take or you could leave is as simple as predicting the potential pain and then placing a value upon it. How much money makes the misery worthwhile? So long as you can answer that question accurately, you can make an offer without fear of negative consequence. Regardless of the decision—you're happy!

"Double it," I blurted.

"You should want that I double my vehdy generous offer? You greedy American pig! I should have it!"

"What the fuck do you mean you should have it?"

"What the fuck do you mean, what do I mean? I mean I should fucking have it. No wonder we are creaming on you Americans. You don't understand the basic operation of dividing by two."

"Dividing by two? What the fuck?" I puzzled. "Oh! You want to cut your offer in half!"

"That is what I have said! I'm about to halve it!"

"I'm about to quadruple it!" I countered.

Obnoxiously forthright people can handle it when you get right back in their grill, and I even find that they positively prefer it. Of course, in this case, we were both calling each other's bluff; it's just that I had him so convinced that I knew he was bluffing, he couldn't possibly call mine. And if he did, I would have no choice but to walk away from the deal. That's crazy fucked up, I know. Essentially what I'm saying is that I was both bluffing and not bluffing at the very same time. It's a good trick if you can pull it off.

"Fine. I will pay you what you ask under one condition."

"This oughta be good," I chuckled.

"Ah hahah. You are a vehdy cynical person. I embrace this about you."

It was the first bit of warmth Paneer had displayed, and his accent was inexplicably more singsongy when he smiled. It was a side of Paneer I'd like to know better. As it turns out, his newfound affability was short-lived.

"You have a knack for upsetting people and having them take notice. I want you to use this skill to make my son famous. You will write about your experience and publish it online."

Motherfucker.

This was a classic bait and switch. Paneer had it all planned out, and I fell for it. Even with doubling his initial offer, I wasn't wild about the concept of writing a book too. Paneer had managed to change the terms on me mid-negotiation, and while I could have surely countered, I decided not to push my luck. I'd already gotten him to double his initial bid, and that was going to put me in a somewhat decent financial position again—one I've not seen for quite some time. Besides, he didn't define "writing about it." It wasn't like I'd have to draft a full-length novel or anything.

"And just in case you are feeling you can slough it off, your book must be a minimum of a hundred thousand vehdy, vehdy entertaining words."

A wry smile came over the Billionaire's face. He'd schooled me, and the motherfucker knew it too. Worse yet, he knew that I knew that he knew it. Which pisses me off to no end, even now.

"I can see by the look on your face that you are not happy with this. Let me tell you not to be a fool. There is a saying in my country, and that is 'Knowledge can only be got in one way, the way of experience; there is no other way to know.' My son can learn everything he must by being at your service for one year as you are paid for the pleasure of his company. And you get a story too. This is a gift that I give to you."

Paneer's little rhyme at the end of his pitch made me chuckle, which may have been my second tactical error given how quickly he closed after that.

"You will get twenty-five percent up front, another twenty-five percent at the end of the second quarter. The remaining fifty percent shall be delivered upon completion of your tenure. Kanish will be there promptly. Thank you vehdy much for your time."

Before I could protest, Paneer hung up the Skype.

I wasn't wild about the payment terms. I was even less enthused with my Intern's estimated time of arrival. What the fuck does "promptly" mean? I was half expecting a knock on the door at that very moment. My phone rang instead. It was India calling.

"Good day, I am seeking Mick Zerman to arrange for the arrival of Kanish Kanish."

It was Paneer's Handler. Kanish was to arrive in a week.

All that I required now was a record to produce—a far easier task than when I began the day. What, with me being fully and properly subsidized? I could now compete with free.

So, *that's* how they do it.

Mixerman

AND THE INDIAN GIRLS SING RAJADUT, DUT, DA-DUT, DA-DUT, DUT DA-DUT, DUT

In the seven days since my initial Skype meeting with Paneer, I've had countless conversations with a veritable parade of Indians, most of them lovely, none of them Kanish. I was beginning to get a little annoyed about that. It's bad enough Kanish allowed his father to initiate contact on his behalf. He should have at least reached out to me within twenty-four hours of the deal being struck.

Most of my many conversations with the Handler were purely a matter of coordination and of no real consequence to our story. I did, however, manage to gather some information. According to the Handler, young Kanish is a legit bedroom recordist—whatever the hell that means. He even used the term *legit*.

Well! My imagination ran absolutely wild as I considered the potential size and shape of a Billionaire's bedroom. At times I found myself day-dreaming about stacks of expensive recording gear, and massive drawers upon humongous drawers of valuable German microphones. I can assure you, should my fantasy prove true, then I will most certainly suggest that Kanish immediately ship all of his high-value recording gear to Los Angeles. This way we could include it in his education!

Then I began to wonder. Is it customary for an Indian guest to bring a gift? And if so, shouldn't that gift be fully commensurate with his wealth? Perhaps young Kanish would bring me a Telefunken ELA M 251, a $24,000 microphone, which I would sell the moment I could, and immediately replace with a $2,000 microphone of nearly equal quality. For those of you who know nothing about microphones, I should probably explain.

There are a short supply of, and a great demand for the Telefunken ELA M 251. As you might expect, this appreciably distorts the value of these rather amazing fifty-year old microphones. And while I will concede that the ELA M 251 is the greatest large-diaphragm condenser microphone ever made, that doesn't make it worth twenty-four fucking thousand dollars. Frankly, I'd be just as happy to pick up a Lewitt LCT 940 and a brand-new car to drive it home in. I'm sorry, but I've been making records for quite some time, and I can tell you that the microphone isn't nearly as critical to a great recording as the Source. Don't believe me? Let me put it this way. The best microphone in the world, whatever that is, will pick up the most torturously atrocious singer with absolute clarity. Once you accept that, then you understand. It's all about the Source.

Of course, if your budget were nearly limitless—if you had say, a billion dollars in your bank account—that would be a different matter entirely. In that case, it might well be worthwhile to have twenty ELA M 251s. At which point, are you really going to miss one? Would this not make a fantastic gift for your new mentor?

Where Kanish's mentorship is concerned, it's his recording experience that bodes well for our journey together. This indicates to me that he has both the interest and the motivation needed for the grueling job at hand. Given this, it seems almost silly for him to work as my Intern, when what I really need is an Assistant. Besides, an Assistant appears far more prestigious to your clients than an Intern. Shit, any schmo can pick up an Intern. You've got to be bringing in the loot to justify an Assistant.

And so, before young Kanish has even arrived, I've made the executive decision to promote him, sight unseen, from Intern to Assistant. I mean, why not? The only difference between the two jobs is the title and the pay. I get paid the same either way!

I'm sure it's no accident that the initial 25 percent installment from Paneer was in my account (and this is no exaggeration), twenty minutes after I'd given the Handler my banking details. The reason I know it only took twenty minutes? Because my banker called me.

I don't have a banker. Or at least, I didn't before today.

An international bank transfer often takes days to clear, sometimes weeks, and I was certainly happy that it could be so easily expedited. I would imagine that someone like Paneer has money all over the world. Which got me to thinking. What do Billionaires do with all their money? I realize much of it will be tied up in various assets, businesses, and markets. But what of the cash?

Just to put this into some perspective, if you have a billion dollars in cash, you could put a million dollars into an account in a thousand different banks. There are fewer than two hundred countries in the entire world. So, if you have a fully liquid billion, then it seems reasonable that you could have a rather large cache of cash accessible anywhere and everywhere, other than perhaps the most remote areas of the planet.

Were I a Billionaire, I'd have all sorts of strategically placed safety-deposit boxes filled with cash, precious metals, foreign currency, bonds, certificates, etc. I'd invest in any financial instrument that could be used to hedge against just about any disaster I could come up with, perhaps even some I couldn't. Currency collapse? No problem, I got lots of gold. Run on the banks? Whatev. I got scads of cash and hectares of land. I'd even fill an entire safety deposit box with vegetable seeds just in case there's an agricultural collapse. And why not? It's not like I'd ever be in danger of running out of money. Hell, it'd be challenging just to spend the interest.

It's quite staggering when you think about it. If you're generating a modest 3 percent interest on a billion dollars, you're accumulating $30 million a year on that money. That means you're hauling in more than $80,000 every day, $3,500 per hour, or $57 each minute. So basically, if you have a billion in cash in a bank account, your net worth is increasing by nearly $1 every second of the day. By the time you finish eating a $10 sandwich, you made $590 in profit after expenses. You could take a day to find a brand-new Range Rover of your liking, and pay for it with the interest you made while shopping. You could fly from LA to Seattle, take an Uber to a studio, purchase their ELA M 251, Uber back to the airport, and by the time you got back home, the mic and your travel expenses would be fully paid for with the interest you'd earned.

And that's just on your spare billion. That doesn't count the other many billions that are surely returning at a far higher rate than 3 percent.

With the initial 25 percent payment from Paneer safely tucked into my account, I was feeling quite liberated. I honestly can't remember when my checking account was this swollen. As a result, there was a spring in my step. A skip in my stride. I was whistling while I worked. Taking it all in. Smelling the roses. Predictably, I started spending like a drunken sailor.

Between paying all my past-due bills, the long overdue repair of some recording equipment, the purchase of a new mattress and linens for my pending houseguest, far too many groceries from Costco for the size of my household, a 70-inch HDTV for my room, a new Mac, a used VW for my son (which freed up my car again), oh, and seven sushi dinners in six days,

I'd already managed to make quite the dent in the initial deposit. And while a little retail therapy is nothing short of invigorating after months of frugality, it's also rather depressing.

At this stage of my life, I should be in my most robust earning years. The problem is that for most of the projects in my career, I wasn't in a position to profit-share. And while I do get some royalties, that particular income stream has shrunk significantly over the years, and not just for me. For everyone.

You see, Producers' royalties have traditionally been based on sales, which are now in a death spiral due to the popularity of Streaming. Why would anyone buy music when they can just Stream it for free? And for a nominal $10 per month you get to avoid annoying commercials too. So, one would buy music and store it locally why?

The problem is that only the Artist and the Songwriter get paid Streaming royalties. And while the rate that Streaming sites pay out to Independent Creators is criticized for being dismally and unsustainably low—which it is—it's really the only area of growth in this business. Which is great. Wonderful, even. Except, as a Producer I don't get paid a dime on royalties from Streams, or radio play, or television licensing.

Sales used to be a lucrative way to profit-share when selling a million albums was a reasonably frequent occurrence. Unfortunately, in all of 2014, there were only two albums that sold over a million copies. Two! That's right. Out of tens of thousands of albums recorded, two sold over a million copies. And one of them was a soundtrack!

Back in the early aughts there were scores of albums certified multi-Platinum on the sales charts. And it wasn't all that uncommon for the most popular albums of that time to sell over ten million copies. But two? Two albums that sold *just over a million copies*? That's a massive contraction, my friends.

I think we can safely declare the CD dead.

This isn't meant as some sort of bitch-fest or "woe is me" story. I'm doing better than most, and my "broke" isn't quite the same as for someone who has limited options and no skill set. I've spent an entire career adapting to changes in technology, so that's certainly nothing new. But how does one adapt to a change in technology that completely wipes away the one revenue stream your entire premise of retirement was based upon? Remember, if current sales dry up, then catalog sales dry up too. Poof. No more royalties.

All that said, at the present moment, my income isn't the big problem. It's my outcome, as Los Angeles is an exceptionally expensive city to live in, more so now than ever. And with record budgets plummeting alongside sales, it has become difficult to survive from the up-front fees alone. To make matters worse, as the economy has slowly recovered, the real estate market has once again exploded. Which would be beneficial if my divorce hadn't forced the sale of my house at the bottom of the market.

Google's relatively new facility in Venice Beach hasn't helped matters, as an influx of even more multimillionaires to the region has resulted in a 300 percent increase in home values there. This has bled down the coast to my neck of the woods in Redondo Beach. Rents throughout Los Angeles are currently at an all-time high, to the point that we are now experiencing an affordable-housing crisis. Frankly, now that my son is a young adult, it doesn't make a whole lot of sense for me to stay in Los Angeles. At this point, I can work from anywhere. Yet here I am. Admittedly, it's difficult to leave moderate weather.

The Sit 'n Sleep mattress delivery truck pulled away, and I was just about to close up the front doors when a black Mercedes-Benz sporting a white Consul license plate pulled up to the curb. An Indian man in his sixties, sporting a white beard and a black suit, exited the car with a clipboard. He was a petite man, but then, most people seem small to me.

"Mr. Mixerman, I presume? I am Rajadut and I work for the Indian Consulate in San Francisco. It is my understanding that you will be sponsoring Kanish Kanish, son of Paneer Kanish, and I would like to go over a few things with you."

"I believe I'm the one being sponsored here, but whatever you need," I replied.

"Yes. I'm sure that you are correct about that. May I come in?"

Unprompted, Rajadut entered the house and proceeded to look around. He wandered from room to room through the first floor of the house as he deliberately marked upon his clipboard. It was almost as if he were planning some sort of event.

"How can I help you, Rajadut?"

"Yes, thank you. As I'm sure you are aware, Paneer Kanish of the New Delhi Kanishes is the patriarch of a vehdy important Indian family. We must be sure that the dots are eyed, and the crosses crossed."

Clearly, he meant "the i's are dotted," which is kind of funny when you think about it.

"I am here to take care of security."

"Security?"

"Indeed."

"What are we protecting?"

"The entitled child of a Billionaire. What do you think we are protecting?"

It was a rather bold statement with undertones of bitterness. Apparently, he was also quite serious. I, on the other hand, was slightly confused.

"Are hoodlums after him?"

Rajadut, who was now tossing my kitchen drawers, stopped momentarily to address me.

"Are there guns in the house?"

"Guns? No."

"What about bullets?"

"Why would I have bullets if I don't have a gun?"

"Are you not American?"

This was getting a bit insulting.

"There are no weapons of any kind here!" I snapped in irritation.

"And what of this?" Rajadut asked suspiciously as he held up one of my kitchen knives. "This is not a weapon?"

"If you think I'm going to kiddie-proof my house for a fucking adult, you're sadly mistaken."

I was growing impatient with the obtrusive nature of his visit. Perhaps sensing this, Rajadut put my large butcher knife back into its protective block, then made his way toward the guest bedroom located immediately off the front foyer.

"You purchased a new bed, I see. This will be perfect."

"You think Kanish will like the room?" I inquired. "I was thinking about decorating the room with Indian tapestries and pillows, you know? There's a store in Little India—that's just down the road in Artesia—and they'll have everything I need to make the room nice and homey for Kanish."

"I wouldn't waste your money. Kanish Kanish will not be staying here. This will be for security."

"Security! Where will Kanish be staying?"

"The Crown Royale Hotel."

Rajadut surely meant the Crowne Plaza in Redondo Beach. *Casino Royale* was the name of a rather bad James Bond film (aren't they all bad?), and Crown Royal is a Canadian whiskey. Still, I didn't bother to correct him.

Putting Kanish up at the Crowne Plaza didn't make much sense for a number of reasons. For starters, it's not all that posh. Not Billionaire posh, anyway. And I really didn't dig the idea of my Assistant commuting from the Crowne Plaza, even if it is just five minutes away.

Frankly, I'd grown excited at the prospect of having a bona fide full-time Assistant, and I'd concocted all sorts of schemes to accelerate his learning curve. I'd even gone out of my way to find a young Indian singer in need of a production so as to be sure our first recording would be of something familiar to him. I was taking this all quite seriously, and I wanted my Assistant living with me—not his bodyguard. I took a moment to register my complaint.

"I don't think you understand. I want Kanish here. Living, eating, and breathing recording," I implored. "It's critical to his education."

"This is not of my concern. I am here to collect information, and I believe I have all that I need for the now. I would vehdy much like to thank you for your time."

The front doors were still wide open, and Rajadut easily slid past me as he made his way to his car.

"Hey, Rajadut," I called out. "Have you ever met Kanish Kanish?"

"I will be meeting him for the first time at the immigration office tomorrow. I will bring him to you personally. You can expect a text from me then. Thank you for your time, Mr. Mixerman."

And with that Rajadut was out.

I closed up the house. The spare bedroom was still in full disarray—not that it mattered: I had no intention of preparing it for security. This would be dealt with upon Kanish's arrival tomorrow. Actually, much would be discussed directly with Kanish Kanish tomorrow, including his complete and total lack of communication.

After all, my pending Assistant will represent me. This is my business, fucked as it may be, and I will run it the way I see fit without an entitled Billionaire or his Handlers dictating the terms.

I'm quite certain I'm entitled to that!

Mixerman

CHAPTER THREE

THE KANISH CONTINGENT

It was a hot Spring day in Redondo Beach today. A rarity. And it meant that the San Fernando Valley had to be baking like a Tandoori clay pot. Which is precisely why I live by the beach and not in the Valley.

I took a moment to watch the termites vacate a hole in my once-solid-wood garage door. One termite after another appeared at the mouth of the small opening and then took flight to nowhere in particular. Admittedly, I couldn't track the little fuckers very far. For whatever reason, the termites absolutely freak whenever the hot inland Santa Ana winds blow into Redondo Beach—an unusual event for the time of year, but certainly not unprecedented. Perhaps the heat would help to make Kanish Kanish feel right at home.

Oh, don't be surprised by that sentiment. I realize I was quite annoyed with Kanish for his inability to pick up the Skype and introduce himself, but you must remember, regardless of his über-upper-class upbringing, he's only twenty-one years old. I really can't expect him to know everything, can I? Why would he need me? And seeing as Producing is largely an exercise in communication skills, it makes sense that this would be Lesson One in our journey together. Always Skype ahead.

Kanish was scheduled to land at LAX at 1:30 p.m., which is precisely the time I received a text from Rajadut updating me on his status.

Rajadut: *Kanish landed. Security to arrive imminently.*

I don't expect that I should have taken that text literally, but for whatever reason, I strolled out the front door as if a security officer was about to pull up—flashing yellow lights and all.

Normally, there would be a line of cars parked in front of the house, but today was street-sweeping day, which people take quite seriously around here. All sorts of crap accumulates along the curbs over the course of a week, and if the street sweeper doesn't suck it up, then it goes directly into the ocean. The Bay is polluted enough as it is.

People were out and about, and there was considerably more activity than I'd ever seen in my sleepy neighborhood. Dog walkers were walking dogs. Meter readers were reading meters. Mail ladies delivering mail. Neighbors cramming cars into driveways. None of which would be worth mentioning were it not for the pitch-black Hummer stretch limousine that pulled up just as I opened the door.

I realize in some neighborhoods, a Hummer limousine would stir up all sorts of excitement. And while I'm sure that some of my neighbors would have happily pelted the behemoth with rotten eggs, it wasn't the Hummer in and of itself that caused the ruckus. No, that would be the four badass Indian motherfuckers, clad in collarless, beaded Sherwani jackets and donning bright-orange turbans, who flew out of the Hummer and scurried to strategic positions all around the house. These were not glorified mall cops, or off-duty sheriffs, or oversized lunkheads. These were Sikhs—martial arts experts from India.

Now, if you're wondering how I might have known that, I happened to watch a BBC documentary the other week called *Who Are the Sikhs?* According to the BBC, Sikhs prefer to wear loose garb, as this provides them tremendous mobility for purposes of killing the enemy with their bare hands and feet. And while it would be unusual for a Sikh to don such restricting garb, it's the orange turbans that are the dead giveaway.

The Sikhs were fanned out around the house, which is perched on a hill on a corner lot, and I should probably take a moment to describe the property to you. The structure is split so that the garage is under one half of the house, and the second floor is above the other half, forming three levels in total. From the garage (sometimes referred to as my mix room), you can walk up a path, under an arboretum to the sidewalk in front of the house. Or you can walk the other direction up the stairs to a large wraparound deck on the backside of the house, where there is a sliding glass door into the dining room. Once you're inside, the living room is on the left above the garage, and the kitchen straight ahead. The hall just before the kitchen leads to the foyer, where you can exit out the front doors, enter the spare bedroom to the right, or catch the stairs to the second floor.

Clearly, Rajadut had come the day before in order to determine the points of entry. The Sikhs had stationed themselves strategically around the property such that there was really no way into the house without them killing you. One of the Sikhs stood sentry by the garage, and while I was thankful to have a permanent guard on my studio, the neighbors were beginning to take pictures with their phones. One rubbernecker even tried to get in a selfie.

Motherfucker!

The last thing I needed was the city up my ass about an illegal business out of my house. And despite the fact that these types of zoning laws are archaic given the Internet, that doesn't change the fact that the city could shut me down. I addressed my concerns to Sikh Number One, who was guarding the front door.

"You guys can't be out here," I whispered to the Sikh. "And that can't stay there," I said as I pointed toward the Hummer.

There was even more debris than usual in front of the house, and I most certainly wanted it cleaned. If the Hummer remained, the street sweeper would have to go around it, and that would leave all sorts of crap in front of the house for another week, and that wouldn't do at all.

Clearly the Sikh understood me, because he raised his hand and waved off the Hummer, which immediately pulled away. I guess there was still a driver in it.

"I was kind of hoping you guys would go with the Hummer."

The Sikh was unresponsive to my complaint, and the crowd of onlookers was growing at an alarming rate. Rather than get into it with a martial arts expert, I sent Rajadut a distress signal in the form of a text.

Mixerman: *911!*

The mail lady slammed down her truck's rear accordion gate, which startled Sikh Number One into a defensive pose, revealing a holstered weapon tucked under his jacket. A handgun, to be more precise. A Glock. Without thinking, I grabbed the Sikh by the shoulders and pushed him into the house as I violently kicked the front door shut. In retrospect, the maneuver was kinda dumbly brave. I mean, forget about the gun, this guy could kill me with his pinky finger.

"Listen. Unless you want an International incident, you all need to get in the house right fucking now. Kanish isn't even here yet, so you don't need to be outside. You understand?"

The Sikh opened the front door and yelled out a command in what I assume was Hindi. Within a moment, all of the Sikhs were in the house and accounted for. I took a moment to perform some damage control.

"Sorry everyone!" I announced. "We're just rehearsing for a film. Nothing to worry about," I said with a nervous laugh.

Being that we were in greater Los Angeles, this was credible enough to break up the impromptu block party. I returned to the kitchen, where the Sikhs were now rummaging through my cabinets and refrigerator, which frankly, I found somewhat rude.

"Rajadut already checked the house for weapons." I sighed.

One of the Sikhs was sorting through the cartons of expired takeout food, which he began to toss into the trash. As forward as that was, he was kind of doing me a favor. I eat takeout on a nearly daily basis, and I can't stand leftovers. To make matters worse, I have a difficult time throwing food away.

Frankly, I'm not so sure it's the leftovers that I can't stand as much as it is preparing them. I mean, the whole point of ordering food, is to eat something good without dirtying the dishes. And since I don't keep a microwave in my home, I require pots and pans in order to reheat food. I mean, I may as well have just cooked a meal for myself. Were I not so atrocious at it, perhaps I would have.

Another Sikh pulled out some instant ramen noodle snacks, which were likely well past their "best before" date, although I have a hard time believing they couldn't be eaten safely a hundred years from now. A third Sikh was heating up some water in my teapot. These guys sure did make themselves right at home.

The front door slammed shut, and the Sikhs snapped immediately into attack mode, as did I, until we all realized it was just Rajadut coming into the house as if he owned the fucking place. Frankly, they all acted like they owned the place. I addressed Rajadut without hesitation.

"Dude. We can't have the fucking Indian Secret Service surrounding my house—and packing, no less."

"I am not Dude, and these are not Secret Service, nor are they Pakis!"

"Not Pakis! Pack-*ing*. As in carrying guns," I explained. "We have to keep everything low-key here. We're in the middle of a residential neigh-borhood, and no offense, but guys with orange turbans surrounding the house are going to freak everybody the fuck out, which is going to cause me problems."

I'd barely finished my admonishment when problems began pounding on the door.

"Police!"

All four Sikhs immediately drew their weapons.

"Holy shit!" I hissed at Rajadut. "Tell them to put those fucking things away! And keep them back here while I take care of this shit show."

I opened the front door to find three Redondo Beach police officers on my stoop and two more on the sidewalk. To make matters worse, their hands were on their holsters. Rajadut's Mercedes was parked in front of the house, and there were three squad cars haphazardly surrounding it—blocking the road from traffic and street sweepers alike.

"We have a report of some unusual activity here, sir. Are you the owner of the house?" the ranking officer asked.

Before I could even reply, Rajadut was gently pushing me aside with the back of his hand.

"Good day, officers. My name is Rajadut Dadut," he said, sounding slightly more British than Indian at that moment. "I am here conducting some official business, and I'm afraid my security detail has, well, freaked some people out, as you might say. Here are my credentials."

Rajadut handed over a document with the words DIPLOMATIC PASSPORT emblazoned across the front of it. It actually said that, right on the passport. Diplomatic! He then handed the officer a blue identification card with the words DEPARTMENT OF STATE featured prominently upon it.

"As you can see, I am an Indian Diplomat, and I am here with the full approval of the US government. You can have your commander call the number on the back to verify, of course."

This motherfucker actually had diplomatic immunity! I thought that was just in the movies. The ranking officer stared at the document, flipping it several times. Clearly unsure of what to do, he excused himself to his squad car. The other two officers remained awkwardly on my porch. Rajadut returned to the kitchen, and the Sikhs were now freely wandering into the dining room, fully visible from the front door.

"Who are the towel-heads?" one cop inquired.

"Really?" I replied with marked disdain.

Redondo Beach has a generally well regarded police force. But anytime you have a unit of more than hundred cops, you can be sure to have the occasional bad apple. Apparently, one of those apples had managed to roll up onto my front stoop.

"Fucking Muslims," he sputtered.

"Excuse me. They're Sikhs from the Punjab region of India," I scolded. "And Sikhism is a religion. So they're not Muslim, not that it should really matter. It's also their ethnicity, and those are turbans, not towels. What the fuck is wrong with you?"

Rajadut was now standing beside me, glowing with pleasant surprise that I knew so much about Sikhs. The ranking officer returned with Rajadut's documents, which he handed back to him.

"Thank you, Mr. Dadut. Please enjoy your time in Redondo Beach."

The three officers jumped into their squad cars and peeled away. Rajadut and I returned to the dining room, where the Sikhs were now fully enjoying my stash of ramen noodles.

"There's no fucking way these guys can stay here," I insisted to Rajadut.

"As impressed as I am with your knowledge of Sikhs, until I get word from Paneer himself, they shall remain."

Rajadut had barely finished his rebuke when the Sikhs inexplicably leaped out of their chairs once again. Their jumpiness was really beginning to unnerve me. I too went into a defensive stance until I'd realized the Sikhs weren't in full battle array. Rather, they were standing at attention. What the fuck?

"Hey, hey, hey! It's a beautiful day in Los Angelay!"

A young Indian lad walked up to me with his arms spread wide. He immediately wrapped them around my body in a full bear hug, pinning my arms to my sides in the process. And although he was shorter than me (who isn't), the young stranger was by no means small, neither in stature nor in personality.

"Mixerman! My dreams have come true!" the strange lad announced as he released me from his embrace and turned his attention to Rajadut. "Raj, did you meet Mixerman? This is the greatest mixer and Producer in the world."

I was so taken aback—this was so not what I was expecting—I was so flummoxed by it all, that even having received pictures of him on the Internet, I still had to ask the question.

"Kanish?"

"Who else!" he shouted with confidence.

Kanish exuded charisma and was about a million times more charming than his father. Frankly, he looked like your typical Major Label executive, what with his perfectly pressed Levi's 550 jeans, leather Gucci slides, Armani button-down shirt, mirrored Porsche sunglasses, and diamond-encrusted Breitling watch, which popped brilliantly off his rich brown skin.

"You and I need to talk," I barked. "Come with me."

"Yeah!" Kanish said as he clapped his hands together in excitement. "We're going to get right into it. I love it! Work me, baby. Work me!" Kanish practically danced as he walked.

I made my way out the front door, and Kanish continued to perform his little dance step as he scatted. There was now a Bentley parked behind the Mercedes. Inside the Bentley was an older Indian couple waiting patiently in the front seats as they stared straight ahead.

"A Bentley?" I inquired dryly.

"You like that? Eat my dust, Rick Rubin!"

"Rick has a Rolls-Royce," I corrected.

"They both come with drivers, do they not?"

Despite the fact that Kanish got the car model wrong, this did make me chuckle. Rick Rubin has been the most successful record Producer in the business for my entire career. He is currently the president of Sony Records, and Rick has had a Rolls-Royce—and a driver—since I moved to LA in 1991. Sometimes I'll see Rick driving his Rolls himself, and while I always wave when I see him, he never seems to recognize me, despite my having recorded for him on several occasions.

"Are you taking me to your studio?" Kanish said, smiling. "I have been dreaming for weeks of the moment that I would first enter your room. Oh, I cannot believe this. I am in absolute heaven. Please. I am dying. Take me there."

I led Kanish down the path under the arboretum to the driveway, and lifted the heavy wood garage door to reveal my room in all its glory.

"Fantastic! It's better than I'd imagined!" Kanish exclaimed. "I love it! The place where all the magic happens. And I am going to work here? Pinch me."

Kanish was so overly effusive and happy, it was ridiculous. It was also infectious. He immediately seated himself in my mix chair and started toying with my Slate Raven MTX—a production desk with a 46-inch touch-screen monitor that is handy for mixing records. Before I knew it, Kanish had Pandora playing from my system.

"So many beautiful colors in this room of yours. And the music sounds fantastic in here!"

Kanish was referring to the Indian tapestries and Turkish rugs that covered every square inch of my room. And while it's true that it does sound fantastic in there, I'm not sure it could be judged accurately with the garage door wide open. In general, it's easier to mix when you have some modicum of isolation from the noisy outside world. Kanish stopped the music and leaned back in my chair in order to take it all in.

"If I become only one tenth as good as you by the end of my career, I shall be happy." Kanish sighed dramatically.

The kid really did know just the right things to say, and I was already warm to him, but we had a problem. Four of them.

"Okay, Kanish, I appreciate the sentiment. Really, I do," I encouraged. "But I want you to come outside here, and I want you to take a look around and tell me what you see."

Kanish eagerly followed me past my truck to the end of the driveway, took in a big breath of air, and then announced, "I see the ocean vehdy, vehdy close by!"

"What else do you see?"

"I see palm trees, without coconuts or figs! I see many, many cars all on one side of the street."

At that moment, the street sweeper made the deafeningly loud slow turn onto my street. The Bentley driver had the good sense to drive away. Rajadut's Mercedes, however, remained.

Motherfucker!

Kanish didn't seem to notice the street sweeper as it made its wide detour around the Mercedes. Nor did he notice the enforcement car following it, nor the guy who got out of the enforcement car to write a parking ticket and place it underneath the wiper blade. I suppose with diplomatic immunity that ticket would never get paid, which only made it all the more annoying to me. Someone should be punished for that. Meanwhile, Kanish was still naming off everything that he could see from the end of my driveway.

"I see houses and yards . . ." Kanish continued.

"Right, okay, now we're getting somewhere. Now, what do those houses and yards represent?"

Kanish considered this for a moment. He was taking it all very seriously and was beginning to repeat my question to himself, "What do these represent?" Without warning, he gave up.

"I'm sorry. I do not know. Please tell me the answer."

"It's a neighborhood."

"Yes, yes, yes, yes, yes! I see what you're saying now! You live in the Hood!"

"Um, no."

"Is this Compton? Am I in danger at this moment?"

Kanish was smiling broadly at the prospect that he was somehow in danger.

"No, Kanish. This isn't the hood. It's a place where people kind of expect peace and quiet, and won't really stand for Sikh sentries with Glocks. You know what I'm saying here?"

"You are certain this is not the hood?" Kanish questioned in disappointment.

"This is definitely not the hood, and unless there's some threat that I'm unaware of, you're really not in any danger here. So I'm afraid the Sikhs are going to have to go."

"Yes, yes, yes. Send them on their way!"

"I've tried. Rajadut won't listen to me," I said.

"Of course he will!"

Kanish called for Rajadut, who was unabashedly eavesdropping with the four Sikhs just above our position at the top of the deck. None of them looked as though they were very sure of what to do with themselves—that is, until Rajadut bolted down the stairs to face me.

"Um. The Sikhs have to go," I said slightly unsure of whether this was what my Assistant expected from me.

Rajadut looked toward Kanish and then back to the Sikhs. At the snap of his finger the four of them flew down the stairs and followed Rajadut up the path, under the arboretum, and into his Mercedes. And just like that, they were gone.

"Are you happy?" Kanish asked. "You must be vehdy, vehdy, happy all of the time. I will not stand for a surly boss!"

The Bentley returned and parked in the spot the Mercedes had vacated.

"Now, what else can I do for you? My wish is your command."

I had half a mind to ask for a million more wishes, but then thought better of it.

It was at this point that I sat young Kanish down and explained to him the gig. He clearly didn't have a care in the world, and while his jubilant manner was endearing, I had to make sure we set some ground rules. I had no idea who the couple was in the Bentley, but the whole elderly-Indian-entourage thing just wasn't going to work.

"Very well!" Kanish agreed. "We shall play small ball, just as you say." Kanish stood up abruptly and walked toward the front of the house where the Bentley was parked. "I will send my driver and chef away."

"Wait. Did you say chef?"

"Oh, not just any chef, my friend. She is a master chef, capable of tastes beyond nirvana."

"Well, maybe a chef would be good to have around. . . ."

Perhaps I'd been a bit hasty when I said "no entourage." We certainly didn't need security, but a driver and a chef? That just seemed . . . well . . . efficient.

It was settled. The chef and driver would stay at the Crown Royale Hotel, and Kanish would remain with me at the house. And whereas his first big lesson was supposed to be one in communication, that didn't seem to be so much of an issue anymore. He communicates just fine. It's the timeliness of his communication that I don't prefer.

Besides, there was really only one thing on my mind. I was going to have a chef and a driver for the year.

Eat my dust, Rick Rubin!

Mixerman

CHAPTER FOUR

THE KANISH CARAVAN

It wasn't long before jet lag got the better of Kanish, who was crashed out before the sun had set. He's fortunate to have slept through the night. I never seem to do that even when I'm not completely lagged.

His chef—a lovely and somewhat round Indian woman in her sixties—arrived shortly after 7 a.m. with some groceries and proceeded to whip up a proper English breakfast. There was no need for me to wake Kanish. The aroma of fresh coffee and bangers was enough to lure even the comatose to the table.

"Is this what Indians eat for breakfast? English food?" I suggested jokingly as I took a bite of a banger drenched in egg yolk.

"I don't prefer Indian food all that much," he replied, still rubbing the grog out of his eyes.

"Really? How can you be Indian and not like Indian food?"

"I like Indian food. But why on earth would I limit myself to one culinary style of cooking? It's not like I spend vehdy much time in India. I have been living in England for the past eight years, after all."

"But the Handler told me that you have a bedroom studio."

"I did have. In London. But I worked mostly with loops. It's nothing like what you do, of course."

"I see. So you don't have a bunch of expensive German microphones then, I take it?"

"I have never used more than one microphone at a time. Why should I need bunches of them?"

Ah, well. It was worth a shot.

After devouring a delicious gourmet breakfast fit for a king, I rinsed the last remains of egg yolk from my plate and placed it in the sink. The kitchen was a mess, and the chef was nowhere to be found. As if by habit, I picked up the sponge and began to clean up. But then I began to wonder how it was that I could have a driver, a chef, and an Assistant, but still have to wash the dishes.

"I take it your chef doesn't do dishes?" I prodded.

"This would be like asking me to do the dishes," Kanish replied absent-mindedly.

Kanish had his face buried in his phone throughout breakfast, and it was starting to piss me off. I find this sort of antisocial behavior far too prevalent these days, and I say that as someone who has actually contemplated ways to physically attach the phone to his hand. So I understand the addiction of connectivity all too well. Far more difficult to understand was an Assistant who doesn't do dishes.

"You know cleaning the dishes is like part of your job?" I pointed out.

"If it is part of my job, then it shall be done!"

"Great," I replied with satisfaction.

I collected Kanish's finished breakfast plate and utensils, brought them to the sink, and gave them a quick rinse. I didn't mind helping out. After all, this was the kid's first day here. Unfortunately, he was still fully engrossed in his phone. Meanwhile, I was growing impatient.

"Well? Are you going to do the dishes?"

"Ridiculous."

"You just said, 'It shall be done!'" I mimicked dramatically.

"It shall be. By the dishwasher, of course."

"And who is going to load the dishwasher?"

Kanish finally lowered his phone, if only to look at me with utter incredulity.

"Load the dishwasher? You just put him in front of the dirty dishes, and that's it."

"Wait, the dishwasher is a person?"

"Who else would it be?"

As if on cue, Sikh Number Four breezed into the kitchen and began washing the dishes with great aplomb. The chef returned momentarily to bark orders at the Dishwashing Sikh, and then turned to Kanish to chatter sternly toward him in what I can only describe as an almost motherly tone. She took a brief moment to glare at me and then left the room in a huff.

"Did I do something wrong?" I asked.

"Oh, I wouldn't worry about it too much. Annapurna was just expressing displeasure with your cooking gear," Kanish replied.

"Yeah, well, I don't cook much."

"Yes, and I do not clean much."

I really didn't mind the direction this was all going. What the hell did I care whether Kanish or a member of his entourage cleaned the dishes? So long as someone washed them, and so long as that someone wasn't me. What was pissing me off was his face in the fucking phone.

"That's it," I proclaimed. "I'm not going to be able to hang with you like this, and I'm instituting a media ban."

"Okay," Kanish replied mindlessly.

"That means you have to put your phone down."

It took another few seconds before that last statement permeated his conscious brain. As if by magic, he lowered his phone again.

"A media what?"

"A media ban."

"What is this media ban you speak of?" Kanish inquired, almost excitedly.

"It means you can no longer look at media on your phone—you have to interact with people instead of your device."

"I do not understand."

"Let me put it this way. I'd sooner spend no time with you at all than allow you to flaunt the fact that there are other things you find more interesting than my company," I said.

Kanish thought about that for a moment and then placed his phone facedown in front of him.

"My apologies. I do not feel this way. I was reading about your gorgeous wine country."

"Oh. Well! Wine country is beautiful. You like wine?"

"I like the country."

"Country, as in countryside? Or country as in the United States?"

"I suppose I mean the countryside, since I have never been to the US before now."

This was staggering to me. He was a Billionaire and he'd never visited the States? Which got me to thinking. Why was I in such a hurry to put Kanish to work? I hadn't had a proper vacation in years, and I now had a Billionaire living with me who'd never even been to California. It just seemed to me, if he was going to live here for a year, then he should at least have some idea of his surroundings. Besides, is exploration not learning? Who is to say what gifts a good road trip might rain upon us?

"Maybe we should take a road trip," I suggested.

"A road trip?"

"I think you need a little tour of California."

"Oh, this would be so vehdy, vehdy wonderful. Yes, yes, yes, yes. Let us do it. I am so excited! This is fantastic!"

Of course, there's no such thing as a "little" tour of California, which is a massive swath of real estate. To give you some perspective, LA County alone is half the size of New Jersey. The county itself only covers 3 percent of the total land mass in the state. That means if you could pick up New Jersey and place it into California, it would cover just 6 percent of the area. I realize that won't be very helpful for those of you who have never been to New Jersey. The point is, California is immense.

Kanish was beaming at the concept of a road trip, but then got serious for a moment.

"But . . ." Kanish started hesitantly.

"Spit it out," I cajoled.

"I am here for an education, and I am feeling quite badly that we are abandoning it before we even begin. There is so much to learn."

"There's no shortage of everyday life lessons that can be applied to producing a record, Kanish."

"You are suggesting that I can learn producing this way?"

"Of course. Producing has more to do with people skills than anything else."

"Ah, you sound vehdy much like my Guru."

"Yeah? Well, while you're with me, I am your Guru."

"Oh, I am so happy to hear of this! Then you will supply me with a daily lesson, just as my Guru does?"

"Your Guru gives you a daily lesson? Even in London?"

"You act as if there is no such thing as Skype."

If his Guru could Skype him in England, then he could Skype him in LA, too, and as much as I would have liked that, it seemed I'd already staked claim to the position. Which was just as well. After all, Kanish was here specifically to learn from me. I supposed the least I could do was indulge him.

"Sure, Kanish. I can give you lessons."

"Every day? You will not take this responsibility lightly?"

"My only responsibility as your Guru is to provide you with a daily lesson, is that correct?"

"At the end of each day, yes."

"Fine. I'll provide you a daily lesson."

"Fantastic! When do we go?"

"As soon as we're packed," I replied.

"Vehdy well. I shall ask Sevaka to load up the Bentley."

"Who's Sevaka?" I asked.

"Our driver, of course."

Apparently, it wasn't just Sevaka coming with. Our chef, Annapurna, and the Dishwashing Sikh prepared for the journey as well.

The Bentley was beginning to look like the Beverly Hillbilly-Mobile, what with two large suitcases and three duffles strapped to the top. It was also going to get a bit cramped in there with five people. At the time, it seemed reasonable to bring Sevaka, Annapurna, and the Dishwashing Sikh, formerly known as Sikh Number Four. But in considering it further, it was clear we'd need another car. And while I did have my twelve-year-old Land Rover available and all gassed up in the driveway, I wasn't wild about putting several thousand more miles on it. Besides, road trips were made for rentals.

The way I figured it was, if you're going to venture through California with a full entourage, you should do so in style. And so I took Kanish to the Exotic Car Rentals at the airport. At first Kanish was eyeing the Tesla, which I advised against, seeing as a 240-mile range between charges really wasn't sufficient for a proper California road trip. In the end, he settled on a brand-new convertible Corvette Stingray in charcoal gray.

And what of Fatties?" Kanish asked with remarkable nonchalance.

"You want to smoke Fatties?"

"Is this not what you and Willy Show do?"

Kanish was referring to my first book, in which Super Producer Willy Show virtually forced me to smoke Fatties with him on a daily basis. A Fatty, or Fatties, as it were, are swollen joints filled with Marijuana—although these days, I just call it Medicine.

Medicine has been legal in California for many years now, and I've had a license for about as long as my THC-drenched brain can recall. It's legal to carry up to an ounce of Medicine, and you can purchase it from special Dispensaries, which are set up like co-ops. Oh, and you don't buy your Medicine. You give a "donation" for it. Yeah. That's not shady at all. Whatever, at least I get my weed.

I pointed Kanish in the direction of the nearest Dispensary, and he screeched out of the rental lot onto the wrong side of the street and then immediately corrected course as he laughed it off. I suppose he was still used to driving in England.

Upon our arrival, Kanish handed me three crisp $100 bills and told me to get whatever that would cover. I was beginning to feel more like his Assistant, but if that meant accepting enough money to pay for a full ounce of Medicine, I was okay with it. For the now, anyway.

Only members may enter the Dispensary, and there are armed guards—mostly off-duty sheriffs looking to make some side cash. I entered the establishment and gave the girl the remaining tatters of my recommendation letter. You see, in the infinite wisdom of our legislature, they don't issue a nice durable laminated card. No. They make us carry a fucking full-sized letter that you have to fold up four times just to get the fat fucking wad into your wallet. Douchebags.

I picked up an ounce of intensely potent California Medicine, which, to be perfectly honest, is a rather large quantity of the substance. Under normal circumstances, that would be well over a month's supply. But when you're on an adventure, you tend to meet other "sick people," and there's no telling how much Medicine you'll need once that happens. I also picked up twenty cookies, each of which had enough THC to level an Elephant.

You have to be very careful with edibles, mostly because there isn't any kind of regulation when it comes to the processing of THC products. That's largely because the US government has marijuana classified as a Schedule I drug, the same as heroin and cocaine, which is absolutely fucking ludicrous and is one of the contributing factors to our staggering incarceration rates in this country. So, while cannabis may be legal in California with a note from a doctor, it's highly illegal in the United States. Which might explain why your board-certified internist won't prescribe you Medicine. You pretty much have to go to an entirely different kind of specialist for that. You have to go to a Marijuana Doctor. That's MD, for short.

Let's think about that for a moment. In order to get a letter of recommendation for Marijuana, you must visit a doctor whose only job is to prescribe that one drug. What do you think the odds are that this doctor, whose entire "practice" relies on patients that smoke cannabis, would turn anyone away? Once a doctor denies a patient seeking marijuana, how long before the word gets out to avoid that particular doctor? I'm not giving my practitioner fifty bucks because I'd actually take her advice as a doctor. I'm paying her because that's how I get my letter. Der.

Of course, back when this was all being debated, the anti-marijuana folks argued that doctors prescribing weed as Medicine was nothing more than a ruse. Which it was and still is. All one has to do as a patient is name the usual adverse effects that are caused by marijuana and the doctor will prescribe you marijuana to fix it. Weed not only causes insomnia and anxiety, it cures them, too!

Now don't get me wrong. Reefer is also quite useful for pain and nausea, among other things, and there's no doubt that there are medical conditions in which the drug legitimately helps matters. I have such a condition; therefore, I'm a proponent, even if the whole doctor thing is clearly a fucking scam. But let's get real here. Given the mind-bogglingly wide array of ailments that Medicine relieves, it's impossible to tell who legitimately needs it and who doesn't. So it's reasonable to allow doctors to prescribe it, even if they're just hacks. Besides, no legitimate doctor is going to prescribe marijuana so long as it's classified by the United States of America as a Schedule I drug. It's just not worth the hassle.

While I call dope doctors hacks, my doctor is the exception to the rule. Believe me, all I really care about is getting my license rubber-stamped. But my Marijuana Doctor is so into it that she actually has charts that show which ailments are helped by which strains based on their chemical composition. Some strains have more CBC, CBN, CBD, and I don't know how they think a stoner is going to be able to distinguish between all of those, but each chemical is effective for treating a specific symptom. I mean, CBD apparently helps with acne. Perhaps that's why weed is so popular among teenagers.

Kanish wanted to eat a cookie immediately, which I prevented.

"I'm not driving, dude," I said. "This much I can guarantee. And you decided to get a two-seater. So if you eat that cookie, then you aren't driving either. At which point you and I are in the Bentley and the Sikh is driving Annapurna in the Stingray. Capeesh, Kanish?"

After I explained what *capeesh* meant, Kanish agreed to wait until we got into Santa Barbara before he'd partake. I, on the other hand, ate a cookie. The ride up the coast with the top down is amazing when you're completely straight. It's nothing short of spectacular when you're practically tripping. Like I said, you need to be careful with edibles.

The Stingray had a killer sound system with bass for days. Kanish was blasting the hip-hop station on satellite radio.

"Is hip-hop your favorite genre?" I asked.

"Oh, vehdy much so!" Kanish yelled over the rushing air of both the wind and the 808 kick drum, which was rattling the entire car with its excessive low-end boom.

"I guess that explains why you never use more than one mic at a time. That's not going to help you much in Bollywood, you know."

"Bollywood! That's hilarious!" Kanish hollered. "What would Bollywood have to do with it?"

Well, that was a surprising response.

"Um, you realize Paneer expects you to return to India to become a Bollywood Producer, don't you?"

"Is that what he told you? Look at me. I haven't lived in India for eight years. Why would I go back? That will not happen. Of this I can promise you."

I didn't dare bring up his Trust. Paneer had made it clear in his confessional that Kanish's inheritance was on the line. His instructions were explicit. Deliver to India the next big Bollywood Producer, or else. But it was far too early in our relationship to have that particular conversation. Ultimately, I would have to explain to Kanish Kanish the terms as told to me by his father, including the ramifications of failure. I already liked the lad enough that I couldn't bear to see him poor.

"I vehdy much came here to work with you because of one album," Kanish volunteered.

"Really! And what's that?"

"*Bizarre Ride II the Pharcyde*. You are the greatest hip-hop Producer who has ever lived!"

First off, I didn't produce that album, and I haven't produced any hip-hop albums to date. The bulk of that album was produced by J-Swift, who last I'd heard was on the streets of LA smoking crack. There was even a documentary about the making of that album, which is kind of odd, seeing as no one spoke to me about it. I was there with those guys every day for eight months.

Bizarre Ride II the Pharcyde was the first album I recorded in Los Angeles. I came here from Boston in my early twenties with several years of recording under my belt, which put me in a good position to find work.

Mike Ross, the president of Delicious Vinyl and the Executive Producer of that album, was working out of Hollywood Sound where I was a freelance recording engineer and Assistant. The Pharcyde was there mixing their first EP with Joe Primeau. Meanwhile, Mike was actively complaining about the studio where he tracked it. So when he told me that he was going to make a full-length album with the group, I suggested that they record with me in one of the upstairs production rooms.

Interestingly enough, I almost lost that gig after the first day, when the group insisted they hold the Neumann U47 as they performed. This particular mic is designed to be hung in a special cage called a shock mount, and it is generally too sensitive to be held without picking up distracting noise on the capture. That said, I was not in a position to say no on our first day working together. And I can assure you, when Mike told me that things weren't working out, I explained to him exactly what had happened.

"Yeah. The fucked-up vocals aren't my fault. The group insisted on holding the U47," I said.

"What! You don't hold a U47!" Mike exclaimed in amazement.

"You and I know that. They don't care about that. And I didn't think it was a good idea for me to be butting heads with them on our first day. And I didn't want to be reporting them to you either. They wouldn't trust me."

Mike was visibly relieved to hear all of this, and he immediately called the group into the production room and played them their vocals from the night before. They didn't have a problem with any of it, so I'm not sure why he bothered with a demonstration. Just the same, Mike banned the holding of microphones during performances, even ones appropriate for the task. He also told them to listen to me, which went a long way, actually. Eight months later, we were finished recording the album.

Now, while I did record the Tiger's Share of the vocals, and even mixed two of the tracks on that album, I was not in any way shape or form responsible for the success of that album—and it was quite successful indeed. It was certified Gold, which means it sold over 500,000 units in the US alone. And while there are plenty of hip-hop albums that have sold many more units, *Bizarre Ride II the Pharcyde* is considered one of the quintessential hip-hop albums in the history of the genre, and you will see it cited on nearly every top-twenty-five-hip-hop-albums list you can find. None of that has anything to do with me. My job was simple. Be there to capture their performances.

"I didn't produce that album, I recorded it," I corrected.

Frankly, there shouldn't have been any confusion in that regard, and it made me wonder just how familiar Kanish was with my discography.

"Kanish, can you name any other Artists I've worked with?"

He rattled off names all right. Tone Loc, Michael Franti of Spearhead, the Greyboy Allstars, and The Brand New Heavies, all of whom I worked with more than twenty years ago. In fact, I don't think I've seen any of them, other than Michael Franti, since that time.

"So all the records that you know from my discography are from my hip-hop days? I asked.

"Is there more?"

"Yeah, like an entire era of records, none of them hip-hop. Is that the only music that you like?"

"Certainly not. I vehdy much like all music. But I truly adore hip-hop."

"Because living in poverty under the constant lure of gangs is something that you can identify with?"

"You are a vehdy funny Guru, you are, Mixerman."

"You realize I haven't worked on a hip-hop album in twenty years?"

"Worry not! I will teach you!"

I was very much looking forward to that.

Between the acquiring of rental cars, the purchasing of Medicine, and a number of other distractions not worth going into, we didn't manage to hit the road until rush hour. A rookie mistake if there ever was one. As a result, it took us five hours to make the two-hour trek to Santa Barbara. Don't ask me how many miles it is—we measure distance by time in Southern California, and today, it was five hours away.

Kanish was still quite lagged, and I continued to trip from that outrageous cookie. So we grabbed a bite to eat and then checked into a seaside hotel to crash for the evening. And although I'd taken some time on the ride to research today's critical first lesson, I wasn't all that confident in the results.

"Good night Kanish," I said as I pushed the card into the reader of my suite.

"You seem to be forgetting something," Kanish said.

"Your lesson?"

"Indeed."

"To be perfectly honest, I'm a little embarrassed, because it's a Buddhist lesson."

"Fantastic!"

"But you're Hindu," I pointed out.

"Yes, yes, but Buddhism has a vehdy long history in India and even in Hinduism. It's perfectly fine to teach me the lessons of Buddha," Kanish encouraged.

"Okay," I said with trepidation. "You're ready for it?"

"Hit me!"

"When the student is ready, the master appears," I intoned.

Kanish smiled as wide is wide. As did I.

"You are going to be a fantastic Guru, I can tell," Kanish encouraged.

We can only hope.

Mixerman

CHAPTER FIVE

THE WOODCOCK'S RESERVE

Shortly after breakfast in Santa Barbara, Kanish and I flew up the 101 to San Francisco. He wanted to find some Gangstah rappers there, and while it's true one can find MCs in every US city, San Francisco didn't make a whole lot of sense as the place to start. Ever since Silicon Valley began moving their operations into San Francisco, the Middle Class has been absolutely priced out. San Francisco is pretty much only available to the über-rich now.

Of course, Oakland is just ten minutes over the bridge. And if you want to find Gangstah MCs, Raider Nation would seem the better place to look. I didn't want to find Gangstahs at all, certainly not in Oakland, particularly since I live in Los Angeles. Even with the Dishwashing Sikh Bodyguard at our disposal, I felt it would be ill-conceived to comb the streets of Oakland in a Bentley and a Stingray looking for Gangstah rappers.

Kanish and I stayed at the Waldorf Astoria in San Francisco and the staff elsewhere. I don't really know where they went, and I found myself wondering just who paid the bills. From what I could see, it wasn't Kanish. Besides, I felt it was a bit early in our relationship to pry about finances. Clearly, someone was paying the bills, and it wasn't me. This is really all I cared about in that regard.

Kanish loved San Francisco, but it was getting quite cold in the city, and he came down with a case of the shivers. As did I. After all, there is no place on earth colder than San Francisco.

Oh, I can hear the snorts and guffaws now, particularly from those of you who live near glaciers. But there is a chill by coastal California capable of penetrating the bone regardless of outerwear. There's a reason why Mark Twain wrote, "The coldest winter I ever spent was a summer in San Francisco." It's deceptively fucking cold here, and the temperature gauge doesn't tell the whole story. The best way that I know to beat the cold ocean air is to head inland. Next stop—wine country.

There are wineries up and down the coast of California, but there are only two counties that make up the area we refer to as wine country—Sonoma and Napa, and they are quite different from one another in culture. Sonomaans like to portray themselves as the ruddy, earthy types, and Napaans are proud to be the highfalutin society types, but when you get right down to it, they're all the same—they cater to tourists.

What most people don't realize is that wineries sell you their stock for the suggested retail price, which is at least twice the margin they get selling it wholesale. This is one of the major ways that wineries eke out a profit—tourists with too much money and an inability to do a simple Google search. Frankly, you're far better off going to the local grocery store for California wines, and will pay considerably less than you would at the winery itself. But then, that wouldn't be nearly as sentimentally satisfying. It would also cause the price of wine to increase.

Kanish and I were starting to get a little tipsy as we vineyard-hopped our way through Sonoma. As it turned out, the wineries were all kicking off their big tourist season and there were special events everywhere, all of which were quite predictably sold out. Under normal circumstances, a sold-out Sonoma would be problematic. We were far from normal circumstances.

Given our level of inebriation, Sevaka was now driving Kanish and me in the Bentley as the Dishwashing Sikh and Annapurna led the charge in the Stingray. Let me tell you, when you drive up to parties unannounced in this particular configuration, strange things happen. They just let you in.

This was especially evident when we decided to join the Woodcock family at their yearly season opening extravaganza—touted in the local Sonoma rag as "the hottest ticket in town." Somehow, Kanish took this as an invitation.

The event was being held on the picturesque terrace of the main estate, and upon our arrival, the party was already in full swing. Of course, I've always found it best to be fashionably late when crashing a party such as this, if for no other reason than you don't have to fight traffic. Sevaka drove through the magnificent iron gates, up the paved driveway to the valet. Much to my surprise, Sevaka rolled down his window to address him.

"Announcing the Prince of Rajkot, India. As expected."

The first thought that flashed across my mind was, *Kanish is a prince*? But that was the Medicine talking. This was just a ruse, of course, one they'd clearly played before.

The Mexican valet clearly didn't understand a word. The short Caucasian man with the clipboard, on the other hand, understood him just fine, and he ran at full gait up to the house. Let me put it this way—the commotion that ensued post Sevaka's announcement was nothing short of entertaining.

The Woodcock family was so taken by the fact that their gala dinner was being attended by Indian Royalty, they cleared a spot for Kanish and me at the family table. The fact that we were both dressed so casually only seemed to make our story all the more believable. Only a prince would attend a black-tie event wearing a Budweiser T-shirt and well-worn jeans.

The Sikh was following close behind, as if Kanish's life might be in danger. This was a good touch, as it made the whole royalty scam all the more believable. Who comes to wine country staffed with a driver, a chef, and a Dishwashing Sikh Bodyguard without a reservation? Royalty was the only logical explanation.

"This is great!" I announced as the staff cleared our places.

"Wait until I tell my father of your remarkable hospitality!" Kanish agreed.

As enjoyable as all this was for us, the same could not be said about the couple we'd managed to displace, who were now seated in the corner at a small table erected just for them.

Kathleen Woodcock—our hostess, perched at the head of the table—was beaming with pride, and was just dying to ask Kanish a question. The moment the waiter placed a napkin into her lap, she nearly burst.

"Tell me about the Taj Mahal! Do you live there?"

"Goodness, no. Do you wish death upon me?"

There was an awkward pause as Kathleen froze in horror at her obvious blunder. Kanish was quick to let her off the hook.

"The Taj Mahal is a mausoleum, and I vehdy much hope I don't live there for many years to come."

The entire table broke out in laughter.

"Long live the prince!" Edward Woodcock, Kathleen's brother, announced as he raised a glass of Cabernet.

Kanish took a big swig of wine and then continued to spin a tale that only someone who grew up in India could muster. He described in detail the palace in Ranjit Villa. He talked about the opulent weddings they would have there, featuring "a parade of diamond-adorned Elephants" and "Princes in full regalia" marching through the town of destitute onlookers. Of course, Kanish didn't bother to mention the destitute onlookers. I just added that.

"Tell us about your bedroom in the palace, Kanish," Kathleen said with great excitement, which I found rather forward, particularly coming from a woman three times his age.

"My bedroom is covered with gold wallpaper. My chandelier with rubies."

I couldn't help but wonder whether that was true. Clearly, he didn't live in the palace—he wasn't royalty, he was Brahman—but everything else he spouted on about seemed at the very least plausible. Kanish continued with what I felt was a rather brilliant touch to the story. He held up his glass such that the rays of the setting sun passed through the wine onto the white tablecloth.

"My whole room turns a spectacular shade of Zinfandel as the sun shines through the rubies."

It was sickeningly overdramatic, what with Zinfandel not actually being a color. It also worked like a charm. Kathleen, who had nearly choked on her own Zin, was clearly enamored by the idea of a ruby chandelier in her bedroom.

"A ruby chandelier!" Kathleen marveled. "Where would one get such a thing?"

"Needless Markups," I said jokingly. And it really was meant as a joke. Why would royalty purchase their chandeliers from a department store? Isn't that a custom item?

"Really! Neiman Marcus carries ruby chandeliers?" Kathleen screeched with delight.

"And flying cars too," I said.

"Yes, yes, yes. This is where I purchased mine," Kanish said casually.

This caught the fancy of Edward, who blurted, "You have a flying car?"

"But of course I do!"

One of the first rules of bullshit is, make sure there is at least a kernel of truth in anything that you say, and when the whole truth works, use it. Otherwise, you risk blowing the charade. I happened to remember a

Neiman Marcus catalog sporting a flying car on the cover many years back. The way I figured it, Kanish must have seen the same catalog.

Meanwhile, the displaced couple was stewing at their corner table. I actually felt bad for a bit, until I found out the guy was a Billionaire. I would have felt terrible had the couple scrimped their pennies to achieve a lifelong dream of dinner with the Woodcocks. In retrospect, given the exclusivity of the event, that scenario seemed unlikely.

According to the chatty lady to my right, the guy was a newly minted Billionaire from Silicon Valley. Apparently, he was rather new to the club, and his net worth was listed at a paltry billion. That's right a billion. By all rights, my Assistant's future many billions should have priority in these matters. I mean, that's how this shit works, right?

It never ceases to amaze me the perks one gets just from being rich. Especially when you bring fame into the equation. I was at the NAMM Show (National Association of Music Merchants) in Anaheim last January, and I watched as CeeLo Green ordered a sandwich. Wouldn't you know it? The manager comped his meal. I paid ten bucks for my shitty fucking sandwich, and the millionaire among us gets his for free. Surely, were the manager to actually means-test this decision, CeeLo wouldn't make the cut. Yet he got a free sandwich.

If you're a celebrity of any kind, you're comped all the time by the Serfs who wish to make an impression upon you. Of course, when the Serfs are all comping everything, everywhere you go, you have to wonder whether any of it impacts anyone other than the peasants who offer the comp in the first place.

The pissed-off Barely Billionaire was starting to make a pest of himself, much to the chagrin of his wife, as he dramatically threw down his napkin and stood up to address Kanish.

"What did you say your name was again?" he slurred.

The Barely Billionaire waved his phone in what I would call a rather taunting manner, and which I must admit, had me a bit concerned. Getting into details like names was going to be trouble, as these sorts of things can be researched on the spot. Kathleen and Edward were visibly upset by this line of questioning, yet they stopped short of doing anything about it. Their eyes darted between the irate Barely Billionaire and Kanish. They were clearly interested in the answer to that question themselves and would live with the embarrassment of their guest verifying the information.

This is the problem with instant and perpetual access to information. One can no longer get away with outlandish bullshit, not without some measure of backup on the Internet. Unfortunately, this was an impromptu visit, and as such, there was no time to properly research our story. Fortunately, Kanish, being Indian, was an expert in such matters.

Kanish announced his princely name, and immediately spelled it for the Barely Billionaire, who frantically entered the information into his phone. I was hit with a stiff shot of adrenaline at that moment, and I began to concoct various exit strategies should our ruse go awry.

The Barely Billionaire stared at his phone as the entire table awaited the results with marked anticipation. After several swipes with his thumb, he turned his phone and held up a picture of a young Indian prince.

"This is you?"

"It certainly looks like me!" Kanish exclaimed in glee.

The table broke out in laughter.

"Thanks, Jim, but we verified him already," Edward lied. Dejected, the Barely Billionaire returned to the Baby Billionaire table where he belonged.

I certainly wouldn't describe the prince as a dead ringer, but Kanish was so confident that no one at the table dared question him. Besides, nearly everyone at this party was white and most certainly couldn't tell the difference between the young Indian prince in the picture and the young Indian Billionaire at the table. That said, the resemblance was quite remarkable.

Edward couldn't contain himself any longer. "Tell me about your flying car!"

Much to my surprise, Kanish did one better than just tell him about it. He actually began to show the entire table selfies that he'd taken in his flying car in London. And were there any hint of a doubt remaining in the minds of the guests as to the veracity of our story, those had now been fully put to rest.

Course after fabulous gourmet course was brought to the table, each with a new tasting of wine, seven courses in all. And although this was the Woodcocks' affair, the outside observer wouldn't have known it by watching it. Kanish was holding court, and had managed to capture the fancy and imagination of every guest there.

Kanish introduced me as his Producer, which made my part easy. I didn't have to make anything up, for which I was quite thankful, as it's not in my nature to do such things. I did, however, have to pretend that I was producing a Vanity album for the Prince of Rajkot, which I found quite demeaning.

Kathleen and Edward were the most wonderful hosts you could imagine, and once the after-party had concluded, Edward helped to load the front seat of the Bentley with three cases of, as he put it, "our most cherished wines." A cursory search of the Internet revealed that the Woodcocks had gifted Kanish thousands of dollars in wine. That said, there's really no telling the true value of the gift, since we would have had to search wine cellars all over the state to find some of these particular vintages. And once again, the person who least needed to be comped was.

"Where are you staying?" Edward asked as he loaded the last case of wine into the Bentley.

"I'm not sure," I replied.

"You don't have a reservation anywhere? You're never going to find a place in the Valley. Everything's booked up! Even the campsites are full."

"I guess we'll have to go back to the City," I said.

"Nonsense! You should stay here tonight, as our guests. We'll provide you a room, Prince," he offered.

Edward then looked down his nose at me and pronounced, "The staff can sleep in the barn."

"Yeah, I'm his Producer, not staff. And I can assure you that I'm not staying in a barn," I replied.

Kathleen apologized profusely for the faux pas and brought Kanish and me up to our respective rooms. The staff were provided with sleeping bags and cots and didn't seem to have a problem with crashing in a barn. After brushing my teeth, I met Kanish in the hall. We faced each other, both of us fully clad in plaid flannel pajamas provided to us by the Woodcocks.

"What is today's lesson?" Kanish asked.

"I can tell you today's lesson, but based on the events of this evening, you already have a firm grasp of it."

"It is never a bad thing to relearn a lesson, my Guru. This is how it remains knowledge."

"Playing the flute to a buffalo is a waste," I said.

"Ah, yes. A vehdy good lesson indeed!"

I couldn't help but chuckle to myself as I replayed the events of that evening. The seemingly exotic and ultra-risky careers of Producers, whether of wine or of music, can become downright mundane given enough time. Kanish played a serenade that Kathleen and Edward desperately required. Me as well.

The kid has a gift.

Mixerman

CHAPTER SIX

THE BLESSED DONKEY

"I wish we had a fucking BMW right now," I complained over the rushing wind.

We were on our way to Mammoth Lake via Yosemite National Park, and the temperature was dropping precipitously as we wound our way through the Sierra Mountains of California. The plan, if you could call it that, was to rent a house there and chill for a few days—literally.

"Why do you wish for a BMW?" Kanish asked.

"Because this thing sucks for cornering, that's why."

"I see what you mean, but I still think that an American car is best."

"Best for faux patriotism, maybe."

"Are you saying that I chose an American car to veil the fact that I'm Indian?"

"I've got news for you. Everyone can see that you're Indian."

Kanish ignored my smart-ass comment. Rather than leave that hanging there, I decided it best to expound upon the thought.

"I think that deep down, you believe you'll curry favor with Americans by driving one of our cars."

"This is what you think?" Kanish replied, completely ignoring my clever use of the term *curry*.

"What other explanation could there be? Surely you've driven BMWs and Mercedes. You can't possibly tell me that an American car competes!"

The top was down, and the windows were up, and we had the heat blasting from the vents in order to counteract the increasingly frigid wind.

"You do not believe that buying American is patriotic?" Kanish asked.

"People buy cars for all sorts of reasons, Kanish. Just as a for instance, I'll reject certain cars just so that I won't be associated with the type of people that tend to drive them.

"Forgive me, but you are suggesting that there are personality traits of people that drive certain cars?"

"Absolutely."

"And what kind of people drive this car?"

"Douchebags," I replied.

"Blurred Lines," was spinning on the satellite radio, which Kanish turned up to full. At first I thought he was annoyed, but then I realized he just loves that song. As do I.

"Blurred Lines," of course, was the mega-hit song from the summer of 2013 featuring Robin Thicke, Pharrell Williams, and rapper T.I. You couldn't go ten minutes without hearing the song that summer, and as a result, it is often held up as proof that there's still money to be made in music. The two main cowriters made millions from it. Unfortunately, that money was at risk from this little matter of a copyright infringement suit.

At issue was the striking resemblance between Marvin Gaye's 1977 hit "Got to Give It Up" and the duo's effort with "Blurred Lines." And while I use the word *striking*, that wouldn't be my term for it. When I listen to the mash-up of those two tracks on YouTube, the similarities most certainly don't rise to the legal definition of infringement.

If you grew up listening to Gaye's "Got to Give It Up," you could very well become irate as you compare the two tracks. They do, after all, use a similar chord pattern and groove, but that's the extent of it. Similar. Regardless, neither the chord changes nor the groove are protected by copyright, and frankly, this is far too outside the scope of what a layman should judge. These cases would be best argued in front of professionals who make music for a living.

Much to-do is made of a Robin Thicke interview in which he admits to pinching the vibe of the track. And while that may seem like one big "oops" to him now since intent comes into play in an infringement case, you really can't blame Robin for mentioning this in an interview. For as long as I've been in this business, an Artist could come right out and state his or her direct influences without concern. It's the lyric and melody that are protected, not the groove, or the vibe, or even the chord pattern. And while it's true that you can also protect certain elements that make a song immediately identifiable—like the guitar riff from the Rolling Stones' "Satisfaction"—in general, you're in good shape so long as you don't rip off the melody or the lyric. Or at least you used to be.

According to Daryl Hall, Michael Jackson confessed to borrowing the bass part from "I Can't Go For That" to use in his '80s mega-hit song "Billie Jean." So, why then didn't Hall & Oates sue for infringement? Because they fucking took the bass line themselves, as did those before them, and those before them. Which is why you can't protect a bass line, or a chord progression, or anything that has to do with feel. That said, Robin Thicke and Pharrell Willimas lost that suit to the Gaye estate. As of this writing, it's in the appeals process.

The problem with juries is that they make all sorts of fucked-up decisions, especially when it comes to something as complicated and nuanced as Copyright Law. That said, the infringement suit itself is nothing more than a distraction as far as I'm concerned. The big story here is the jaw-dropping $7 million that Universal Music Group spent to promote the song.

Let me repeat that.

The Universal Music Group spent *$7 million to promote one song*, performed by two proven and currently hot commodities in Robin Thicke and Pharrell Williams. From a songwriting standpoint, it was about as close to you can get to a guaranteed hit. Yet they spent $7 million to promote it!

Granted, this figure includes expenditures to send Robin Thicke around the world to perform the record, including his infamous public dry hump of Former-Miss-Disney-Innocence #19, also known as Miley Cyrus. Even so, that's a lot of jack to promote a song that's already hitting on all cylinders.

I hate to be the one to point this out, but if Universal has to spend $7 million to ensure that "Blurred Lines" blew up sufficiently, then all you Independent musicians out there trying to break your song really don't have a shot. Even if I were to halve that promotional figure to $3 million—even if I were to bring it down to a million—tell me, how is an Indie Artist supposed to compete with that? How long must the odds be before it's not even a worthwhile gamble?

The song was coming up to T.I.'s rap in the third verse, which meant my favorite line was approaching, Much to my surprise, Kanish yelled it out with me.

In a hundred years not dare, would I,
Pull a Pharcyde, let you pass me by!

"You see! You are vehdy famous from this song!" Kanish laughed.

The lyric was a reference to the song "Passin' Me By," which was the hit single off the album *Bizarre Ride II the Pharcyde*—my first Gold record as a recordist. Kanish was once again giving me far more credit than I was due.

"I'd be willing to bet most people have no idea that line is even in the song, Kanish."

"You are vehdy much missing my point. Your work is rehashed and regurgitated into the lexicon."

"It's being regurgitated, all right."

"Why do you deny being part of something so great? No matter how you discount your influence, you must remember, had you not been there, the results would not have been the same."

Had I not been there, the results would not have been the same. It was difficult to argue with that logic, but Kanish was now confusing the influence of a creative force with a facilitating one.

"Look, I don't discount my contribution to the Pharcyde's first album."

"But you do!"

"No. I don't. I was the only one who was straight for the large preponderance of that album, and I know what my role was on it as a facilitator. I was just there to keep the technology out of their way and to capture their brilliance, over and over again, until they were happy. I never gave them any advice on what was good. I never made suggestions. I just shut the fuck up and captured them, and tried to keep the technology out of their way, nothing more and nothing less."

"Perhaps so, but at the end of the year, you were an important part of a work with great relevance to society."

"Relevance to society? Please. You realize the song is about them getting their hearts crushed in high school, right?"

"And what could be more relevant than that?"

A line of ten cars was now crawling up the mountain—a silver Prius leading the parade. I was half expecting a marching band and some onlookers, and even with no particular schedule, I found myself becoming aggravated by the pace. I'm not sure what it is about Prius drivers, but for some reason, they seem content to be the ones in this world who constantly fuck up the free flow of traffic.

I've driven a Prius, so I'm familiar with the car, and while it is certainly a dog where pickup is concerned, it is nowhere near as slow off the line as

Prius owners would have you believe. It's almost as if the Prius driver views the actual destination as irrelevant. All that really matters is that one use as little gas as possible. Perhaps someone should tell all the Prius diehards out there that they would use even less gas if they'd just stay at home.

You know, I don't begrudge someone driving slowly. What pisses me off is when people drive obliviously. And this is the big problem with many Prius drivers—I find them inexplicably oblivious. I mean, if you're going 30 miles per hour in the left lane, on a road that people generally travel at 50, and if car after car passes you on the right and then whips aggressively in front of you, then that would be the very definition of oblivious. If only there were a passing lane.

You see, mountain roads generally only have one lane going each direction, and that would be the case here. In California, if you have five cars or more stacking up behind you on a single-lane road, you're supposed to pull over at a turnout. These small areas of shoulder appear every few miles or so on the mountain roads, so as to promote the free flow of traffic. This particular Prius had neglected to pull over at the last two turnouts. As a result, drivers were now laying on their horns.

"Prius drivers are such fucking Douchebags!" I exclaimed.

"You vehdy much like this word, *Douchebag*, don't you?"

"It's a Jersey thing."

"A Jersey thing?"

"That's where I grew up. In New Jersey. It's a popular word there."

"To douche is to bathe. You know this?" Kanish pointed out.

"Yes, in French. But we have a very complicated relationship with the French. We even changed the name of their fries to Freedom."

"But wouldn't a better insult be to call someone an Enemabag? I would vehdy much prefer be called a Douchebag than an Enemabag, let me tell you."

Kanish had me laughing at this line of reasoning, flawed as it was. I'm not sure how *Douchebag* came to be such an effective slur, but people sure do seem to understand that you don't like them very much when you call them that. I just didn't understand where this was coming from.

"Is there like a campaign against the word *Douchebag* or something?" I asked.

"A campaign? What do you mean by this?"

"Like, you know, if you use the word *retard* these days, some people get all bent out of shape."

"Ah, yes. But you use that term in your books."

"I used it in my first book. But the backlash to that word is . . . I mean, you'd think it was a fucking racial slur. So I've stopped using it. Now I just refer to anyone below an IQ of 80 as *Rrritarded*."

"*Rrritarded*? How is this different?"

"*Ritard* is a musical term which means to slow down. So now I use the term *Rrritard*. This way, I'm not offending anyone."

"It's interesting when you think about it," Kanish pondered. "The *Rrritards* seem to have more protection than black people in this country."

It was a good point. *Rrritards* weren't being shot and incarcerated at an alarming rate.

I understand defending the defenseless, I suppose. But hysteria breaks out the moment anyone mutters the term *mentally retarded*. Even a phrase as innocuous as *to retard one's progress* seems to get a rise out of the more sensitive types. I had a woman flip out on me once over that phrase, which is absurd. To retard progress means to slow it down. The object in that sentence is *progress*. We need to protect progress? Meanwhile, you can't turn on the radio without hearing the word *ho*. Not that I care about that word either, but the verbiage police really need to get their priorities straight. *Ho* is demeaning to half our population. What percentage is *Rrritarded*?

The only people who feel better about removing that word from the list of approved speech would be those who care for the mentally *Rrritarded*. What-fucking-ever! The *Rrritards* themselves are oblivious to all of it, and I have a problem with people telling me that I'm being hateful by using a term that quickly and easily describes a person in need of permanent assistance. That's *Rrritarded*!

The green Prius finally made use of the turnout. Unfortunately, there was a red Prius next in line and fully prepared to take over the Douchebag patrol. Kanish had had enough. He swerved into the left lane and gunned it up a short stretch of straightaway. Well! As crappy as the Stingray was around corners, it sure did like straightaways just fine. We passed the entire line of Douchebags in a flash.

"Let me ask you this," Kanish said. "Did you keep them happy and relaxed?"

"The *Rrritards*?"

"The Pharcyde."

Ah, he was back on the Pharcyde again.

"Of course I did," I replied.

"Did they like you?"

"Sure. But I was never close with them or anything. They weren't inviting me to go out with them after recording. I never went to clubs with them."

"I don't understand. You say clearly in your Zen books that your most important job is to keep the Artist happy and relaxed because this has an effect on performance."

As appreciative as I was of Kanish's attempts to place my involvement with that album as historically significant, that's the last thing I wanted. The Music Business isn't about the past. It's about the here and now. It's about relevance. And relevance has a very short shelf life, more so now than ever. I can assure you, an album that I recorded twenty-two years ago doesn't qualify as current or relevant.

Bizarre Ride II the Pharcyde is, and always will be, an important feather in my cap. And while it's true I wouldn't have gotten the gig were I not exceptionally aggressive—and I'll take all the credit in the world where that is concerned—I really just happened to be in the right place at the right time.

"You know, Kanish, timing is a very important component to success, and when it comes to timing, there's often an element of luck. You know?"

Of course, I was saying that to the son of a Billionaire. A Billionaire's Heir, as it were.

Let's face it, when it comes to opportunity, Kanish would have considerably more than I ever did. Certainly out of the gate. When you have to work just to survive, which surely describes the large majority of us, this limits your options tremendously in life. Immediate need always gets the priority over creative outlets, and only those who view creation as an integral part of their survival will find a way to accomplish both. But if you can literally devote all of your time toward a goal of your choosing, without any concern toward basic fundamental needs, then the only thing that can really stop you is your own self-discipline.

Discipline is an important virtue to have when it comes to creating art. It's easy to create when everything is going smoothly. It's those times when you must overcome problems that pure drive comes into play. To create requires a mental fortitude in which confidence manages to keep the upper hand in the unending war against self-doubt.

I imagine it would be more difficult to muster artistic discipline from a position of wealth. There is surely a certain unavoidable apathy that comes from such a position. Drive is born out of need. The question wasn't whether Kanish has talent—he has it in spades in the form of charisma and charm. And people skills are of far more consequence for success in the Music Business than musical talent. But what kind of creative drive does he have?

One thing is for sure, Kanish will always have plenty of opportunities—and opportunities are the lottery tickets in life. Of course, unlike actual lotteries, skill and preparation have great influence over the winners and losers in this game. Which goes right back to timing. Once an opportunity arises for which you're fully prepared, chances are, you're going to come out ahead.

We pulled up to our Airbnb, which turned out to be a rather palatial residence tucked into the mountain at about 9,000 feet, and with a killer view of the lake. There were four bedrooms and a couch, and I was glad that the staff wouldn't need to sleep on the floor of a barn again. Sevaka and Annapurna didn't speak much, and the Sikh might as well have been a mute, but strangely, I was starting to really like them.

The staff caught up to us an hour later in the Bentley packed full of groceries. Annapurna grilled up the most stupendous ribeye steaks, corn, and potatoes, followed by a delicious salad. The dining room table was massive, and so I invited Annapurna, Sevaka, and the Dishwashing Sikh to join us. This surprised Kanish, but he didn't dare protest. Of course, no one said a word the entire awkward dinner.

I rolled a Medicinal Fatty as the Dishwashing Sikh cleaned the kitchen. Annapurna and Sevaka retired for the evening, both of them to the same room. Kanish and I moved to the deck so as to enjoy our nightcap.

"Are Annapurna and Sevaka together?" I asked.

"They are married," Kanish replied, before immediately changing the subject. "You have thought about today's lesson, I hope, Guru Mixerman?"

"Oh, I have today's lesson all right, but you're not necessarily going to understand it."

"Tell me!" Kanish busted.

"If god blesses a Donkey, it can become a wrestler."

Kanish pulled from the Fatty and then proceeded to nearly cough out a lung. By the time he could breathe again, his eyes were a deep glassy red, and swollen from tears.

"This is not a lesson," Kanish wheezed.

"Sure it is," I replied.

"But the meaning is that even the most useless person can become great."

"You're assuming that a Donkey is useless."

"I know the meaning of an ancient Hindu proverb."

"That may be true, but are you suggesting to me that a Donkey isn't a useful animal?"

"There is machinery that can do the job in a tenth of the time. That makes the Donkey indeed useless."

"I doubt there was machinery when this proverb was written, Kanish."

"You make a vehdy good point, but the Donkey is still considered useless."

"You're focusing too much on the Donkey."

"So you are saying I am blessed, then?"

"I'm suggesting you can be and do whatever you want, Kanish. And I'm going to help you figure out exactly what that is."

Kanish didn't last long after that. Between the mountain air, the altitude, and the Fatty, he was faded, and crashed out on his bed fully clothed.

It was about time for me to have a discussion with Kanish over who he is, and what he is to become. It was clear that god had no designs on Kanish being my Assistant. This was not his lot in life. What was unclear were god's intentions with me, and I say that as an agnostic or perhaps an atheist, whichever one requires less effort. If Kanish isn't a blessing, then I contend there's no such thing. And as much as this is Kanish's journey, I'm not sure he isn't just along for the ride.

Mixerman

CHAPTER SEVEN

FOR SALE: BILL OF GOODS

While it's quite possible that I flubbed yesterday's lesson, I will say in my defense that proverbs are fraught with problems, as they require human interpretation. The moment you bring perception into the equation, all bets are off. To make matters worse, metaphors borne from India don't always translate well. I mean, if god blesses a Donkey and it becomes a wrestler, I would have to know that Hindus view Donkeys as useless and wrestlers as great. I, not being Hindu, read that and think it's a lesson in opportunity. If god blesses you, whether with talent or a bankroll, you can pretty much do what you desire, the caveat being that you must operate within your talents and your bankroll. In Kanish's case, both seemed in high supply.

I might also point out that there's another Hindu proverb that states: "If you need a job to be done, be prepared to fall at the feet of a Donkey." Which makes one wonder, who would fall at the feet of a useless animal? If the Donkey can help get a job done, and you're prepared to fall at the Donkey's feet, then it can hardly be considered a useless animal, regardless of protests from Kanish.

To make matters worse, I'm searching for these proverbs on the Internet, and for those of you who haven't figured it out by now, you can't rely on some of the information you find there. Believe it or not, people make shit up, and as a result, I really have no idea whether I'm reading a proverb that was written by some schmo today, or by some schmo from a thousand years ago.

To be perfectly honest, I had half a mind to toss yesterday's lesson as presented in this diary and make one up that wouldn't be such an embarrassment. That would make me no better than the assholes who invent shit on the Internet. And since the misunderstanding was merely an issue of translation, I've decided to keep the lesson as is, even if that means I must endure the sniggers of a billion Hindus. I could only be so lucky.

I'd given quite a bit of thought to all of this last night. In particular how opportunity relates to talent. This can happen when you smoke an exceptionally powerful Fatty—you often find yourself pondering. At least, I do. I shouldn't assume this happens to others, but I dare say it is a known side effect of Medicine. Some would call it the purpose.

No matter what your background, if you have talent and the drive to go along with it, you can achieve some modicum of success in the Music Business. If you have something to say, and a good way of saying it, and if you can tap into just the right cultural vein at precisely the right time, people will react. That will never change. That's how art works. But only the Creators are in a position to strike that kind of chord. Even when this business was at its most robust, that was a long shot, which is why some of us became Producers.

As a record Producer I act as a facilitator. I help the Creator to deliver her carefully honed message in the most musically effective way possible. I also get many bites at the apple in this regard. If one record doesn't work out, there's always the next. Even the most successful Producer has more duds than winners; it's just that no one has ever heard the duds, and nearly everyone the winners. As a result, it can be rather deceiving to review a Producer's discography. The only names that will pop out are the familiar ones.

As much as I pshaw Kanish's attempts to elevate my stature on a project that I recorded well over twenty years ago, we can't discount the opportunity the album has generated for me over the years. Just by virtue of the fact that *Bizarre Ride II the Pharcyde* was awarded Gold status by the RIAA (Recording Industry Association of America), I went from a $10-per-hour house engineer to ten times that, literally in a matter of a day.

Regardless of success, the more time that passes after an album's release, the less power that album has to directly convert into gigs. A successful and beloved record made decades ago is judged within the totality of my career, which is expressed in the form of a discography. Current records prove my relevance. Older records verify my longevity. Of course, if you're just getting started, then you need to learn what you're doing first.

Most recording professionals who got into this business before the mid-aughts were mentored to one degree or another. Recording was a trade passed down from master to student. Those days are over. Mentoring in this industry is all but dead, as large, for-profit schools have taken over the job of preparing our next generation of recordists and Producers for an industry that is already fully saturated. It really doesn't matter what the intentions are of a for-profit school: if the institutions are spitting out more students than a particular trade can sustain, then they are by their very nature predatory.

The problem is that we don't have an organization that attempts to restrict the number of recording trade graduates exported into this industry. You would think that NARAS (National Academy of Recording Arts and Sciences) or AES (Audio Engineering Society) might provide this service so as to protect their membership from oversaturation. They don't. And while the US government is now starting to crack down on for-profit trade schools, it's probably too late.

The recording Industry is currently littered with thousands upon thousands of newly minted graduates desperate to make a living producing music. Predictably, this has managed to suppress prices, often below a living wage. Some would argue that the job market will eventually correct itself. Perhaps it will. But at what cost? A certificate from a recording school is not transferrable to any other school or job, and a "correction" in this case would have to look more like a mass exodus. I mean, if you peruse the long lineup of former A-list mixers now teaching master classes, it's pretty clear that there's more money in teaching recording than there is in the industry itself.

Here, Mixmaster #10, let me give you thousands of my hard-earned dollars so that you can teach me in under a week how to succeed in a business that even you can't make enough money in anymore.

That doesn't bode well.

Meanwhile, because music is so readily accessible, it appears as if opportunity abounds. One can find an endless supply of new songs being generated by Independent Artists looking to be the next viral sensation. But as I've already pointed out to you, if it requires $7 million to blow up "Blurred Lines," then an Artist's only feasible chance to break is to get in bed with the Major Distributors. Same as it ever was.

All of this got me to thinking about opportunity outside of this business, particularly as it relates to my nineteen-year-old son in comparison with Kanish. Surely a Billionaire's Heir would have far more opportunity available than my son, just by virtue of his wealth. But money alone isn't enough to fulfill a prophecy of success, certainly not if we're to measure success in terms of happiness. Of course, sociologists suggest that money has no influence on one's overall contentment in life. Even if you buy into that crap—and I don't—I have no doubt that most of us would risk bliss in exchange for an ungodly sum of money. I mean, if wealth has no bearing on our happiness—if it truly comes from within—then you may as well take the money, right?

The big problem with a windfall of funds is that it doesn't necessarily come with an education. That's the social contract of the Trust Funder. The money is handed down along with the tools necessary to prosper, and that's mostly a function of education. I mean, were I a Billionaire, teaching my child high-level money management and business would be my number one educational priority. Delivering an enormous sum of cash to someone who hasn't even been taught to count change let alone assess risk is an absolute recipe for failure.

This is why the professional sports leagues provide mandatory classes on money management. Because very few of their young athletes coming in (especially the teenagers) have the tools necessary to deal with that kind of income. Hell, most of us don't have those tools, and if it's proof you're looking for, you need only to look at the dismal financial record of mega-lottery winners, many of whom ultimately return to their natural state of destitute bliss.

I don't denigrate someone who suddenly wins millions and then proceeds to lose it all. The pressure must be intense, as everyone in your rapidly expanding sphere needs help and has two friends who need even more help, each of whom has two more friends, in what ends up an endless procession of friends and family in need.

You find out that your second cousin is diagnosed with cancer and can't afford the surgery. You're hit up by an in-law who wants to go back to school so he can provide for your favorite nieces and nephews, all of whom desperately need braces. Your newest, bestest friend has a great idea for an invention and wants you to invest in his sure thing. You hand out far too many loans, none of which have any structure or any feasible path for repayment. Your investment portfolio is wiped out one Monday because you didn't understand how to properly hedge your bets in the market. Then there's the thousands upon thousands of charities that hit you up, most of which are totally worthy causes. And so you give and you give and you give, and you forget to make, because that's not how you were programmed.

You're not the moneymaking kind of animal. You spent your childhood watching money go out faster than it came in, and that's familiar to you.

While the cost of Kanish's education at Eton and Oxford was a pittance for a Billionaire, I would say it came at a much higher price. Kanish had spent his early teenage years without his father's influence. Obviously, I have no idea how Paneer is as a father, nor could I possibly judge. All I know is that I couldn't imagine sending my child thousands of miles away to boarding school at the age of thirteen and for the remainder of his teenage years. But then if I were an Indian Billionaire, I might feel differently about that. And although my son won't start off with the financial security afforded to a Billionaire's Heir, he most certainly has the one advantage that he can't rightly lose: American citizenship.

There's a reason why we love to declare the United States the land of opportunity. Because opportunity isn't a handout. It's a moment to prove yourself. It's the American Dream. If you work hard, you can succeed in life, regardless of whence you came.

Of course, that's utter bullshit.

I mean, we have essentially segregated an entire swath of the population, jailed half their fathers, and funded many local economies on the backs of the poor through insidious taxes in the form of oppressive fines manifesting as veritable debtors' prisons. As if that's not enough, we have refused to provide our inner-city youth the tools necessary to succeed in life through a relevant education. And we do all of this as if slavery and segregation never happened. Fifty years after the civil rights march in Selma, we continue to perpetuate this travesty upon our young black and brown children, and it all becomes nothing more than a self-fulfilling prophecy. How could it not? Yet we still have people insisting all you have to do is pull yourself up by your bootstraps. What if you don't even have boots?

Anyone who says there isn't a caste system in the United States is absolutely delusional. Practically speaking, and barring the occasional exception to the rule, you have very little shot of rising more than one caste above that of your parents. Even that's a feat. Immigrants who own businesses are the most successful at this, and that has little to do with work ethic. I mean, picking produce twelve hours a day, seven days a week is the very definition of a work ethic. Yet it pays less than the minimum wage. Merely working hard doesn't pull you out of poverty. Owning a successful business does.

The problem is that what we constantly see around us doesn't necessarily match reality, which distorts our perception of things. For instance, you can't watch television, or pick up a magazine, without exposing yourself to well-known multimillionaires. In fact, if you take a moment to write down all the names of the millionaires and billionaires that you hear about every day, and if you compare that list to your Facebook friends, the millionaire column will surely have the greater number of names. Seriously, try it. I'll do it too.

Hillary Clinton, Bill Clinton, Gwyneth Paltrow, Paris Hilton, Will Ferrell, Chris Matthews, Rachel Maddow, Kevin Spacey, Al Roker, Brian Williams, Kobe Bryant, Moses Malone, Charles Barkley, Larry Bird, Magic Johnson, Michael Jordan, Eli Manning, George Stephanopoulos, Barack Obama, John Kerry, Larry Johnson, Derek Jeter, George W. Bush, Poppy Bush, Chris Rock, Kanye West, Sting, Jude Law, Madonna, Kevin O'Leary, Daymond John, Mark Burnett, Barbara Corcoran, Robert Herjavec, Ashton Kutcher, Stephen Colbert, Jimmy Fallon, Tom Hanks, any and every Kennedy, Donald Trump, David Koch, Charles Koch, Rupert Murdoch, Sheldon Adelson, Oprah Winfrey, Mark Zuckerberg, George Soros, Paul Allen, Mark Cuban, et cetera, et cetera. The last ten are Billionaires, and this list is entirely off the top of my head. I can easily surpass my personal acquaintances with known millionaires.

Between the carnival barker nature of our society—in which the winner, winner, winners are pronounced and paraded about with great fanfare so as to perpetuate the dream—and our overt obsession with wealth as a society, it appears as though more than half the people in our lives are rich. And yes, clearly, we can consciously separate the reality of those that we interact with personally from those whom we merely watch from a distance. But make no mistake, the American Dream appears alive and well when half of the people that you can name are millionaires, and it doesn't matter whether you know any of them personally.

Really, this illusion is probably worse now than ever, because we live in a world in which Facebook allows us to hoard past acquaintances like trinkets in the junk drawer. These people have about as much direct interaction with us as the millionaires who are trotted before us on the newsstands, on the radio, on the television, at the stadium, in the movies, in the bookstore, and of course, in Congress. The fact of the matter is, you can almost certainly name more winners of the American Dream than you can personal friends, even if you include all of your acquaintances.

This means, every time we see yet another famous person on TV, we are likely watching someone who is the beneficiary of the American Dream. And some of those Dreamers may even have a good story about how they rose from poverty to achieve their accomplishments, which is often held up as evidence that you, no matter who you are, or from whence you came, with hard work, can become a bona fide multimillionaire.

No, you really can't. It's a mirage. A charade. A farce. An illusion, in which a long shot is presented as if it's even odds.

To make matters worse, when you look at how the media treats and discusses matters of income inequality in this country (let alone the world), the argument that it's good for 1 percent of the US population to control the predominance of the wealth is, most inexplicably, given equal time and weight as the argument that 99 percent of the country is getting royally screwed.

Until the 99 percent says, *"Enough,"* none of that is going to change.

Frankly, I shudder to think about just how bad an economic calamity we must face before we wake up. Apparently, the last collapse wasn't enough.

It was a lazy day on the mountain. Which is fine with me. After all, I'm experiencing a kind of financial freedom I haven't had in quite some time. Not only do I have the year covered, I don't even have to pay any expenses.

Should that trend continue, I may actually get ahead.

Now, that's a dream I can buy into.

Mixerman

CHAPTER EIGHT

THE CODE SHACK

Kanish was engaged in a rather agitated conversation. I have no idea what was being said, partly because it was six in the fucking morning, but mostly because he was speaking in Hindi gibberish. And although I couldn't make out a word, the inflection reminded me of the tone my son sometimes takes with me. Either Kanish was ignoring good fatherly advice, or Paneer was just being his usual domineering self. Perhaps a little of both.

I rubbed the crud from my eyes as I poured myself some coffee and then sparked up the remaining nub of last night's Fatty. To wake and bake is not usual for me, but I had no responsibilities today, and calls from Billionaires tend to unnerve me. Kanish declined my attempts to pass the Fatty, and then screamed into his phone one last time before ending the call abruptly.

"And how's Paneer today?" I asked.

"As per usual," Kanish replied.

"Loving?"

"Overbearing!"

Annapurna handed us each a piece of bacon and then turned her attention to the omelettes. Sevaka was loading up the Bentley with bags, and the Dishwashing Sikh was meditating on the side deck.

"I take it you're done with the mountains?"

"I'm finding myself restless," Kanish said curtly.

"Is everything all right?" I asked.

"Everything is fine."

Everything was not fine. Kanish, who was normally as bright as the sun, was dour and intent. As he packed his duffle in the middle of the floor he voiced a request.

"If it's okay with you, I'd like to head back to Redondo."

"Sure, Kanish. Whatever you like," I replied.

As we made our way down the mountain, I tried every fatherly trick I knew to open Kanish up, but to no avail. He was deep in thought, and my prodding was ineffective. Not that I kept at it long. The frigid mountain air and the morning Fatty conspired to knock me out, if only briefly. When I returned to consciousness, Kanish was once again on the phone.

"Yes, yes, yes. I will be there in three hours," Kanish concluded.

"There's no fucking way you'll be in Redondo in three hours," I said.

"Ah, you're awake!" Kanish replied.

He seemed in much better spirits now.

"Kanish, what the fuck is going on, dude? You're all over the map here with your mood."

"My apologies. All is better now. There has been a slight change in plans, however."

"What's that?"

"I must run an errand."

We were in the middle of the Sierras and on our way back to Redondo. What kind of "errand" could he run? And why were we heading back the same way we'd come, through Yosemite National Park? This was about as roundabout a way back to Redondo as I could imagine. Kanish must have sensed my confusion, because he addressed it straightaway.

"We are headed to your Silicon Valley. I have a business there and I must pick something up."

Just as he said it, we passed a family of bears foraging for berries on the side of the road. Kanish got so excited he pulled over. Or at least he started to until I reminded him that we were in a convertible with the top down, and much like 500-pound Bengal Tigers, bears are dangerous. With that crisis averted, I addressed the business at hand.

"You have a business in California?"

"I own a Corporation, yes."

"So, that's why you can stay in this country so easily!"

You see, when you own a business in the US, you can live in the US. There are no lotteries. There's no asylum. There are no visas. There are no workers' programs. You are the workers' program, because you're ostensibly bringing jobs here. And when you bring jobs to America, you get to live in America.

How does that motto go again? Give us your tired, your poor, your huddled masses yearning to breathe free—but only in limited supply. In the meantime, send us all of your wealthy, thank you very much. Of course, that's part of the reason why people are getting priced out of Los Angeles. Every wealthy person on earth wants to own a place there, and so it distorts the property values, which affects the price of everything.

"This is your business in name only?" I asked.

"I do not understand name only."

"Meaning you don't run it."

"Goodness, no. My father vehdy much wants me to, but as you know, I'm going into music now."

"What kind of a business is it?"

"Let us call it a jobs program."

Well, that sounded nice.

We made our way through San Jose and into the Silicon Valley. Siri directed Kanish through a veritable sea of industrial parks with sprawling bright-green, perfectly manicured lawns in front of enormous Industrial buildings. It was precisely what I'd expected the Silicon Valley to look like.

Then, as if someone had flicked a switch, the scenery changed from sprawling to barren. From alive to dead. From beautiful to eerie. We now found ourselves smack-dab in the middle of an industrial ghost town, the likes of which I'd never seen. The grass was brown, the buildings shuttered and abandoned. And aside from the occasional burnt-out car, the expansive parking lots were empty. What the fuck?

We drove several miles through the unsettling dead zone before Siri announced, seemingly out of nowhere, that we had arrived. Arrived where exactly?

On the left, in the distance, was a massive warehouse. It was lined with loading docks designed for the back ends of tractor trailers to cozy up to. But there were no trucks to be found, and all of the metal roll-up doors were shut. Kanish made the trek across an expansive silver, faded parking lot, littered with divots and painted with the undersized parking spaces from another era. Only a lot designed in the '80s would be drawn like this.

Of course, small parking spaces were a direct result of the late-'70s oil crisis. I'll never forget those interminable lines for gas. I was just a young lad at the time, but old enough to remember sitting in the oppressively hot backseat of my mother's car as I sucked on fumes for hours. At the time, we were all told to get used to it. Oil was a finite commodity, and we were on our final drips of the stuff. This would be the new normal, we were told. As a result, the Japanese started pumping out smaller cars, which we bought up to replace our large American gas guzzlers. With smaller cars so popular, developers could install more spaces. I guess we found more oil, because fifteen years later SUVs became the new breed of gas guzzlers, and developers were forced to redraw the lines of their parking lots to accommodate the beasts.

Undersized spaces or not, parking wasn't going to be an issue in this lot. There wasn't a car in sight.

Kanish was attempting to read from scribbles on the back of the rental paperwork. They were written in Hindi, and I wasn't going to be of much help with that. He drove directly to the left corner of the warehouse, made the right turn along the significantly narrower side wall of the building, and then turned right once again to the back of the structure, where we saw our first signs of life. Cars. Five of them, all American.

The rear of the building was butted up against a greenbelt of high-powered electrical lines. The five cars were parked neatly against the warehouse adjacent to a set of opaquely tinted Industrial doors. On each side of the doors were two potted trees, and just past that was a makeshift patio with an assortment of planters, none of which matched, not in size nor color, most of them overflowing with cigarette butts. The whole place was absolutely littered with butts.

To the right of the double doors was a handicapped parking space with a sign.

RESERVED

KANISH KANISH

CEO

Kanish took his reserved spot, jumped out of the car, and looked at me expectantly. I accepted his invitation and followed him to the door, which buzzed as he pushed on it.

We were greeted immediately by a follically challenged Indian man in his late fifties, impeccably dressed in a double-breasted pin-striped suit. His name tag displayed his title: FOREMAN. Frankly, he looked more like hotel security. Whatever. As if in a trance, I walked right by him.

I can assure you, were I to have taken a month to write down a list of everything that might be held in a warehouse large enough to house two jumbo jets, the scene I'd witnessed wouldn't have made the list. It wouldn't have made anyone's list, for that matter. The gargantuan room was filled for as far as the eye could see with row after row of tightly connected desks. Upon each desk was a laptop computer. In front of each laptop an Indian—every one of them young and male.

There had to be a thousand young Indian men in that room. How the fuck did they get there in five cars?

I found myself wandering past corn rows of Indian workers, all of whom were typing furiously. The ticker-tack of plastic computer keys was nothing short of deafening. The uniformity of the room disconcerting. Occasionally an Indian worker would look up briefly, deadpan, without ever missing a keystroke. One Indian man smiled at me, and I took that as an invitation to look at his screen.

It was code. Computer code.

I was now half a football field from Kanish, who was shaking hands with the Foreman. Without warning, an industrial whistle blew, and the roller doors surrounding the structure began to raise. Between the whistle and the doors, it sounded as though a train were coming through. The Coders unceremoniously stopped their typing, got up from their chairs, and made their way to the exits, as did we.

There were throngs of Indians spilling off the back patio. They were speaking in Hindi as they smoked their cigarettes, many of them watching us in fascination as they chattered, others stealing momentary glances. Still others paid us no attention whatsoever.

"How the hell did all those Indian Coders get here?" I asked as I got into the passenger side of the Stingray.

"They came from India, of course."

"No shit, Kanish! There's five fucking cars for what has to be a thousand people."

"We bus them, of course."

"From where?"

"All will be understood soon. We have one more stop to make, and then we will be on our way."

The Foreman started up a blue Ford Fiesta and called out to Kanish in Hindi. We followed him in the Stingray, first across the vast parking lot, and then even deeper into this bizarre industrial wasteland somewhere in the middle of the Silicon Valley.

"You want to explain to me what the fuck that was? That room?" I snapped.

"Yes, my apologies. My father is vehdy distressed with the expenditures thus far, and he wanted to know what I was spending money on, and of course, I had to tell him that we were traveling. He is vehdy angry at you right now, let me tell you."

"That's wonderful news," I replied sarcastically.

"He is certain that we are lollygagging."

"Lollygagging?"

"It means to fuck around."

"I know what it means! I'm surprised *you* do."

"You discount my British education."

After what turned out to be a rather short jaunt around a sizable block, we drove up a private road leading to an abandoned school. The entrance of the school was tagged in big spray-paint letters: HOOVERVILLE. Kanish pointed to the tag and spoke sternly in Hindi to the Foreman, who instantly became apologetic. He even started bowing and shit.

The moment we entered the building, I was hit by the unmistakable stink of curry. Don't get me wrong. I love curry. But it still stinks. The Foreman pulled out a rather robust set of janitor's keys and opened the administrative offices. Kanish followed him. I made my way down the main hall.

I took a peek through the narrow panel of chicken-wire safety glass of the first classroom. It was filled with fifteen army-style cots, each with a duffle bag placed on top. The next classroom looked the same. And the next. My walk turned to a trot as I glanced into the rooms one after another, every former classroom a makeshift dorm.

The stench of curry was surely coming from the cafeteria, but I needed only to follow the cacophony of pans and the nonsensical chatter of female Hindi voices in order to find it. The large dining room was bustling with middle-aged Indian women in saris preparing food. A corpulent woman wearing oven mitts struggled mightily with an overfilled serving tray.

In retrospect, I probably should have been a bit more stealth, because the moment the woman saw me she dropped her tray with a spectacular splatter and began squealing a distress signal in full Hindi wail. This set off even more chatter and excitement. One of the women picked up a pan, another a serving spoon, and yet another a ladle. The three of them began to approach in a rather threatening manner. Fearing for my life, I hightailed it down the hall the same way I'd come, and nearly bit it on the final turn as I tripped awkwardly over a hard-shelled briefcase on the floor. Thankfully, Kanish caught me.

"It is time for us to go," Kanish said as he picked up the briefcase.

It was indeed. The sound of Sari-clad women armed with kitchen utensils was rising in intensity. Both Kanish and the Foreman looked at me in marked confusion.

"I think I startled the girls," I confessed.

The Foreman left us to take care of the angry mob of Hindu hens. We made our way out of the school.

The Bentley had finally caught up with us and was parked next to the Stingray. Sevaka, Annapurna, and the Dishwashing Sikh were there waiting patiently, as was their way. Kanish laid the briefcase in the boot of the Bentley and opened it to reveal many neat stacks of $100 bills, each wrapped with a purple $5,000 band.

"Nice, huh?" Kanish said. "A hundred k."

"I don't think you want to keep that money anywhere near the Medicine, mate."

Kanish stared at me momentarily, closed up the case, and, without saying a word, moved it over to the Stingray trunk.

"What the fuck kind of business are you running, exactly?" I asked.

"It's cheaper to bring Indians over here to code than to pay your American workers. It's a jobs program. The men work for a few months and then return home, and the cycle repeats."

"An Indian jobs program, you mean."

"Precisely."

"But they're obviously coding remotely. Why not just let them work from India?"

"Because the companies with whom we contract require some face time with their team."

"This is how Paneer made his billions?"

"Goodness, no. This is just one business out of many, many businesses. And yes, it was started by my father, but I am currently the majority share-holder, and listed as CEO. Admittedly, I'm nothing but a figurehead. But that does not mean I can't raid the petty cash!"

"That can't possibly be legal," I admonished.

"What can't possibly be legal?"

"None of it. Taking petty cash for personal use certainly isn't legal, and a warehouse storing that many people can't be legal."

"I am fully aware that I must return the petty cash—this will not be a problem. As to the warehouse, clearly, you have never been in a factory, and surely you've never been to one in India. And we aren't 'storing people,' as you say. It's a safe place to work and we have the full blessing and investigation of the local officials. There is proper ventilation and many exits, which are always unlocked. There are regular, mandatory breaks throughout the day. I can tell you, those Indian men would be fortunate to make two hundred rupees a day were it not for this kind of opportunity. That is the equivalent of three to four US dollars. This is what you wish for them? Poverty?"

It was true. I have never been in a factory, let alone to one in India. I suppose I couldn't get over the shock of it.

"And the school?"

"We bought the school when the city agreed to rezone it as a hotel. It's perfectly legitimate. It has electricity and plumbing. We installed the required number of bathrooms with many showers. We get inspections. The whole nine meters."

A seemingly endless procession of yellow school buses passed us on our way out, each bus filled to the brim with hungry Indian workers, all of whom waved excitedly at us as they chanted. *Kanish. Kanish. Kanish. Kanish.*

"So, then what's the $100K for?" I asked.

"Well, let me just say that sometimes Paneer gets quite angry, and he just cuts me off."

"He just cuts you off? Like one day you have billions, and the next you've got nothing?"

Kanish laughed as he fishtailed around another turn.

"I never have access to billions. Is that what you think?"

"What the hell do I know!"

"The hundred thousand allows us some freedom to operate without my father following the money trail. He will continue to pay for the Crown Royale Hotel and the staff. As for me, I must survive on my own for the moment."

Survive, indeed.

The sun was fully set by the time we reached Monterey. We rented another palatial Airbnb near Cannery Row—a place made famous by John Steinbeck in his book titled same. Kanish paid for the place in cash, of course.

"I vehdy much feel that it is my turn today to provide the lesson," Kanish said as he sparked up the Fatty.

"That would be good, because I have no idea what today's lesson should be."

"Are you ready?" he asked.

"Hit me."

"It is not wise to live in water and be an enemy of the crocodile."

"That's your lesson for me?"

"That is your lesson for me," replied Kanish.

As weird as that might seem, it was actually quite clever. Kanish could surely tell that I had been affected by the scene—by the Code Shack, as he called it. To him, it might have been perfectly acceptable. To me, it looked more like a sweatshop so that greedy Corporations didn't have to pay $70 an hour to American Coders.

"Now," Kanish continued. "Would you like to know my lesson for you?"

"So we're exchanging lessons now, and you're delivering them both? Sure, what's your lesson for me?"

"Learn the skills of accepting and forgiving and move on."

Child.

"You don't think that I accept you?"

"I believe you found the Code Shack unsettling because it's not what you're used to here. But my culture is different from yours."

I took a toke of the Fatty and pondered this for a moment.

"Okay, Kanish. Here's my lesson for you then. A leopard never changes his spots."

"What's this? What are you saying?"

I stood up and put my hand on Kanish's shoulder.

"I'm saying I absolve you of your sins, my friend."

I couldn't be disappointed in Kanish for being the product of his environment. As distressing as I found the mega–boiler room and the make-shift dormitory—as disillusioned as I was—from the relative standpoint of being Indian, there was nothing wrong with it. As Westernized as young Kanish is, the cultural divide between us is vast.

That said, at the end of the day, it isn't my job to fix the broader global economic issues of our time. The young Billionaire's Heir is in a far better position for that than I. My job is to teach young Kanish to Produce.

Work on that front begins tomorrow.

Mixerman

CHAPTER NINE

Nobody Beats the Rev

We had breakfast in Monterey, a beautiful and quaint upscale coastal town with remnants of an edge from another time. It's best known as the setting for John Steinbeck's popular book *Cannery Row*, a story set around the sardine-canning industry.

For much of the early twentieth century, fishermen pulled sardines out of Monterey Bay by the ton—a quarter million tons per year at the height of World War II. The idea that the Monterey Bay might one day run out of sardines was preposterous. That is, until it did. Now you see them, now you don't. By the 1950s, the local fishing industry summarily collapsed, destroying the livelihood of an entire town in the process. It was unsustainable.

This was a cautionary tale. A warning. That our resources are finite and require replenishing for purposes of sustainability. It's also a lesson we've yet to properly heed. The fish are back, I'm happy to say, but now we have other more pressing issues to deal with here in California. Like, we may be running out of water.

Years of drought have taken their toll on California's water reserves. The Sierra's snowpack is gone. Most of our aboveground reservoirs are now dry lake beds. And while it's true that we have one of the largest underground aquifers in the world running beneath the San Joaquin Valley, that water is currently being pulled out of it an alarming rate. Satellites allow us to track the rapid change in underground water mass. What has yet to be determined is exactly how much water is left.

To make matters worse, water shortages are not relegated to California. Groundwater is being depleted throughout the world. HBO's *Vice*—the best news program on television—recently reported that without significant changes, India likely has only fifteen years of underground water left. If that's true, we're in big trouble. There isn't a person on this planet that won't be affected by such a calamity.

Part of the problem is, there are large swaths of overpopulated India that do not have infrastructure for the removal of sewage. As a result, the rivers and reservoirs in those areas are noxious with human waste. An unsettling percentage of India's population is literally surrounded by human shit. Meanwhile, and much like California, the farmers there are also pulling groundwater at an unsustainable rate.

Scientists are now warning us that all the aquifers in the world could go dry one day. Meanwhile, the world's largest reserve of potable water is wasting away into the Arctic Ocean, yet we continue to do nothing about the problem. It's all related, of course—the ice melting and the water tables disappearing. Personally, I'm more concerned with running out of fresh water than I am with the effects of rising salt water.

We had two routes available to us for our return to Redondo. We could head inland and haul ass on the interstate through miles of monotonous farmland. Or, if we preferred a magnificent view painted by Buddha himself, we could take the winding coastal route above Big Sur. At times the road runs a thousand feet above the Pacific Ocean, and it has to be the most mind-meltingly majestic and awe-inspiring ride you can take. And so with the top down and the weather gorgeous, our path was clear—we took the coastal route.

Along with the spectacular views comes some danger, of course. Erosion is a part of daily life in California, and as a result, sometimes rocks submit to gravity. Sometimes an entire section of road falls into the ocean. Parts of Palos Verdes—the Peninsula that forms the natural southwest corner of Los Angeles Bay—fall into the water all the time. Just ask Billon-hair Donald Trump.

In 1999, Donald Trump rescued the Ocean Trails Golf Course from bankruptcy after the eighteenth hole slid from the edge of the Peninsula into the Pacific Ocean. Three hundred meters of fairway and the entire green—gone. And just a week before the course was set to open, too. Trump reportedly purchased the distressed property for a paltry $26 million—$100 million less than it cost to build the course.

The eighteenth hole was repaired at a cost of $20 million, making it the most expensive golf hole ever built. Frankly, I'm surprised Trump got off that cheap. This was a massive geotechnical project that required 1,250,000 cubic yards of earth mixed with other materials in order to promote stabilization. According to Trump, the eighteenth hole is precisely where he would want to be in the event of a California earthquake. That's where I would want him to be too. Personally, I'd rather be in a different State, but then, I lived through the Northridge tumbler, and so I have some concept of what a powerful quake feels like. I doubt Trump does.

Then there's Paseo Del Mar, another rim road located on the San Pedro side of the Peninsula. A twenty-five-foot portion of that road slid down the cliff in 2011. As a result, the pavement ends rather abruptly as you make your way along the peninsula to San Pedro. There is some talk of taking down the safety fences and rebuilding, but there's even more support for just giving up. The land is unstable. Not because of man, but regardless of him. They can build another road farther back, but it's still going to end up in the ocean in the foreseeable future. At what point is it not worth trying to maintain? Apparently, this point.

Kanish drove the Stingray with great aplomb around the dangerous hairpin turns on the top of Big Sur. Honestly, though, I could have walked faster. Somehow, we once again found ourselves behind a fucking Prius.

"Douchebag!" Kanish yelled in frustration.

Mile after mile we crawled behind this Prius-driving Douchebag. There was nowhere safe to pass along the serpentine stretch of coastal road, and it didn't matter how closely Kanish rode his ass—the Douchebag refused to pull over. As a result, I had time to come up with a Ditty, which I sang to Kanish the moment I'd perfected it.

> *Just another Douchebag driving in a Prius*
> *You drive so fucking slow, I know you see us*
> *If you'd pull over, that would free us*
> *Just another Douchebag driving in a Prius*

"I love it!" Kanish yelled. "My turn!

Kanish repeated my chorus back to me almost exactly as I had sung it to him.

"How the hell did you do that?" I asked.

"Do what?"

"Repeat my little song back perfectly like that?"

"I don't know. I learn things quickly. Is that unusual?"

"It's certainly impressive."

"We should make this song!" Kanish exclaimed.

"You mean record it?"

"Yes!"

"But it's nothing but a Ditty."

"A Ditty? What is this Ditty you speak of?"

"A Ditty is a short simple song."

"Ah yes! This is indeed a Ditty. Which we shall now turn into a hit song!"

Kanish and I began to sing the Ditty as loud as we could without actually screaming. There is no doubt the Douchebag in the Prius could hear us. I know because the passengers in the two cars behind us were now joining in on the serenade. It wasn't long before the entire mountain was in full chant, and the Douchebag really had no choice but to finally pull over.

"You see!" Kanish exclaimed. "It's a vehdy effective song! Those people behind us were singing it too. Not only could it be a hit, but perhaps it will also alter the driving habits of Prius drivers."

"We can only hope."

While the concept of shaming Douchebags driving in Priuses all over the world over was admirable, what I really wanted was a conversation with Kanish about his goals, particularly how they related to the Music Business. I'd been putting off this conversation for the better part of four days, and I wasn't to be sidetracked again.

"Let me ask you a question, Kanish"

"Please do. I love your questions! They are so revealing!"

"They are? Never mind. So, my question is this. What are your goals?"

"My goals," Kanish parroted.

"Yeah. What do you see yourself doing ten years from now?"

"I have no idea!" Kanish exclaimed excitedly, as if he were happy about this.

"You have no idea? Why are you here working with me? What's the plan?"

"Ah! Now I see where you're driving at. The plan is simple. To learn to record."

"Why do you want to learn to record?"

"So that I may make music."

"For what reason do you want to make music?"

"What do you mean, for what reason? To make moneeeey, of course! Why else would I make music?"

The way Kanish drew out the word *money*, he sounded like Kevin O'Leary, one of the "Billionaires" from the hit TV show *Shark Tank*. According to the Internet, Kevin O'Leary is really only a third of the way to his first billion, which certainly explains why he did the show. He could use the money, if not the notoriety. Fame, after all, is the ultimate aphrodisiac for money.

Kanish gave the wrong answer. You don't go into music for the money. You didn't when I was a lad, and you most certainly don't now. Of course, when I entered this industry you could actually make good money as a technician, particularly in the upper echelons of the business. That's why I moved to LA—for proximity to the big Artists and their big Labels. There was a time when some technicians—like mixers—could even command a percentage of the sales, often called points. These days, those kinds of agreements wouldn't be worth the paper they're written on. Without sales there are no points, and without the possibility of profit sharing, good luck ever retiring.

The investment necessary to build a proper commercial studio today is far beyond the prospects of any real profitability. All you can really hope to do is to break even for long enough that the real estate value allows you to profit. As a result, commercial studios have become the playthings of the pleasantly rich. Kanish was nowhere near pleasantly rich. He was filthy rich. As far as I'm concerned, filthy rich puts him in the Mogul's domain.

"There is no money in music, Kanish."

"That is a ridiculous notion! You don't know where to look!"

"Okay. You're right about that. Correction. There is no money in recording music anymore. It's just a job. You really aren't a candidate for a job. There will be a time in your life when you're making more interest in an hour than you could ever get paid recording music. You know what I mean?"

"I see . . . I should be a mixer!"

"Not a mixer either."

"I'm graduating to Producer already?"

"Well, maybe Producer, but really, I think we can set our sights just a bit higher."

"Tell me! What is higher than a Producer? I will set my sights as high as the farthest visible star!"

He could be such a fucking enthusiastic card.

"I think you should be a Mogul, Kanish. More specifically, a Music Mogul."

Kanish snapped his head and stared me down, which was brilliantly theatrical, but perilously dangerous, seeing as we were still teetering a thousand feet above the ocean. I reminded him to keep his eyes forward.

I'd given all of this plenty of thought, and the fact that he was already scheming on how to turn a little Ditty into a hit only bolstered my point. Kanish was meant to be a Mogul. He has the money, he has the interest, and he clearly has the hustle. If that doesn't describe a Mogul, I really don't know what does.

Of course, anyone who suggested to her childhood career counselor that she wanted to be a Mogul would surely be admonished on the spot. You can't just willy nilly make up jobs that don't exist. And besides, one doesn't set out to be a Mogul, one just is. It happens naturally. Over time. And while it's true that it's rare to achieve such Mogul status, given the circumstances, it was most certainly a goal worth pursuing.

Let's face it. Ultimately, with Paneer's blessing, Kanish could fund any music that caught his fancy. He could even put the same kind of monetary weight behind a track as that of the Major Labels, if he chose. All Kanish would need was just one of his father's $42 billion. Just one, and the kid would have to be considered a major player in the Music Business. After all, in the grand scheme of things, music isn't all that expensive to make and promote. It's the videos that cost a fortune.

"You really think I'm Mogul material?" Kanish asked sheepishly.

"I think if your interest is music, then you may as well skip all the other steps, and jump right into becoming a Music Mogul."

"What does a Music Mogul do?"

"A Music Mogul makes money making music, of course."

"But that's my goal."

"Precisely."

Kanish remained deep in thought as he drove down the 101 South, due east through the San Fernando Valley. The sun was scorching, and I couldn't wait to get over the mountain and into the basin on our way back to Redondo.

"So you don't think that I should learn to record and produce?" Kanish asked unsurely.

"Why would you? You can hire people to do that for you."

"What will I do, exactly?"

"You make it all happen."

"But how do I make it happen?"

"Well, the first thing you need to become a Mogul is to find a great song."

"I see."

"And then you find an Artist to perform the song."

"And what if the Artist wrote the song?" Kanish asked.

"Sometimes the song and Artist come together, sometimes you have to put them together. Either way, once you have your song and your Artist, you hire a Producer to record it. Then when you get the record back, you either shelve it and try again with another song and Artist, or you spend obscene sums of money to promote the shit out of the record until it's reached enough people to garner a reaction."

"It's that easy?" Kanish asked innocently.

"Sure it is!"

It's not even remotely that easy, and frankly, I felt like I was in high school the way I was explaining this. I don't care how much money you have—you can't spend your way to a hit on any old song. The track has to be catchy, relevant, and ultimately must invoke a widespread viral reaction. All promotion offers is the opportunity to reach enough people to get a reaction in the first place.

"I have made a decision," Kanish announced. "I would vehdy much like my first song as a Mogul to be the Douchebag Song."

"Dude, that song is kind of a joke, you know?"

"This is no joke, let me tell you. These drivers of Priuses can really be Douchebags."

I couldn't argue with that.

"Look, Kanish, It's not a song without a full lyric."

"This is not a problem. Besides, I am certain the Pharcyde will want to write their own rhymes."

"Oh my god."

"Oh my god what?"

"Oh my god, you think that we're going to get the Pharcyde to perform this Douchebag Song!"

"Why not?"

"You see? You're Music Mogul material. I should introduce you to Willy Show," I said half-jokingly.

Willy Show, the former Super Producer, is currently the president of Easter Island Records. I've made a number of records with and for him in a variety of capacities, and if anyone could explain Moguldom, it was Willy. Kanish was busting at the mere mention of him, and insisted—much like a spoiled child—that we go to him immediately. Still, I found the reaction somewhat endearing.

"I'll tell you what. Take the exit coming up, and we'll drop by Mel Odious Sound and see if Willy is in.

Mel Odious Sound is a commercial multi-room recording complex a block from the ocean in Santa Monica. The complex is owned by a Silicon Valley quarter-Billionaire named Mel (of all things). I've never met Mel, and don't expect that I ever will, as I don't believe he's ever there. Even if he were, I'd really only worked at the studio complex once, and that was with Willy Show himself.

Countless hits have been recorded at Mel Odious Sound over the years. But Mel, much like everyone else, seems to have far more sales awards for past successes than for current ones. The complex has several large recording and mix rooms, and there are also a number of production rooms, which are really nothing more than suites much like the one in my garage. It's just that having a suite in a high-end multi-room complex offers considerably more prestige than a garage. My good friend Rev has a room there, one that I've been eyeing for quite some time. Prestige has value, after all.

Kanish and I pulled up to Mel Odious Sound, and just as we'd relinquished the Stingray to the valet, a voice came from above. It was the Rev himself, in all of his corpulence, catching the ocean breeze as he smoked a cigarette on the balcony of his production room.

"Mixerman!" the Rev called out.

"Hey, Rev! I was just checking to see if Willy Show was here."

"I don't think he's here today."

"Typical."

"Come on up!"

The historic building is enormous and about as old a structure as you'll find in LA. The interior decorating in the joint was, kitschy, oversized, egotistical, and had to cost more than the acoustical build-outs in some of the rooms. The fifteen-foot walls were adorned from floor to ceiling with Gold and Platinum records dating back to the '60s. Frankly, the place looked more like a Hard Rock Cafe than a studio.

Multi-room complexes like this used to bustle with musicians and Producers, but these days they seem to cater more to the TV executive. That's purely for survival. I'm sure Mel would have preferred that it remain a music facility. But at the end of the day, rich people won't tolerate losing money, even from their hobbies.

The receptionist confirmed that Willy did indeed have a session, but that he wasn't expected. This was no surprise, as he didn't get the name Willy Show for nothing. So I took Kanish up to see the Rev instead, who was waiting for us at the top of the dramatic, *Gone with the Wind* staircase.

The Rev is an icon in the Music Business. He's also one of the most likable guys you'll ever meet, and has a wonderfully skewed way of viewing the world, but I suppose that would describe most Producers.

It didn't take long for the Rev's small talk to morph into full-bore venting. The grind of the business was getting him down, but this was nothing new, or isolated. That's just the way things are these days. Kanish began to show signs of boredom, and the Rev, being a good host, engaged the lad.

"I think I saw Lil Wayne walking through here with a watch just like that. Are you an Artist? A Producer?" the Rev inquired.

"Kanish is my Assistant," I interjected.

"Yes, yes, yes," Kanish agreed. "And Mixerman is going to make me a Music Mogul!"

Said like that, it seemed ridiculous.

"A Music Mogul!" The Rev beamed in amusement. "That's very interesting. So, how does one become a Music Mogul?"

"You find a vehdy good song and Artist and then you promote the living shit out of them, of course! Is this some sort of test? I'm familiar with your work. Surely you know all of this already."

"You know my work?" the Rev replied with interest.

"But of course. You are my best friend's favorite Producer!"

"I am! Well, that's nice to know. Isn't that nice, Mixerman? So, have you found an Artist yet?"

"As of this moment, I have only the song. I am currently looking for a rapper to perform it."

"Well, I can't help you there, I'm afraid," Rev said resignedly. "Have you seen any of the rooms yet?"

"I have not! Please! Take me there!"

I'm sure that Kanish would have preferred a personal tour by the Rev, who instead called down to reception and summoned one of the Interns to take him around the place.

"Show him Studio X for sure," the Rev instructed the Intern.

The moment Kanish left, the Rev pulled me toward him, as if Kanish had superhuman hearing or something.

"You know, that watch costs nearly as much as that Stingray he's driving. I smell money. What gives? He's a Trust Funder, isn't he? Are you fucking kidding me? Holy shit, you got yourself some Vanity fucking Trust-Funder record. And what the fuck is that Music Mogul shit? That's not even a thing!"

"Sure it is."

"You and I both know that the only reason that might be a thing is because this guy is loaded. So, what gives? You gonna get this kid to pay mid-aught money for all your little pet projects? Or are you just gonna make his Vanity album over the course of years for obscene money? Don't bullshit the Rev, now."

Vanity albums are self-funded albums that have no chance of ever being heard. Typically, they are funded by someone who is either rich, famous, or both. While it's true that just about every LA Producer has been hired to make at least one Vanity album, they are not the kind of projects you necessarily admit to. They merely pay the bills, and within the industry itself, there is a stigma attached to Vanity albums—one that tells all of your peers that you've just about given up on life in general—an intolerable accusation, if there ever was one.

"He's a Billionaire's Heir!" I scolded. "And I'm not making his Vanity album, thank you very much. Who the fuck makes albums anymore, anyway?"

"It's okay, dude. Vanity albums are good work if you can get it. I don't judge you."

"Seriously, he's here as my Assistant."

The Rev sparked up another smoke and exhaled out the balcony door.

"So, how much do you pay your Assistant then?"

"That's the funny part. He's paying me."

"He's paying you! Son of a bitch!"

I don't believe I displayed it openly, but I cringed as I said it. Something about an Assistant paying me sounded so fucking wrong. And although on the surface the Rev's line of interrogation may have seemed rather forward, it's one that I should have expected. It's also probably one I should have answered a bit less truthfully. The fact of the matter is, the Rev got my Goad. How dare he accuse me of making a Vanity album? Who the hell did he think he was?

"A Billionaire's Heir," the Rev pondered. "That's fucking awesome. Where do I sign up for that shit?"

"I guess you'll just have to find your own," I quipped.

The Rev took a final drag from yet another butt and then doused it in an overflowing ashtray. He was clearly deep in thought, perhaps even scheming.

Fuck me! Why the hell did I tell the Rev? I realize you wouldn't think it to read this—the way he managed to herd me into the admission that my Assistant was a Billionaire's Heir and all. Really, I like the Rev, but I don't actually know him all that well. I don't even really know what records he's worked on, other than one, and I hate it, so why should I know about any of the others? For whatever reason, the Rev just feels comfortable whining in brutal honestly just how shitty life is, and somehow he expects me to be equally forthcoming. As if my Billionaire's Heir is anyone else's business.

"Do me a favor, Rev, and keep that under your hat, willya? I don't actually want it getting out, you know? I mean, what would people think about me running around with my very own Billionaire's Heir?"

"Of course, Mix. Come on. Who am I going to tell?"

"Thanks, man, I can't tell you what a relief that is."

"So, I take it he's funding your projects then?" the Rev asked.

"Well, it looks like he might be funding a song that I came up with. It's really just a Ditty, though."

"Son of a bitch! You just offer up a Ditty and he wants to fund it like it's a song? I gotta get me one of them Billionaires' Heirs."

Kanish returned exuberant from his studio tour.

"This place is fantastic!" Kanish exploded. "I must work here!"

"Yeah, you should," the Rev encouraged. "Let's listen to some music, shall we?"

Oh my god! The phrase "let's listen to some music" is as old as suggesting to a girl in college, "Let's study in my room." Neither is an innocent invitation to be taken at face value, and both involve ulterior motives. Quite simply, "Let's listen to some music" was code for "Fund my project!" And frankly, it's dirty pool. I expected more from the Rev—what with him edging in on my action like that. This was my Billionheir, and everyone else could fuck off.

"We'll have to take a raincheck on that, mate. We're pretty road worn, and it's time for us to be heading home."

"Sure, sure. Of course! Listen, kid, I know how hard it is to be new in town. If you ever want to come up and visit, I'll play you some music. You know?"

"Oh, I would vehdy much like that!" Kanish exclaimed.

And with that heartwarming invitation, I grabbed Kanish and we exited stage left. I was just glad that he followed my lead. Had Kanish been in the mood to listen to Rev's music, we would have surely been there for hours.

Kanish and I smoked our late-night Fatty on the rear deck. It was nice to be home.

"Perhaps tomorrow we'll hear back from Willy," Kanish said.

"We didn't even leave him a message."

"I'm certain the Rev will tell him. He has a vehdy big mouth, don't you know? Now, tell me. What is today's lesson?"

"A slip of the tongue cannot be recalled."

#oops

Mixerman

CHAPTER TEN

Show Me the Money!

Since the days of piano rolls, the Music Business has been riddled with unscrupulous charlatans—the sharks of the sharks—for whom even a relatively shrewd investor is nothing more than chum. It's even worse than ever, as the lack of sales has put legit Producers into a veritable feeding frenzy for any project that's funded. It's gotten to the point that it's almost a waste of time to discuss music before determining the budget, since nine times out of ten there isn't enough money to fund the first day of recording anyway. Optimism runs amok and delusion abounds in this industry at the moment. Far more so than usual.

I bring this all to your attention to explain my seemingly paranoid freakout at the prospect of Rev homing in on my Billionheir. Surely, Kanish could make his own determinations as an investor. But this is the Music Business, after all, and I feel some responsibility for the lad. It's not that he can't fend for himself. Clearly he can. But without a firm understanding of how the money flows, investing in music is nothing short of foolhardy— more so now than ever. Regardless of how shrewd young Kanish proves to be, at this particular juncture he is under my tutelage, and I won't allow him to make bad investments—and I say that as someone who absolutely abhors the word *tutelage*.

I don't want to get too bogged down with all of the complexities of how people get paid in the Music Business, partly because it's arcane, and mostly because it's in an absolute state of flux given the rapid changes in technology. I have literally spent hours researching how Streaming services like Spotify, Pandora, and YouTube pay Independent Artists and Songwriters, and I can tell you that it's nearly impossible to decipher, and is completely dependent on their revenues. How nice for them. And here I have to operate with risk.

Setting Streaming aside for the moment, there are really only three major revenue flows in the Music Business—sales, Publishing, and touring. And while it's true that Streaming sites pay out some Mechanical Royalties that would fall under the umbrella of sales, they are currently insufficient to rely upon. Given the massive overhead, touring is also an unreliable profit center. That leaves but one viable place to earn money in music. Publishing.

Publishing is the writer's share, and it's the only share worth discussing at the moment. It's where the big money is in this business, which is why the Major Labels have pretty much stopped fucking around with anything other than pop Artists. Bands require patience, effort, and time, and once they break, there is no guarantee the band can follow up their success with another hit song. And so it makes far more sense for a Label to align with Songwriter Producers and then swap out Singers like fashion plates. Make no mistake, these are indeed Singers and not Artists. The difference? A Singer delivers a message. An Artist has something to say.

Now, there are two halves to Publishing. There's the Songwriter's half, and the Publisher's half. The Songwriter can surely administer her own Publishing, and thereby maintain 100 percent ownership of her song. But there are a number of advantages to signing with a Publishing company. For starters, a Publisher can help a Songwriter get her songs placed with Major-Label Artists. That alone can make a Publisher worthwhile, but that's not the only advantage. There's also licensing, which can be quite profitable. Especially if you're the Beatles.

When a large portion of the Beatles' catalog went on the market in 1985, Michael Jackson outbid Paul McCartney and snapped it up for $47 million, making Jackson a 50 percent stakeholder in most of McCartney's early songs. That means Michael Jackson's Publishing company was retaining half the total Publishing revenues, while McCartney and the Lennon estate would split the other half between them. Just as an aside, some people estimate the catalog to be worth well over a billion dollars today. Given the current state of things, I'm dubious.

In order for a song to be heard in a television show or a movie, the Publisher negotiates what's called a licensing fee. In the case of the Beatles, that can be quite hefty, which is why you rarely hear their songs in movies or on television. The Beatles' catalog is often considered prohibitive, even for Studios willing to risk hundreds of millions of dollars at a time. Then there's the television networks, who prefer to take advantage of all the desperate

Independent Artists these days by licensing their songs for as little as $500 in total. And that's for a hit show that reaches millions of viewers and might even be syndicated. So why would Songwriters accept such a shitty one-sided deal? Exposure.

When it comes to pop music, the Songwriter Producer makes the most sense for everyone involved. For starters, a Songwriter can justify making a record speculatively because there's a huge potential payoff should the song become a hit. The Labels prefer this arrangement because they get to hear the produced track before their Singer even performs it. And the Singer loves to work with the Songwriter Producer because she can be involved (even if just a little), as a cowriter. For a Singer, a cowriter credit is as good as gold.

Given this, an established Singer—that is to say, one who might be considered a Superstar—could easily command half the writing credit (if not more) without contributing anything of substance beyond her vocal performance. Why? Because the Superstar can nearly guarantee the song will be a hit just by singing the fucking thing. One hundred percent of nothing is nothing. Fifty percent of a shitload is half a shitload. And a hit begets more hits.

Meanwhile, Independent bands and Singer-Songwriters who write their own material are often unwilling to even discuss paying a Producer's back end out of their Publishing, despite the fact that they rarely have a budget worth a damn. So, let's see if I've got this straight. You want me to Produce you for what amounts to nothing more than a stipend as you offer me no real opportunity to profit-share should you succeed from my efforts? Kindly fuck off.

As a result, many bands and Songwriter Artists are choosing to Produce themselves. In fact, it seems as though everyone and his sister refers to themselves as a Producer. Recordists are Producers. Musicians are Producers. Singers are Producers. Artists are Producers. Even the damn Intern is a Producer. Which is kind of strange when you think about it. Why would anyone and everyone want stake claim to a title that clearly no longer has any real value?

Along with pop music, there are really only two other genres within which it currently makes any sense for someone like me to Produce—EDM (electronic dance music) and hip-hop. The Producer position in those genres is paid as a Songwriter because the track is considered half the song.

Which makes me wonder, why the hell should I work with Artists making anything other than pop, EDM, or hip-hop? Those are the only genres in which I can currently profit as a Producer, and that's because they include a stake in the Songwriting.

I'm not sure why I thought it would be a good idea to bring Kanish to Mel Odious Sound yesterday. Bringing a Billionheir to a large recording complex full of Producers is like opening a bag of chips at a seagull convention. It wouldn't be long before every Producer within earshot swooped in to aggressively pitch his latest and greatest pet project, most of which would likely prove unprofitable.

Rev is obviously going to pitch a project, and it very well may be something amazing. But as I've pointed out, in order for Kanish to make a profit, he would have to pick up half the Publishing—a non-starter for the Rev. He's not a Songwriting Producer, so he likely doesn't have a sufficient portion of the Publishing to share. And even if he did, no seasoned Producer is going to give half of their equity in a song in order to basically secure a small loan from an outside investor. There's no upside.

For starters, Kanish has no channels of Distribution beyond Streaming, which is already available to anyone and everyone who wants it, and which is currently only profitable for the Major Labels and the stockholders of the Streaming services themselves. Everyone else is getting screwed. And please don't quote me the Douchebag Big Tech Billionaires running big Streaming Corporations. They are literally lining their pockets with the would-be earnings of Artists and Songwriters alike. What they claim as fair is anything but.

Frankly, I don't think we should be comfortable with Spotify taking a 30 percent margin off the top, and then disbursing the Tiger's Share of the remaining 70 percent to the Major Labels who have already negotiated top dollar for access to their catalog. This has resulted in nothing but some remaining scraps trickling down to the tens of thousands of Independent Artists out there who just want to make a living. You can't make a living off scraps, or even a trickle, for that matter.

Mark my words, we are currently witnessing the greatest heist in the annals of the Music Business, and that's saying something given its history. Can you say Napster?

Stunningly, the only place that Songwriters can make sufficient Performance Royalties is radio—a medium that is coming up on its hundred-year anniversary. To make matters worse, the Major Distributors still have radio all locked up, and without airplay, there's no hit. So even now, more than twenty years into the Internet revolution, the odds of breaking through the artistic cacophony without Major-Label Distribution are impossibly low. So much for the Internet leveling the playing field.

At this point, only Congress can solve the problem. And despite the fact that Streaming has been around since the mid-aughts, Congress has done nothing to deal with the issue. Why? Because it's far cheaper for Big Tech to line the pockets of lobbyists and fund the campaigns of politicians who gladly ignore the issue than it is to pay Artists and Songwriters a fair rate for their work, my friends.

Same is it ever was.

Just so I'm clear, there is a debate to be had as to how much Song-writers and Artists should be paid for Streaming. A radio Spin can reach millions. A Stream rarely reaches more than a few listeners. Clearly, a new method of calculation is required. But that doesn't mean that we should just sit by as the Big Tech Douchebags rob an entire generation of royalties all so they can sell their Streaming Corporation for billions down the line. I mean, that *is* the end game, after all. At which point, profit for the new majority stockholder will be all but impossible. How will anyone get paid then?

Annapurna cleared our dinner plates from the table and the Dish-washing Sikh went straight to work cleaning up the kitchen. Most of the day was spent resting from our extensive road trip. Normally, I'd have clothes to wash and errands to run, but when you have a full staff, these sorts of things are taken care of for you. Which left me plenty of time to consider Kanish's harebrained scheme.

While Kanish's idea to pitch the Pharcyde on a Ditty that I currently own 100 percent of the Publishing on was most certainly an interesting proposal, I found a number of problems with the plan. For starters, each member of the Pharcyde—Fatlip, Slimkid3 (pronounced *Slimkid Tre*), Romye, and Imani—is surely locked into deals with Labels and Publishing companies. Just getting them to perform the Song would require multiple permissions and clearances. Further problematic, the Pharcyde would rightly want half the overall Publishing for themselves. I'm certainly not opposed to giving up half the Publishing, but let's face it, that would get halved again upon landing a Distributor. Which might all be worthwhile, but it does significantly dilute the shares.

Then there's the word *Douchebag*—a term generally used by white boys from Jersey, not black guys ostensibly from the Hood. Even if the Pharcyde were comfortable featuring the word in their rap, I highly doubt that Douchebags driving in Priuses is a Hood sort of problem.

Logistics could also prove problematic. In my experience, working with the Pharcyde can be similar to herding butterflies. But then, they probably still think of me as the wide-eyed ponytailed kid who worked for the studio. Neither characterization would be fair to make this many years later.

Kanish and I retired to the side deck to enjoy our usual late-night Fatty.

"I've been thinking about it," I said. "Let's make the Douchebag Song."

"You mean you will call the Pharcyde?" Kanish yelled enthusiastically.

"Maybe. I mean, we can certainly try, but I'll warn you now, it could be prohibitively expensive to even attempt to get involved with them. The lawyers' bills alone—"

"This is wonderful news!" Kanish interrupted.

I'm not sure how "prohibitively expensive" was wonderful news, but then, I was talking to a Billionaire's Heir.

"We also need a Plan B," I said.

"Yes, yes, yes, a Plan B. I love it. Tell me it!"

"Well, if we can't get the Pharcyde, or even part of the Pharcyde, I think we should find a young, talented, up-and-coming rapper and break off a piece of the Publishing for his rap. Here's the bottom line. You've got $100K cash at the moment. Actually, a bit less at this point. "

"Ninety K, but you act as if I cannot get more money."

"Wait. I thought you were cut off."

"That is temporary, let me tell you. All that is required is for you to say the right things to my father."

"Kanish, am I supposed to call your father?"

"You do not call Paneer. Paneer calls you."

"Ah. Okay. Well, let's deal with the capital you have available now. Since we're only cutting one song, even bringing in the Pharcyde, $90K is surely plenty of money to get the product made. But it's definitely not enough money to garner radio play, and as an Independent entity, Streaming doesn't pay out enough to us for us to parlay a profit. So we're going to need Distribution."

"Distribution?"

"That's right. We're going to need a Major Label involved to make this profitable. The good news is that if the Pharcyde is attached, it may be easier to attract a Distributor."

Kanish and I spent the next while discussing the Music Business, in particular the flow of money. It was a crash course, which included the history along with the current realities. I'm happy to report that Kanish understood the basics, which is what I would expect. I mean, if a Billionaire's Heir can't follow the money, who can? That said, I still had concerns.

"About the Rev and his offer to play you some music," I said.

"You don't need to worry, you know."

"I don't?"

"You are my Guru. I'm not going to just hand out money for projects such as this without the counsel of my Guru."

"That's good to know," I replied.

I couldn't have been prouder of young Kanish than I was at that moment.

"Now, tell me!" Kanish goaded. "What is today's lesson?"

I'm not sure what he thought the past two hours were, but Kanish expected something a bit pithier, I suppose. Even at this early stage in our time together, I'd read so many Buddhist and Hindu proverbs that they were practically spilling out of my ears. And while I probably could have come up with something better, this one happened to be on the tip of my brain and seemed entirely appropriate.

"If the mind be fixed on the acquirement of any object, that object will be attained."

"Excellent! It shall be done!" Kanish replied.

I don't doubt it for a second.

Mixerman

CHAPTER ELEVEN

WAKE UP CALLING

Early-morning calls suck in general, but they're especially sucky when they come from irate Billionaires. I suppose most of you will just have to take my word on that.

"Mr. Mix! Mr. Mix! Wake up! It is Paneer on the Skype. He must speak to you urgently!"

As I'm sure you can imagine, I wasn't very happy to be woken up at all, least of all by the pounding at my bedroom door—and I do mean pounding. It wasn't tapping, or knocking, poking, scraping, scratching, or pecking. It wasn't clawing, rapping, patting, flicking, or, god forbid, stroking. There was no attempt to gently get my attention so that I might fade softly from blissful dream state to full consciousness. No, this was fucking pounding through and through.

What the fuck! Did something happen to Kanish between two and four in the morning?

Thankfully, it was Sevaka at my door, as I was buck naked, and I'm not sure Annapurna would have survived the shock given the height differential, among other things. Sevaka was holding his iPhone 6 with an angry Paneer on the Skype. Of course, Paneer always looked angry to me. You'd think having $42 billion would tend to put him in a better mood. Just saying.

"Hold the fuck on!" I yelled as I slammed the door.

I immediately picked my skivvies up off the floor and put them on, opened the door again, and grabbed Paneer out of Sevaka's hand.

"What the hell, Paneer?"

"If you expect me to apologize for waking you after you have been screwing me so much, you are vehdy, vehdy mistaken."

"Whoa, wait a second. Screwing you? How the hell am I screwing you?"

"You are taking my son Kanish for a ride. Literally and figuratively, both. You gallivant all over California when you are being paid to teach him! Tell me, how is traveling learning?"

"How is it not?" I replied.

You know, there is a definitive culture shock that comes with moving to California, and although that shock was surely softened for young Kanish—what with the presence of his cook, his driver, and his Dishwashing Sikh, and let us not forget his Guru—I still needed the kid to assimilate. That said, it was useless debating this point with Paneer. The way I figured it, he just wanted to push me around a little bit. Apparently, he wasn't done.

"I would ask you," Paneer continued, "do you realize how much you have spent on this trip? I get the bills, and I look at them vehdy, vehdy closely, don't you know. Kanish is my only child, and I will not have you taking advantage."

"Really?" I mused. "You actually look at the bills? So how much did we spend?"

I'd been wondering this for quite some time now. Between the Stingray rental, the gas for two cars over thousands of miles at $4 per gallon, hotels, Airbnbs, and meals for five people three times a day, not to mention the entire floor of the Crown Royale Hotel (oops, just mentioned it), the burn rate on this session had to be rather impressive.

"You are asking me how much you spent? You should know how much you spent!"

"No, I shouldn't."

"Of course you should! You are in charge!"

"Okay, first of all, Paneer, your son is an adult, so I don't actually have any control over what he does. I can only guide him."

"How dare you speak back to me!"

"How dare you speak back to me!" I parroted.

In retrospect, I may have been a bit bold talking to Paneer in this manner. Enduring an occasional outburst was going to be part of the gig and I understood this going in. I suppose given my relationship with Kanish, I wasn't feeling particularly vulnerable. The way I figured it, even if Paneer were to fuck me over, Kanish would certainly meet his father's contractual obligation. Of course, at the moment, Kanish was cut off.

Honestly, my goal wasn't to get into it with Paneer, but rather to shock him long enough that I could explain some things, and it seems the tactic worked. Paneer was visibly taken aback and clearly didn't know how to react. Frankly, if I hadn't been operating on a total of two hours sleep, I might not have been quite so aggressive, but as it turns out, I did manage to get his fucking attention.

"Paneer, I need you to listen to me for a moment. You have an incredibly gifted son, who I really like, by the way, and who wants to learn how to produce records. The best way for me to teach Kanish how to produce is on music that he likes. I already know what I like. We know what you like. He needs to figure out what he likes. Otherwise, he'll fail. Okay? So, the first step is to find a project the kid can really sink his teeth into, you know what I mean?"

"What is this? I do not know what you mean! What is this sinking of teeth?

"In other words, you need to let go a little."

"Let go? You make no sense. How do I let go with sinking teeth? Explain yourself!"

I'm not sure why I said it, or where the hell it came from exactly, but at that particular moment, I felt it best to talk in proverbs.

"Knowledge can only be got in one way, the way of experience; there is no other way to know."

This was a particularly potent one because it came from Swami Vivekananda, an influential Hindu spiritual leader at the turn of the twentieth century. Most of the proverbs that I've memorized come from Buddha himself, although I must admit, some of them are likely made up by unenlightened idiots on the Internet. The point is that I managed to smack Paneer square in the nose with some straight-up Hindu wisdom from the swami himself.

"Ridiculous!" Paneer exclaimed. "I told you this exact thing the first day I spoke to you!"

I knew I'd heard it somewhere before. Fortunately, I had another one ready to go.

"Fine," I said. "You cannot travel the path until you have become the path itself."

"What is this?" Paneer scolded. "You're speaking to me in Hindu Proverbs?"

Kanish quietly entered my room and took a seat in my favorite red wing-back chair. The whole fucking house was up now, which is what happens when your driver nearly knocks down your door. Not that I could be mad at Sevaka about it. He worked for Paneer, so he was just doing what was expected of him. Annapurna was kind enough to bring me some coffee. It was like a party in my bedroom. Oh, joy!

"You insult me!" Paneer yelled.

"No. I don't insult you. I speak truth," I replied in my best broken American.

"What is it that you tell me? That I should trust you?"

"That would be a good start. I mean, you only gave me twenty-five percent of the money up front, so I'm pretty much trusting you, aren't I?"

None of this seemed to make an impression on Paneer, as evidenced by his rather blatant threat.

"Let me make this vehdy, vehdy clear for you, Mister Mixerman. You have two weeks to show me some results or I will pull the plug on your gravy train!"

And with that, Paneer hung up the Skype. I handed Sevaka his iPhone and he left with Annapurna. Kanish was visibly upset.

"I am so vehdy, vehdy sorry about that. No one deserves Paneer's ire."

"Don't worry about it, Kanish. I can take it."

"But what will we send him? He is expecting to hear Bollywood music."

"Maybe we can just send him some Hollywood music and pretend it was a misunderstanding."

"You are not helping matters."

Between only two hours' sleep and Paneer's vibe-sucking ways, it took us some time to get going today. To make matters worse, I was still recovering from our road trip. We were also running low on Medicine, so we organized a trip to the Dispensary, where I picked up another ounce of the stuff.

Kanish was quite down at the prospect of losing his Mogul Internship so early in our time together. As such, he was pressing me to reach out to the Pharcyde. Time was of the essence, as far as Kanish was concerned, but there really was no point in approaching the Pharcyde about the Douchebag Song without a track to play them. Programming the production was the first step.

That afternoon, I began to muck around with some beats, if for no other reason than to come up with a direction for the song. Kanish, however, was injecting his opinion a bit too readily and was giving me no room to maneuver. I'm not sure why I was bothering anyway. The first step in any

Moguldom is to learn that you can hire others to do the grunt work for you. I felt it best to lead by example.

"Here. You program the beat, then," I said. And I took my rightful place, horizontal on the back couch.

I was exhausted from only two hours' sleep and was in desperate need of a nap. I was also feeling a bit news-deprived after our trip. So I plugged my earbuds into my iPad and streamed my favorite news commentator—Rochelle Meadows.

@RMeadows: "We have a big show for you today, lots of stuff to tell you about, but first . . . this is Senator Crou d'Etat, and as you probably know, he is running for president. He announced that just last week, and since that time—since Senator Crou d'Etat announced his bid last week for president of the United States—there has been some question as to whether he could raise enough money to mount a credible run. I'll spare you the dramatic pause. As it turns out, the answer to that question is, yes.

"Now, on your screen is a man, a very wealthy man, who you may or may not recognize. And you may not have ever heard of him before—that is, unless you're in politics. Then you definitely know this man. His name is Rodney Cursor.

"According to *Forbes* magazine, Rodney Cursor is a Billionaire, a ten-times-over Billionaire, and he has pledged his support for Senator Crou d'Etat in the past, but has yet to make an official endorsement, which usually comes in the form of a donation. Mr. Cursor has stated on numerous occasions that he believes in Senator Crou d'Etat's desire to, quote, 'permanently shut down the US government.' Which makes one wonder exactly what the Senator would be in charge of should he win the presidency. But hey, at least he's standing on principle, right?

"Today, Billionaire Rodney Cursor has now reportedly put his money where his mouth is. More than reportedly, actually. According to Rod Cursor himself, he has donated $50 million to the Crou d'Etat friendly Super-PAC Citizens for Shutting Down America. Now that's an endorsement!"

Next thing I knew, I was in the front car of an old wooden roller coaster, clinkety-clunking my way up the first big climb. Senator Crou d'Etat, of all people, was sitting next to me.

"So, what are you running for?" the Senator asked.

"Are you talking to me?"

"Do you see anyone else on this roller coaster?"

"You realize I think you're a total Douchebag, right?"

"If half the people don't hate you, you're doing something wrong. You know that. So what are you running for?"

"Running for? Do you mean like running for office?"

"That's right."

"I'm not qualified to run for anything."

"Sure you are! There's only one qualification, and it begins with an *m*. What is it?"

"Making no sense?" I quipped.

"Come on, now. Think about it. An *m*."

"Mixerman?"

"Money! You already have your own Billionaire. Well, in your case, a Billionheir, as in the Heir of a Billionaire, but that's close enough to the real thing. The point is, my friend, you're way ahead of the game."

"But aren't we supposed to be hiding the fact that we have Billionaires?"

"It depends on what you're trying to achieve. If you want everyone to know that you're a force to be reckoned with, then you flaunt your Billionaire."

"Huh. You think I should flaunt my Billionheir?" I asked.

"You already did when you told Bigmouth Rev all about him. And asking the Rev to keep it under his hat, that was a nice touch. You may as well have paid him to blab it everywhere."

"But I really don't want anyone to know I have a Billionheir."

"Then you'd better get yourself a Prius, my friend. The Bentley is a dead giveaway. Besides, the cat is out of the bag, and once a cat is out of the bag, it's just about impossible to get it back in."

"Why is that?" I asked innocently.

"Because you've lost control of the situation, of course."

The Senator and I were still in the front roller-coaster car as we ascended, and now the Pharcyde were magically in the two cars behind us, and they were chanting the chorus of the Douchebag Song, although it was better than before. It wasn't the lame little poem or Ditty it had been. The Song had blossomed into something much hipper. It was more Pharcyde-like in its nature. What's more, the Pharcyde were rapping to the most compelling track I'd ever heard—but then, those always come when I'm dreaming, it seems.

"What a lovely song that is," Senator Crou d'Etat said. "Such an excellent message."

"And what message is that?" I asked.

"That the tree-hugging doomsayers are always getting in the way of good old American progress, of course. Do you realize how many jobs there would be if we'd just use more oil?"

"Are you high?" I asked incredulously.

The roller coaster made its final clink at the precipice of the steep hill, and entered into its first big descent. Fatlip inexplicably began screaming my name.

"Mixie! Mixie! You forgot your seat belt!"

As the roller coaster maintained its downward trajectory, I was ejected out of the car, almost gracefully. For a moment, it was as if I could float like a feather. Without warning, and much like a cartoon character, I began to plummet.

The g-forces from the fall woke me just in time to experience the painful jolt of the floor. Kanish was standing over me. Ebullient.

"Mixie! Mixie!" Kanish yelled. "It's Willy Show! It says it right here on your phone!"

"It's dark out," I said. "How long was I out?"

"A long time. What are you waiting for? Answer it!"

I was far too groggy to be accepting phone calls, but much as it is with Paneer, you don't reach Willy, he reaches you. Half asleep or not, I was taking his call.

"Hey Willy!" I exclaimed with feigned energy.

"Mixerman!" Willy said in his highbrow British accent. "Did I wake you?"

"Not at all. My Assistant did that."

"Quite right. Bloody well right. So sorry to interrupt your nap time."

I was thankful for the small talk, because I was completely fucking out of it. Can't people call me when I'm awake? I switched the phone to speaker.

"I heard you came by to visit me the other day," Willy said. "I'd love to see you. Why don't you meet me in my room at Mel Odious Sound tomorrow? Say two?"

Kanish immediately began to jump up and down and around in circles like he was a human fucking pogo stick.

"Yeah, yeah. Two tomorrow is good," I replied with one finger pressed against my ear in order to drown out the commotion.

"Great. And bring your friend. The Rev mentioned him. What's his name?"

"Kanish," I said.

"Yes. Kanish. "Of the New Delhi Kanishes, no doubt. You know I love Knishes?"

"Most people do."

"Excellent. I'll see you both tomorrow then."

Kanish was still circling like a pogo stick and began chanting a Ditty of his own.

"We have a meeting with Willy Show! We have a meeting with Willy Show! Bring your friend! Bring your friend! We have a meeting with Willy Show! He loves Knishes! Willy loves Knishes! We have a meeting with Willy Show!"

The fact that Willy had called me back to invite me to the studio was not all that remarkable. But to invite Kanish? Specifically? Why the fuck would he be so interested in meeting my Assistant? Yes, yes, of course, the big plan was Moguldom, but until such time, Kanish was still my Assistant, and I found the whole damn thing suspicious. Willy was a stand-up guy. But to invite my "friend" just to say hello? That was beyond basic etiquette. My "fuck me" meter was going off big-time. Clearly Rev opened his trap. But that still doesn't answer why the hell Willy would want to meet Kanish.

Don't get me wrong. I don't mind Willy being aware that my Assistant is a Billionaire's Heir. Like Senator Crou d'Etat told me in my dream, sometimes you want to flaunt your Billionheir. What pisses me off is the Rev blabbing to Willy about my Billionheir when I specifically asked him to keep it "under his hat!" Of course, according to my subconscious, that was by my own design.

Kanish was now bear-hugging me as he continued his incessant jumping. I refused to join him, and he finally gave up and released so as to continue pogoing on his own.

"Dude. What the fuck? You need to chill out. Have a Fatty or something."

"Do not even try to make me calm down from this excitement! I am going to meet Willy Show—the greatest Producer in the world!"

"Hey, you said that about me!"

"You're not seriously going to put your discography up against Willy Show's, are you?"

It was dark out, and I never really recovered from my nap. Annapurna whipped up a fabulous dinner, as usual, and then Kanish and I retired to the porch for our evening Fatty and its corresponding lesson.

"This was a vehdy good day, my friend," Kanish said. "Tonight, I will supply the lesson."

"What is it?" I asked as I administered my Medicine.

"Every day is a lucky day for an industrious man. Only fools wait for a lucky day."

It was a beautifully poignant and well-delivered message that revealed a deep emotional maturity. Then Kanish began pogoing circles again. This time, I joined him—both in pogo and in chant.

We have a meeting with Willy Show!
We have a meeting with Willy Show!
Bring your friend!
Bring your friend!
We have a meeting with Willy Show!

Mixerman

CHAPTER TWELVE

BILLIONHEIRS BE BLUNT

I'm not sure why Kanish was so excited to meet Willy Show, or how he thought he was going to parlay a meeting with him to his advantage. Of course, I still can't figure out why the hell Willy—the president of a Major Label—would want to meet Kanish in the first place.

What was Willy playing at?

Then there was Kanish, who was nothing short of furtive all morning. For starters, he left the house early and alone, which he never does. Then, upon his return, Rajadut came by for a brisk in-and-out meeting, all of which was rather hush-hush and dripping with paranoia. Then Kanish locked himself in his room for the better part of two hours. Meanwhile, I couldn't find the fucking Medicine anywhere.

"Kanish! Where's the Medicine?"

"You are looking for your Medicine?" Kanish replied in a hushed tone through the crack in the door.

"Yeah," I muttered. "Why are we whispering?"

"And why would you need Medicine this early?"

"What the—? Because I want to bring Willy a blunt? Why are—"

"You mean those super Fatties one makes with Medicine in a cigar wrapper?"

"You know what a blunt is, Kanish. Dude. What the fuck are you up to?"

"I do not understand this 'up to,' as you say. I believe, however, there are some prerolled emergency Fatties in the Medicinal cabinet. Perhaps you could extract the Medicine from those for your blunt."

"You can't put ground Medicine in a blunt, Kanish. It'll fall right out."

"I did not realize this."

For those of you unfamiliar with blunts, they're relatively easy to make. You cut a cigar down one side, replace the tobacco with large buds of Medicine, and then use your saliva to crudely glue the folded-over cigar leaves. Given the size of a Blunt, they are the preferred method of delivery for dispensing copious doses of Medicine to a rather sizable posse. They're also useful for smoking out Willy Show. After all, no one on earth could possibly smoke more Medicine than Willy, and I'm really not sure the man even gets stoned anymore.

Kanish dropped his guard momentarily and the door opened a bit to reveal his attire. He was wearing a beautiful black three-piece suit, adorned with a light-green tie.

"You're overdressed."

"I'm dressed for success!"

"In LA that means you look borderline homeless. Never mind. I'll just give Willy one of the Fatties. We should probably think about leaving soon."

Sevaka had the Bentley all gassed up and ready to go. Frankly, I would have preferred to take the Stingray, as I really didn't want to draw more attention to ourselves. But even going bluntless, you can't expect to come out of a meeting with Willy Show in any condition to drive. Given the circumstances, the Bentley seemed the better call.

Sevaka dropped us off in front of Mel Odious Sound. Rev was, once again, jovially peering down at us from his perch.

"You guys meeting Willy?" the Rev inquired from above.

"Yes, yes, yes. Isn't it fantastic!" Kanish replied.

"Come on up after your meeting, okay?"

The receptionist escorted us to Studio W, where the music was blasting out of the Bigs—pop music, and it was nothing familiar. Willy was on the back couch with his eyes closed, and a young man—a Producer—stood with his back toward us in front of the 80-input mixing console. Both of them were deep into the music, and neither seemed aware that we'd entered the room. That is, until the music stopped abruptly.

"Can I help you?" the young Producer quipped.

"Mixie! How are you?" Willy greeted as he pulled himself awkwardly from the couch. "Guys, this is Juno. He's producing this EP for us."

We all exchanged introductions and hugs along with the usual niceties before getting back to our small talk.

"Who's the singer?" I asked.

"We call her Allaire."

Willy motioned with jazz hands as if he were magically presenting the name Allaire in midair.

"Just . . . Allaire?" I said, mimicking Willy's jazz hands motion. Then Kanish joined in on the fun.

"Allaire," Kanish parroted. But the way he moved his hands, I swear it almost made a swooshing sound.

"Yeah. Allaire," Willy repeated as he attempted to get a bit more swoosh out of it.

"That's her stage name, I take it?" I asked. "Allaire?"

"We had no choice! Her last name is Rumplestiltstein, of all things. How the fuck would I market that?"

"Huh. That sounds pretty tired," I replied.

"A total snooze-fest!"

"You may have a sleeper on your hands."

"She's like a dream."

Kanish had a strange smile plastered on his face, and his eyes darted back and forth between us. He was clearly struggling to understand what the fuck we were going on about. I found out later, of course, that Kanish didn't understand the whole Rumpelstiltskin reference. That would make things difficult, I suppose.

Juno was now vibing us out. I don't criticize him for this. After all, I know how annoying it is when people invade my room while I'm trying to Produce a record. We were clearly in his space, and I don't begrudge him for using Mind Tricks designed to chase us away.

"I think Juno's trying to work," I said.

"Yeah. Come on. We'll go into my office," Willy replied. "The mix sounds wonderful, Juno. But I think we could use just a tad more vocal, if you wouldn't mind."

Willy pushed on the heavy soundproof door, which opened up into the expansive wood tracking room of Studio W. In the middle of the room there were four oversized red suede beanbag chairs arranged symmetrically around a stark white shag rug. Between two of the chairs was a small decorative midcentury side table, upon which sat a plastic '70s ashtray complete with a fan for sucking up the smoke. A quick test revealed it to be in working order. Between the other two beanbag chairs was a fully stocked beer refrigerator, the kind you'd find in an old SkyMall catalog. On top of the SkyMall fridge was a Beats by Dr. Dre Beatbox.

Kanish released the button on his suit jacket and plopped down into one of the beanbag chairs like he was eight. Willy followed suit, as did I.

Kanish, without fanfare, reached into his interior jacket pocket and pulled out a cigar—or what looked like a cigar—and handed it to Willy.

"Holy-fuck-what-have-we-here!" Willy exclaimed as if he had just sneezed a word.

"It is customary in my country to bring a gift to an important meeting," Kanish replied. "I present to you, the One-Ounce Blunt."

Just to be clear, an ounce of Medicine is enough to get twenty 400-pound rappers perpetually high for more than a week. It was a ridiculous amount of Medicine to put into a single delivery device, and it was housed in a Cuban Cohiba cigar wrapper of all things!

"The wrapping is completely intact . . ." Willy said, almost in a trance. "How did you do that?"

"Let me tell you, it took quite some time, and a few attempts to get the tobacco out of one of those things without ripping the leaves," Kanish replied.

"Why, this is the most amazing thing I've ever seen!" Willy marveled. "It's beautiful!"

I was stunned and I didn't know whether to kick Kanish for upstaging me or to hug him for being so brilliant.

"Please accept this gift from both of us," Kanish finished.

A hug it is!

"Well, that's a very . . . nice . . . gift."

Willy was losing his train of thought as he peered quizzically at the cigar. It was perfectly formed and jam-packed with weed. And I do mean jam-packed. Like, the thing looked as if it had been hand rolled with the Medicine right in it. But how?

"Filling it with Medicine was not so easy either, I should say," Kanish started. "It took me an hour just to grind it all."

"You ground it?" I laughed.

"This is astounding," Willy marveled. "Why have I never thought of this?"

"I even clipped the end for you."

Willy rolled the cigar in front of his face in absolute fascination. He couldn't get over it. Neither could I, frankly. I still can't. How does one successfully extract the tobacco from a hand-rolled cigar and then manage to replace it with so much finely ground weed that it can't escape? And how the hell did Kanish find a Cuban cigar? I have to get mine from Jersey City.

And then I realized. Of course! Rajadut supplied the Cubans. That's why he was at the house this morning.

Willy sparked up the Blunt, which caught fire immediately and generated a massive plume of smoke. He drew in what had to be an enormous dose of Medicine, and then handed the blunt to Kanish, who did the same before passing it to me. Willy got up and reached in the beer fridge to pull out some Stella Artois. I flicked on the ashtray fan, which did almost nothing to clear the thick fog of smoke filling the room.

"Kanish," I said, "this is a big day. You invented the One-Ounce Blunt, dude."

"I figured what the hell! It grows on bushes, does it not?" Kanish replied.

"It most certainly does!" Willy said as he handed us each a beer. "So, tell me what you guys have going on."

"Going on?" I asked.

"Why are you here today?"

Why were we here today? Didn't he invite us?

The Medicine kicked in almost instantaneously, and I was having a little bit of a problem coming up with an answer to his question. We'd stopped by the other day to say hi, so that I could introduce Kanish to a real-life Mogul. I didn't actually have a reason for being there other than that. Really, the only thing we had going on—if you could even call it that— was the Douchebag Song, and I certainly wasn't going to bring that up.

"I am vehdy glad you asked this," Kanish interjected. "We are presently preparing to record the Douchebag Song with the Pharcyde!"

This was about the time that I was on the floor nearly coughing out a lung. The sheer surprise of the statement caused me to suck Stella Artois down my windpipe.

"Are you all right?" Willy asked as he patted me on the back.

"I'm fine," I croaked. "Please. Continue."

"Well, tell me about the Douchebag Song, then, Kanish. It sounds fascinating."

"I can do much better than that. I can play and sing it for you!"

"You can?" I said in surprise.

"I'd so love to hear it," Willy replied.

Kanish pulled out his phone and connected it to the Dre Beatbox on top of the SkyMall fridge and hit play. The sound of the boom box was quite atrocious. I can't believe Dre got three cents for that piece of shit, let alone three billion, but then that's branding for you. The track, on the other hand, was compelling, and also strangely familiar. It took me a moment to place it.

"That's the track from my dream!" I exclaimed.

"This is the verse beat," Kanish said with a glare. "This would be the first Pharcyde rhyme in here, which they would write, of course. And then coming up is the chorus, which would be performed as a group vocal."

The verse beat continued until there was a momentary drop. When the drums returned, Kanish began to rap, of all things.

Just another Douchebag
Another Douchebag
Another Douchebag
driving in a Prius
You know you see us
How you gonna beat us
when you're driving in a Prius?

"I love it!" Willy exclaimed.

"So do I . . ." I said.

"You wrote the chorus then, I take it?" Willy asked Kanish.

"Mixerman wrote the chorus. I have made some vehdy minor improvements upon it. And I programmed the beat, as well."

"I love the track! It's really catchy. And the Pharcyde are in?"

"That is the plan!" Kanish beamed.

Willy took a sip from his Stella and then asked to hear the track again. Kanish performed the chorus several more times for us. It wasn't long before both Willy and I began to join in, at times interjecting responses to Kanish's calls, as if Kanish were our MC and we were his posse.

"Mixerman. You've been holding out on me. I didn't realize you were a Songwriter."

And here I thought that I was a Ditty writer, but sometimes in this business they're one and the same. Apparently, this was such an occasion. Kanish sat up as much as one can in his beanbag chair as if to indicate intent. Oddly, Willy and I both followed suit.

"Here is what I would like to propose, Willy, if I might call you that," Kanish began.

"Let's have it."

"As you can hear for yourself, Mixerman here is an amazing Song-writer, and I—"

Kanish paused for dramatic effect.

"—am Music Mogul material."

I snorted quite loudly at that comment and immediately sucked it back in as best as I could. Willy was clearly taking all of this quite seriously. Kanish continued his pitch.

"I'm not sure whether you know it or not, but I am in a unique position to fund this project. With the Pharcyde performing the verses, and with Mixerman's fantastic chorus, I think we have a vehdy good opportunity to produce a huge smash hit the world over. This is my plan."

"I see," said Willy.

"There is just one problem," Kanish continued.

"And what's that?"

Willy was on the edge of his beanbag, as was I.

"We need Distribution. And since you're the greatest Producer who ever lived, there is no doubt in my mind that you can recognize that this song has the word *hit* written all around it."

Willy sparked up the blunt again and took a drag. His lung capacity was impressive, and he held his breath for what must have been an hour. Of course, my Assistant had basically just asked one of the most heralded Producers in the history of the business for a Distribution deal based on an incomplete demo of an embellished Ditty, and although I could count on Willy to let the lad down gently, the anticipation was nothing short of torture. Finally, Willy released his breath in order to address young Kanish.

"It's true, you know," Willy started. "You can't seem to drive anywhere without some Douchebag getting in the way these days. And those Prius drivers can be the worst Douchebags of them all."

"So many fucking Douchebags!" Kanish agreed.

"I think you may strike a nerve with this one, boys."

"Fantastic!" Kanish exploded. "When can we get started?"

Willy rolled out of his beanbag chair about as gracefully as one can, and without so much as a word made his way over to his satchel, which was perched upon the nine-foot Steinway piano in the corner of the room.

Upon his return, he plunked back down in his chair, rummaged through the bag, and methodically removed several stacks of $100 bills. Each stack was wrapped with a labeled purple band—$5,000.

"Here's what I'd like to do," Willy said as he handed five stacks of bills to me and five to Kanish. "That's $50,000 to get you boys started. I'd like to set the two of you up with a Distribution deal. We get fifty percent of everything. So we're equal partners in this venture. Now, if the single generates more than $5 million in revenue, then that will trigger a full Label Distribution deal, including a large capital investment from us. Then you can go and sign more Producers to your Label and make us all money."

"Wait," I interrupted. "Did you say sign more Producers?"

"Did I? When?"

"Just now. You said that we could go sign more Producers."

"Ah, right. Producer. Artist. Is there a difference anymore?"

Although this was a point that I had made the other day, it was still surprising to hear it from Willy Show. And I probably would have spent more time on the subject had it not been for what he said next.

"If everything goes the way I expect, we're talking an eight-figure deal here, boys."

Eight figures?

Eight figures?

EIGHT FIGURES!

I began to work out the zeros in my head, but no matter how many times I worked it out, the lowest qualifying figure I could come up with was $10 million! The highest, $99 million.

"Did you say eight figures?"

"That's right," Willy replied. "In the meantime, you guys go finish this Douchebag record and bring it back to me so we can get it out there. You have complete autonomy on your creative decisions. Whatever you guys think will sell. In the meantime, we'll let the lawyers hash out the contractual details. Sound good?"

"It's like music to my ears!" Kanish exclaimed.

Mine as well.

The scene unfolded in front of me like a crazy movie mixed in with a dream and topped off with a dollop of fantasy. Kanish just manifested a fucking Distribution deal. For us! Based on a Ditty of all things. My Ditty. Who knew this was how it all worked?

Juno's voice came over the monitors in the room.

"I'm ready for you to listen to this, Willy."

"I have to run, boys. Bring me something soon."

Willy swiped up the partly smoked blunt from the vacuum ashtray as he returned to the control room. Kanish stuffed all of the $5K stacks into his suit jacket and we made our way back into the hall, where we ran into the Rev.

"Hey, boys!" the Rev exclaimed. "How'd your meeting go?"

"It went fantastic!" Kanish replied.

"Good to hear! Come on up!"

Kanish was more than happy to follow the Rev up to his production suite. I, on the other hand, needed to empty my bladder, which I found nothing short of inconvenient, given the circumstances. Regardless of Kanish's assurances, I didn't like leaving him alone with the Rev. Not yet, anyway. To make matters worse, my bathroom run took longer than expected (shit happens), which wouldn't be worth mentioning were it not for what I witnessed at the top of the staircase some minutes later. The Rev and Kanish were on the landing, shaking hands exuberantly, as if they'd just come to some sort of agreement.

"Thanks, Kanish," the Rev bubbled. "This is so great. I really appreciate it. Thanks for setting this up."

Motherfucker!

The Rev gave each of us a hug, and then immediately herded us down the stairs and out the front door to the waiting Bentley. Rev went to the driver's side of the car, stuck a $20 bill into Sevaka's breast pocket, and then tapped it for good luck. Without a word, Sevaka pulled the bill out of his pocket, crumpled it up, dropped it on the ground, and drove away.

Kanish didn't say much at first. He just smiled smugly, as he should have done. I, on the other hand, was stunned. What the fuck just happened?

"So?" Kanish asked. "Am I Music Mogul material or what?"

"You most certainly are Music Mogul material, Kanish. Of this there is no doubt. But if you don't mind me asking, what was that shit with the Rev?"

"What shit is this that you speak of?"

"Please. The hug."

"Ah, yes! He wanted me to invest in an Artist, of course. But you and I have our dishes full at the moment, and so I merely gave him a connection to a friend of mine who would love to learn how to Assist."

Kanish pulled the $50K in bills out of his suit pockets and placed them on the seat between us.

"This friend of yours," I started. "Is he a Billionaire?"

"The son of a Billionaire, yes. How else is Rev going to make any money?"

It was a good point.

"Would you like today's lesson?" I asked.

"Vehdy much so."

"This one comes from one of my college professors at Rutgers University, William 'Prof' Fielder. He was one of the first great crossover jazz and classical trumpet players."

"Hit me with it."

"As the prof used to say: There are three evils in life: Passing the blame. Excuses. And 'I can't.'"

"Yes, yes, yes, yes. This is a vehdy good lesson."

We drove in silence for a while, the Medicine still in full effect. I gazed out the tinted window at the poor people that had to operate their own cars. The saps were stopping and starting in fits on the crowded freeway as we traveled freely down the newly minted toll lanes. Driver after driver craned and squinted as we passed them by. All of them seemed desperate for a glimpse of us through the dark, tinted windows of our Bentley. It felt like success.

"Of course, there might be two lessons today," I suggested.

"Two lessons! How could I be so lucky? And what is the second?"

"Money is the root cause of unhappiness."

We laughed the entire rest of the way home.

Mixerman

CHAPTER THIRTEEN

MANIFESTING AARDVARK

When I told Kanish that we needed a Distribution deal, I didn't think in my wildest dreams he would manage to acquire one in less than forty-eight hours' time. Who would? I mean, it's absurd. How the fuck does a veritable dilettante walk into a meeting with a Ditty and a prayer and walk out with a Distribution deal?

Of course, the deal that Willy offered includes half of our Publishing, which I wasn't too happy about. But fuck it. The Ditty isn't going to make money as I sing it in the car. And it's certainly not going to go anywhere without airplay. Besides, I would need more than a few screws loose to turn down a deal that featured an eight-figure performance bump.

Just so we're clear, Willy was starting us off with an Artist's Distribution deal, which is essentially a straight-up record deal, which is certainly more than adequate given our goals. It's the eight-figure Label Distribution deal that's the jewel here. This is what any and every Producer that ever lived covets most. This kind of deal is typically reserved for world-famous Artists and Producers in a position of leverage. It's a way for a Label to keep their most profitable talent happy, and it's quite ingenious, when you think about it. The Distributor gives an Artist or Producer a whole boatload of money to fund projects that will make the Distributor, the Artist, or the Producer even more boatloads of money.

I was busting.

Normally, when something extraordinary like this goes down in my life, the first person I call is my best friend and fellow Producer, Aardvark. Unfortunately, I'd been trying to reach Aardy for the better part of a month, to no avail. Last we spoke he was heading for India, of all places, and as a result he has been completely off grid. So how does one reach the unreachable Aardvark? Why you Manifest him, of course. That's right, you Manifest Aardvark.

Quite simply, Manifestation is the act of making things happen. Manifestation can be as simple as asking for what you want. It can be as complex as a state of mind.

Plainly, Kanish had Manifested a Distribution deal, and this was no matter of pure luck. He wasn't there to meet Willy Show for the thrill of it. He wasn't there so that he might brag to all of his buddies at home. The kid came into that meeting with a goal, fully prepared to pitch and close a deal. Not only did he program an amazing track, he also turned a veritable nursery rhyme into a well-designed rap. Then, without fear, without hesitation, with no concern for his ego, he pitched the whole thing to one of the most powerful men in Music. And why not? What's the worst that could happen? He says "no?"

An important component to Manifestation is fearlessness. You can't be afraid of the results, and you most certainly can't be scared of the word *no*. I understand, it's a brutally intimidating word, but in the Music Business, it's a syllable that one best become accustomed to. That said, Kanish revealed some real chutzpah with his proposal.

I would have never thought to ask Willy for a Distribution deal, certainly not without having an Artist fully committed to the project. So I had no intention of bringing up the Song, or the Pharcyde, for that matter. Frankly, I know better than to approach Willy for Distribution on anything other than a fully realized track with an Artist attached. But then, that's the thing about Manifestation. Sometimes "knowing better" just gets in the way.

Manifestation also requires some modicum of faith. I'm not speaking of the usual dogma proselytized by shamans and pontificators who would have us all believe in a meddlesome and micro-managing higher power. That kind of faith makes no sense to me whatsoever. After all, to give credit to a higher power for my own Manifestations would be to shun personal responsibility for it.

And please don't confuse Manifestation with the power of positive thinking. This is not an exercise meant to help deal with the negative influences of self-doubt. Manifestation is the refusal to leave opportunity purely up to chance. It's an aggressive stance in which destiny is treated with disdain, and self-accomplishment is given its credit due.

All of that said, there are caveats to Manifestation. That is to say, rules. The primary rule being that you can't Manifest something you're not in a position to make happen in the first place.

Suppose I should want to become the president of the United States. This would be a ludicrous goal, seeing as I'm not currently in a position to become the president. I can't Manifest that. I can, however, Manifest something smaller. Like a run for mayor, which I can then parlay into a run for State Legislature, which I could then Manifest into a successful run for Congress, or governor. If the results of those Manifestations align, then I might one day find myself in a position to Manifest the presidency. Of course, I'd be too old by then. Manifesting is time-consuming business.

In regards to yesterday's Manifestation of a Distribution deal, I would argue that I too deserve some credit. It was I, after all, who convinced Kanish that he was Music Mogul material. Granted, I was only telling him that because he had the capital to become one. I had no idea he had talent too. But you have to admit, he's come a long way in his first two weeks. We both have. I mean, we started this journey as Intern and Mentor. It wasn't until we came to the Guru–Mogul relationship that things really started to happen. Now look at us. We're in position for an eight-figure Distribution deal!

This is not to take anything away from Kanish. The kid was making his own breaks, and if you want to get ahead in life, that's what you do. Frankly, Kanish and I have been Manifesting machines lately. And since Manifesting opportunity begets more opportunity, I was now actively Manifesting my good friend Aardvark. I was in need of his counsel.

It was the middle of the afternoon, and I was taking a much-needed nap in the comfort of my own bed. I hadn't slept much the night before given our meeting with Willy. And I didn't dare turn on the news, the din of which would have surely put me to sleep. I really don't think I could take another news-inspired dream with Senator Crou d'Etat. It kind of freaked me out.

Once again, I was awakened by pounding at my bedroom door. This time it was Kanish.

"Mixie! Mixie! Wake up! Your sidekick is here!" Kanish announced.

"Not this shit again!" I huffed. "Who?"

"Aardvark, of course! Who else could qualify as your sidekick?"

"Aardvark!"

I threw on yesterday's pants and T-shirt, whipped open my door, and ran at full gallop down the stairs.

I suppose from Kanish's perspective as a fan of my books, Aardvark would indeed be my sidekick. After all, Aardy has been involved with nearly all of my creative projects to date. He produced *The Daily Adventures of*

Mixerman Audiobook: A Dramatization (which I can guarantee is like no audiobook you've ever heard). He produced several hours of supplemental videos for me, which are now available in digital versions of my Zen and the Art Of series of books. Still, as much as I enjoy the term *sidekick*, when it comes to Aardy, he will always be my Producer.

Showing up unannounced was not at all unusual for Aardy. Had he arrived while Kanish and I were out of town, he would have likely just driven to meet us wherever we were. Such is the unconventional dedication of an Aardvark. In fact, that's exactly the word I'd use to describe him— *unconventional.* Followed by *nomad, philanthropist,* and *Renaissance man.* All of which make him interesting, which is really the only true prerequisite to being my friend.

Kanish and I ran through the front door, down the sidewalk, under the arboretum, and onto the driveway, directly in front of the wide-open garage. I had indeed Manifested Aardvark!

Aardy sauntered out of the garage with his hands held out wide, as if he were seeking some sort of explanation.

"Habs suck? You can't just call me?"

Aardy was referring to a Facebook post that I'd made this morning in order to Manifest him. As it turned out, it worked!

Aardy, who is ten years my senior, was wearing his usual skullcap constructed from a red bandana. His curly silver hair flowed out of it to his shoulders. The only time I'd ever seen him without his skullcap is far too scandalous to discuss here. Suffice it to say there are some women in this world that prefer Aardy bald. He wore his favorite Manchester United shirt with the usual pair of khaki shorts, red socks, and white tennis shoes and gave me a great big hug, which was out of character for him, given that he's from Canada.

"Where's the Goddess?" Aardy asked in bewilderment.

"Somewhere in the Antarctic Ocean, I believe."

My girlfriend, known as the Goddess, was in the middle of a grueling 120-day transglobal single-handed yacht race. In other words, she sails alone for thousands of miles at a time, and you have to be pretty fucking badass to do that. The Goddess, however, is a story for another time.

Aardy had a perfectly rolled cigarette in his hands, and although I don't smoke these days, I certainly didn't mind taking a puff or two when he was in town.

"You met Kanish, of course," I said as I took a drag off the filterless bat.

"I did," Aardy replied. "You know, I love Knishes."

"Most people do," I said.

"You don't see Knishes much out here, do you?"

"I wonder why that is?" I said as I passed back the smoke. "Where have you been?"

"I've just come back from India, oddly enough. I'm contemplating another Eight-Thousander."

An Eight-Thousander is a mountain with an elevation of greater than eight thousand meters above sea level. For the Americans out there, that would be nearly five miles. And yes, Aardvark is a mountaineer.

There are fourteen Eight-Thousanders in the world, most of them in the Himalayas. Everest is the most famous of them, given that it has the tallest peak. Statistically speaking, however, it's one of the safer Eight-Thousanders to climb. In fact, it's a veritable factory for amateur climbers, and it can't possibly be considered the prize it once was. Well over three thousand people have reached the top of Everest and lived to tell about it. In contrast, K2, on the border of China and Pakistan, has only been successfully ascended but a few hundred times.

"Which mountain?" I asked.

"Annapurna," Aardy replied.

"Perhaps it's time you and I discuss your will and testament."

While I have some idea of Aardy's financial situation, it's murky at best. He doesn't have to work—this much I know. But he's not fabulously well to-do, either. He lives rather modestly, and his BMW is the only item of status that he owns—aside from his free-spirited way of life, I suppose. Much of his time is spent in some of the poorer regions of Africa, India, and Asia, where he attempts to divert sustainable water to villages. Much of his charitable work can be dangerous, like the time he found himself facing AK-47s in Tamil Tiger territory in the northern part of Sri Lanka. But that's his story to tell.

Aardy got out of the Producing game somewhere around the 2008 crash, and I have to say that his timing was impeccable. Now, I wouldn't go so far as to suggest that Aardy is retired. He still produces records that interest him, and, as I've already pointed out, he produces my projects. He also happens to be an author, and there is nothing better for writing than to experience extreme situations. But climbing Annapurna? That was a fool's mission.

You must understand, I wouldn't climb an eight-foot rock, let alone a mountain. All of my knowledge regarding climbing comes from Aardy in conjunction with the National Geographic Channel. That said, you don't have to be a climber to know that some ascensions are far riskier than others. There are nine mountains with a higher elevation than Annapurna, none of them quite so dangerous. Climbers who dare take on Annapurna face a 40 percent chance of death.

"I kid! I kid!" Aardy replied. "I met your lovely chef Annapurna by the Bentley out front, and I had the name on the brain, I suppose."

Aardy was beaming as he said it, and between the crazy smile plastered on his face and the dripping sarcasm, I knew exactly the subtext: *I don't know what the fuck kind of crazy-ass shit you've managed to Manifest here, but I like it!*

I let Kanish tell the story, which started on the mountain with the Douchebag driving a Prius, and ended with the Manifestation of a Distribution deal. None of it addressed how Kanish had come here, or the details of our arrangement, and I didn't bother to interject. I don't think Aardy really believed any of it, as evidenced by what he said once Kanish had finished.

"Well, that's quite incredible," Aardy blurted. "Really. Anyway, Kanish! Do you play darts?"

To the outside observer that may seem like a rather random question, until you see my mix room. You see, the dartboard is placed prominently and directly in front of the mix position. People could actually play darts as I mix were I to ever allow it. As it turns out, I don't.

The dartboard is well-lit from above with halogen spotlights and mounted with precision and exactitude on a four-by-four-foot backboard of seasoned wood planks. Below the backstop is a wall of custom-made acoustic panels shrouded tightly in colorful Indian scarves. On each side of the planks are two massive whiteboards, which are used for keeping score, among other things. Darts is serious business around here, particularly when Aardy is around, although it's not quite what you might expect. You see, Aardy and I don't throw three darts one at a time toward the board like most people. That's only good for traditional dart games, like Cricket or 301. We throw four darts, two in each hand, all at the same time. The name of the game? California Beaver.

Aardy lived with me for a spell a few years back, and we would play darts at night. I supposed he was sick of my dominance in traditional darts, and so he invented a game he called California Beaver. At first I wasn't into the game, but Aardy was persistent, and it wasn't long before I was finally hooked. We've been developing and refining the game ever since.

The rules aren't written anywhere; they're mostly in our heads. They're also constantly changing, which makes for some rather interesting debates. It never gets to fisticuffs or anything, but there have been times when we didn't speak to one another for the better part of an hour over a Beaver disagreement. Outsiders have accused us of making up rules on the spot, which I certainly wouldn't put past Aardy. As for myself, I'm far too scrupulous for such chicanery.

There are very specific rules when it comes to tossing your Beaver darts. A player must stand square to the board, toes to the line, and hurl the darts such that they all arrive at virtually the same time. That's easier said than done, even for someone who plays traditional darts. As far as scoring is concerned, the outer double and the inner triple rings come into play, as do the bulls—all of which can have an exponential effect on the score. As a result, we start the game at 1,001 and count backwards from there.

In order to force skill into the match, there are all sorts of specific combinations that offer game-winning scoring opportunities. Yes, I'm saying that Aardy and I have some modicum of control over the darts such that we can actually call a game-winning shot. Just try to stand square to a board from the line and throw four darts into a desired location. It takes a bit of practice.

Aardy introduced Kanish to the game, and Kanish was instantly enamored with it. He was also in desperate need of some practice, as the darts kept colliding in midair and dropping to the floor.

"This game is fantastic!" Kanish exclaimed. "Why have you not shown this to me?"

"I don't really play darts when Aardy isn't around," I replied.

Aardy picked up the keys to his Beemer and gave me a nod before addressing Kanish once again.

"You keep working on that, Kanish," Aardy encouraged. "I'm going to take Zerman here to pick up some vodka martini supplies. It seems to me there's a celebration in order."

"Yes, yes, yes. I will practice throwing until you return," Kanish replied. "But before you go . . ."

Kanish stopped momentarily, pulled out a $5,000 wad from his pants, and slipped off three $100 bills.

"We need Medicine."

To which I pulled out my own wad of $5,000.

"I've got it," I said with a fist-bump and a smile.

Aardy peeled out of the driveway in his black BMW 330ci convertible, as per usual, nearly leaving his bumper behind in the process.

"All right. What the fuck is going on?" Aardy asked.

I dished the whole story, starting with the crazy call from Paneer, followed by the strange inspection by Rajadut, to the near international incident with the Sikhs. I told him about the road trip, including the gala affair at the Woodcocks', and of course he was absolutely floored by the visual of the Code Shack and the abandoned high-school dormitory. I even explained my crazy, fucked-up goal of transforming Kanish into a Music Mogul, and the way he'd somehow managed to Manifest it. And as if on cue, we found ourselves stuck behind a Prius. So I took the opportunity to sing the newest version of the Ditty.

"I like it! But a Distribution deal?" Aardy questioned.

"Which automatically turns into a Label Distribution deal," I said. "But only if it's successful."

"Define successful."

"Dude, we only need revenues of five million to kick in that deal."

"That's a lot of revenue!"

"Not if your dad's a Billionaire, it's not. I mean, if spending $5 million gets us a $90 million Label deal, then why not just purchase the records ourselves?"

"Wait. The Label deal is worth $90 mil?"

"I have no idea. It could be $10 mil, it could be $99 mil. All I know is Willy said eight figures, and there are a great many eight-figure deals that would make it worth our while to purchase five million copies of our own record."

"Dude. Eight figures?"

I can assure you that the word *dude* is not normally in the day-to-day cadence of my friend Aardvark. This was a direct result of my influence.

"Eight fucking figures!" I exclaimed. "You can bet your ass I'm going to do whatever I need to to make that shit happen. You know?"

"I would imagine so."

Aardy drove to BevMo!, where we picked up four bottles of Crystal Head vodka and five jars of pimiento-stuffed martini olives. He then drove me to the Dispensary, where I picked up an ounce of Medicine before we returned home. Kanish was still working hard at his Beaver technique.

"It looks as though you've coughed up some Hairy Beaver there, Kanish," Aardy pointed out.

"What is this this you are saying? Hairy Beaver?"

"You have a dart off the grid, and that's Hairy, so no score for you on that toss."

"That doesn't score?"

"All the darts have to be on the grid to score," Aardy said.

I went upstairs to make us all some vodka martinis as Aardy and Kanish played Beaver. Annapurna was in the kitchen preparing us all a veggie-tray snack with some kind of clever curry-flavored dip. She brought the platter down to the boys. I returned with three perfect martinis.

"Cheers!" Aardy toasted. "Congratulations on your big score, boys."

We all clinked glasses, and took a swig of martini.

"Oh," Aardy said. "Oh my. That's some Spinalblifia there."

"Spinal what?" Kanish asked.

"Spinalblifia. It's the sensation you get from a perfect Mixerman martini."

Spinalblifia is also a totally made-up word, but then, all words are made up. Aardy took another sip of his martini, and then launched into a summation of events.

"So, let me see if I've got this straight. Mixerman, you wrote a hook—a chorus lyric. Kanish here wrote the beat and made some alterations to the lyric. And without even a demo, you have been offered Distribution for one song as Artists."

"Producers," I interjected.

"Call me crazy, but I think it would be best if we just stuck with the term *Artists* for now. I think it's going to get quite confusing if we don't adhere to the old model when referring to Artists and Producers."

"Fair enough."

"So, if you hit the five-million mark in revenues for your song, you trigger an eight-figure Distribution deal, at which point you can sign more Artists. Does that about sum it up?"

"It does, indeed," I replied.

"I see. So you're partners in this?"

This was a good question. Kanish didn't write the Song. He improved the Song, which is what the Producer's job is. He didn't hardly change the words at all; he just kind of mixed them up a little. He did, however, program the beat, and as I've already pointed out, in hip-hop, that's half the Songwriting.

"Clearly, you don't have an answer to the question of partnership, so let's move on to the next one. Who is the Artist?"

"Mixerman is the Artist," Kanish volunteered.

"But I thought the Pharcyde were the ones rapping," Aardy questioned.

"They are," I replied. "I guess we're all the Artist, then."

"Yes, yes, yes. I am also the Artist, as are the Pharcyde," Kanish said.

"Right," Aardy continued. "So, you're all the Artist, all six of you. That's interesting. And are the Pharcyde also going to be Songwriters?"

"They're going to want to write their own rap, so yes," I replied.

"And what percentage are they going to get for that?"

"I don't know. We haven't spoken to them yet."

"What do you figure you're going to offer them?"

"I guess half," I said.

"Half of the Writer's share? Willy is already taking the Publisher's share, right? So, if you divide fifty by half, that's twenty-five percent for you guys, and twenty-five percent for the Pharcyde. That gives you and Kanish twelve point five percent each, and it gives the four Pharcyde members six point seventy-five percent each."

"That sounds about right," I replied.

"What happens if they want an even piece? There are four of them and two of you."

"Well, I don't know about Kanish, but I certainly wouldn't be interested in that."

"I can tell you I would vehdy much not be interested in that either," Kanish concurred.

"And who is the Producer?" Aardy asked.

"I am the Producer," Kanish said. "And the Mogul."

"Me too," I replied.

"You're a Mogul as well, Zerman?"

"Well, yeah. I'm helping to run this organization, right?"

"And what about the Pharcyde?"

"They'll want to be Producers too, I would imagine."

"They most certainly are not Moguls!" Kanish exclaimed.

"I see," Aardy began. "So Kanish is the Mogul, the Producer, the Artist, and the Songwriter. Mixerman is the Mogul, the Producer, the Artist, and the Songwriter. And the Pharcyde are the Producers, the Artists, and the Songwriters. Is that right?"

"Correct," Kanish replied.

"Well, it's pretty clear to me what's going on here," Aardy concluded.

"What's that?" I asked.

"You have too many hats."

"Too many hats?" Kanish questioned.

"That's right. And you need help. What you need is a manager."

Aardy went straight into his pitch.

"First, I don't think it makes a lot of sense to approach the Pharcyde on this. They're a bit long in the tooth."

Of course, I'm older than the Pharcyde by just a little, so what does that make me?

"You need an injection of youth into this project. And you want to find a rapper who won't cost you a fortune in Publishing. The Pharcyde will likely insist on at least half the Publishing, possibly more."

"But the Pharcyde are famous," Kanish argued.

"When was the last time you bought a Pharcyde record?" Aardy asked.

Neither of us seemed to have an answer for that.

"Even if I were to agree with you that the Pharcyde was the best choice here, you guys need someone to take care of all the details. There's going to be contracts, and lawyers, and other Labels to contend with—as many as four—one for each of the Pharcyde. And then, you also need to form a Corporation, and before you do that, you have to sit down and hammer out an agreement stating who is doing what and how the revenue is going to be split. At the moment, it seems like you guys are all things in this venture, but the details have to be very clearly spelled out before you enter into an eight-figure deal as partners."

Aardy was right as usual, and the more we discussed it, the more complicated it all became.

"You two are the Creators, and you need someone taking care of the business," Aardy pointed out. "Here's what I would propose. I think you should let me manage you."

"And may I ask you," Kanish started, "how much this would be costing us?"

"A modest fifteen percent."

I was good with that, but then, I trust Aardy with my life. Kanish, on the other hand, who has already revealed himself to be rather shrewd, stopped throwing darts to consider the offer briefly, then rendered his decision.

"Here is what I have to say to this. For my part, and I cannot speak for Mixerman here, I will happily agree to this arrangement for the Douchebag Song. If you do a vehdy good job, then I would wish to discuss your involvement in the Label Distribution deal at that time. Does this sound reasonable?"

"I'm good with that," I echoed.

"Excellent," Aardy proclaimed. "I'd say it's time for another martini!"

"First, you need an advance," I said.

I pulled out the $5K wad from my front pocket and chucked it over to Aardy.

"There's your first ten percent,"

Kanish threw him his wad as well.

"There's another ten percent. We'll take the change now, thank you vehdy much."

Aardy placed the wads on top of the Raven MTX, stepped to the dart pitch, held up four darts and began to offer his own commentary in the customary British accent.

"Aardvark lines up his shot. Yes, he'll be shooting two bulls to end the game, folks. It's a bold decision, one that only a champion the likes of Aardvark would make, but then, that's why he's known as the Father of Modern Beaver."

The darts flew through the air in a dangerously tight pattern. The two top darts landed simultaneously in the red bull, the other two in the smallest part of the 19.

"Lights out, Beaver!" Aardy exclaimed as he ran down the street with his arms held high in victory.

"Are you ready for today's lesson, Kanish?"

"Vehdy much so!"

"Ask and you shall receive."

Mixerman

CHAPTER FOURTEEN

MC SKANKY O, YO!

There are few things in this world as difficult to acquire as a Distribution deal. You wouldn't know it from reading this story.

I've given all of this quite a bit of consideration since my last entry, and I can assure you, had I walked into that meeting with Willy Show alone—had I somehow mustered up the gumption to present Kanish's most fucked-up proposal for Distribution on an unfinished Ditty with a totally hyped-up promise to involve the Pharcyde—he would have outwardly questioned my sanity.

Furthermore, Manifestation techniques are insufficient to explain Willy's offer. The whole "ask and you shall receive" principle really doesn't fly here. Kanish wasn't in a position to Manifest a Distribution deal of any variety.

Yet here we are.

Clearly, I was at the meeting. Yes, I have a relationship with Willy, and have proven to him time and time again that I can deliver a record that he can sell. But to offer a $50K advance? He most certainly could have thrown considerably less cash at us for the same result, and he knows it. He could have just as easily handed us $10K and told us to go make the record and it would have been enough to get the job done. I mean, Kanish outright told Willy that he was in a position to fund the project. He started off the whole pitch telling him so.

And just in case a $50K advance isn't baffling enough, for good measure Willy throws in a $5 million trigger which converts our little 360 deal into a full-fledged eight-figure Label Distribution deal. Why on earth would Willy offer us that? Is the chorus of the Douchebag Song really that catchy? It's not like there were other buyers in the mix.

I'm sorry, but no matter how I slice it, no matter how many angles I look at this from, I simply come to the same unavoidable conclusion: None of this would have happened were Kanish not a Billionaire.

Of course, he's not actually a Billionaire. He's a Billionaire's Heir, which is wholly different from a Billionaire. A Billionaire can't get cut off. A Billionaire's Heir, on the other hand, can. And at the moment my Billionheir's money spigot is in the off position. At this point, Kanish is down to his last $120,000, and I shouldn't have to say it, but $120,000, a significant sum of money for most of us, does not a Billionaire make. Not even close.

Suppose you were paid $120,000 in cash every single day of your life starting today. It would take you just shy of twenty-three years to accumulate your first billion, and that's assuming you're not spending any of it. You'd also need a mattress the size of a two-meter-square room, and that's assuming you're stuffing it with neat stacks of $100 denominations.

Now, if you decided to invest your daily $120,000 payments, and you did so shrewdly, then the pace at which you acquired wealth would quicken considerably. With that kind of guaranteed daily income, banks would beg you to borrow money from them, and it wouldn't be long before that daily $120K installment would be enough leverage for billions in secured loans. With billions in real assets on the books, you would be a Billionaire, despite a paltry income of only $120,000 per day. You see, wealth is judged not by what you have, but rather by what you owe.

As usual, I digress.

There's no doubt, the kid put together a great track, and I love his improvements to the chorus. But one track doesn't prove long-term talent. Certainly not to Willy. And since he went out of his way to invite Kanish to that meeting—a person he wouldn't even know existed were it not for the fat-mouthed Rev—it's pretty clear to me that he already knew Kanish was loaded. Which brings up the next question.

Why the fuck would that matter?

All I know is that the moment I got me a Billionaire's Heir in my back pocket everything became way fucking easier. Were it not for my impromptu road trip with Kanish, I might never have come up with the Douchebag Song. And while in its current form the Song amounts to nothing more than a lottery ticket, it also came with a $50,000 guarantee.

Aardy stood before the whiteboards, absentmindedly tapping his teeth with the half-chewed cap of a dry-erase marker. He was taking his new role as manager quite seriously, and he'd turned both whiteboards into brainstorming boards full of to-do lists and ideas. He was so full of ideas, he'd barely left a space for scoring Beaver.

"So," Aardy said as he returned the marker to its ledge. "I've been giving this all its due consideration, boys, and there's lots to do. But first things first. We need a rapper."

"We're not even going to approach the Pharcyde?" I asked.

"We shouldn't close the door on any possibilities, of course. But I'd like to hear some of the talent out there for myself. We should go to some clubs tonight."

"Clubs? What clubs?"

"I don't know. Hip-hop clubs."

"We can't just search for rappers on the Internet like the rest of the world? We have to go out to clubs?"

"You can't judge stage presence on the Internet. Besides, we should really look for a freestyler. Those are the best rappers."

"I am so vehdy excited!" Kanish interjected. "Finally! We go to the Hood!"

I'm not sure why Aardy was under the impression that freestylers made the best rappers. Writing well-thought-out rhymes is an entirely different skill set from riffing them off the top of your head. And while both are useful skill sets, in general, I prefer the former ability when it comes to making a hip-hop record. That said, Aardy was right. And as much as I wanted to avoid the Hood, it would be best if we checked out rappers in person.

"I do know one local rapper," I said absentmindedly as I searched through my contacts. "He's a Blasian rapper from Torrance who goes by the name of MC Skanky O. He's big on the freestyle battles."

A friend introduced Skanky O to me some years back, and for some reason I seem to run into him around town with some frequency. Every time I see the dude, he hits me up to be his "Produsah," because, you know, he doesn't know how to make beats. Other times he knows how to make beats, he just can't afford the gear. Sometimes he has both problems.

All of that is total bullshit, of course. The whole hip-hop movement started with the idea that you shouldn't need money to create art. Hip-hop was born from the streets of the inner city, and embodies all media disciplines, including visual art, writing, dance, and music. The only thing that you need in order to perform hip-hop is your brain and your voice. All that matters is the flow. So I'm not buying any of his excuses. Skanky's problems had everything to do with fear.

I know Artists (although I'm not sure we should call them that) who have been so debilitated by fear that they make the same album perpetually for years. Over and over again. The paralysis comes with all sorts of rationalizations, all of them tired, none of them valid. One may as well never make a record in the first place if one is never able to finish it. A record that isn't finished isn't art.

Never completing a work is the very definition of playing it safe. You see, if you never put yourself out there, you never have to face harsh criticism. Unfortunately, ridicule is the fare of adulation, and for most people, that's far too steep a price to pay. One doesn't "want" to be an Artist. One either is or isn't one.

Skanky was a good rapper, with good flow, and he had a solid ability to tell a compelling story in rhyme. Unfortunately, he was incapable of finishing a record. I know, because I helped him to produce a track once, and the record came out great. Or at least I thought it did, until he hit me up a year later to try again. Not only didn't he play the track for anyone beyond close friends, he wanted me to entirely redo my production. Setting aside the fact that he wasn't paying me, why the fuck would he come to me for another production if he didn't like the first one? I already helped him to deliver the song the way I thought it should be. Even if I was getting paid, I ain't making the track again just because he refuses to move forward.

All of that said, as annoying as I find Skanky on a number of levels, he's not without his redeeming qualities. At the very least, he would know where the live hip-hop clubs were.

"Call MC Skanky O," I said into my iPhone.

"Calling MC Skank E Yo." Siri replied.

"This guy can help," I said to Aardy and Kanish as I placed the phone on speaker.

Skanky picked up on the very first ring.

"Yo, wat up, wat up, my brothah?" Skanky greeted.

"DJ Mixerman in da house, yo!"

"Word up. Thanks fah callin' me, yo! What up?"

"Yeah, yeah, I'm lookin' for the best live hip-hop clubs. My friends and I want to check out a good show."

"Aw man, da best clubs are undahground, yo! Dey don't exist, know what ahm sayin'? Dey move around an' shit. But I can take you, Yo! I be battlin' tonight! Gonna get my freestyle on, know what ahm sayin'?"

"Word. You want a ride?"

"Thatta be da bomb, yo! Hit my cell at midnight."

"I'm just gonna pick you up at midnight, aight? Text me your address."

"Aight. Dat works."

"I'll be in the beige Bentley," I said.

"Haha! Word, yo! I'll be waitin' by my Rolls-Royce."

"In a minute."

"In a second."

Kanish and Aardy were staring at me like I had two heads.

"What? You need me to translate all of that?" I asked.

"He freestyles!" Aardy scolded. "Why are we not using him?"

"He's too old, too unknown, and he's a major pain in the ass."

"But he freestyles!"

Annapurna entered the garage with a tray of breakfast burritos, which the three of us devoured in short order. Aardy continued to strategize in front of the whiteboard. Kanish tossed Beaver darts toward the board with no regard for Aardy's safety. And I considered the ramifications of a trip to the Hood.

"We should probably bring all of the Sikhs with us tonight," I said.

"What do you mean by all of the Sikhs?" Aardy asked. "There's one by my count."

"Oh, I guess you don't know. There's three more Sikhs staying at the Crown Royale Hotel."

"Really. And how many people fit in a Bentley?"

It was a good point, and I started to do the math. We had the four Sikhs, Sevaka, myself, Kanish, Aardy, and MC Skanky O, for a total of nine people. While the Bentley could comfortably hold five, and the BMW four, Kanish Kanish inexplicably wanted to bring the Stingray—which is costing him a fortune, by the way. He might as well buy it.

In the end, we decided the best course was to take three cars. Two Sikhs in the Beemer, two Sikhs in the Stingray, and the rest of us in the Bentley.

Kanish was once again acting suspiciously throughout the day. He kept leaving to run "errands" and spent quite a bit of time alone in his room. He came down to play a game of Beaver at one point, but the moment either of us pried, he feigned as if he couldn't understand basic American and headed back to his room. The last time Kanish was so clandestine, he invented the

One-Ounce Blunt. I was hopeful that he was preparing something equally as useful.

This left Aardy and me to fend for ourselves, and despite Aardy's pleas, I was not going to dress the part of a hip-hopper. I was going as a Producer, and would wear my usual Producer clothes—unfaded jeans and a T-shirt. Kanish as well. It was Aardy who was in desperate need of some gear. Golfing attire just wouldn't do.

As I'm sure you can imagine, a lily-white, golf-loving Canadian the likes of Aardy is about as far removed from hip-hop as one can get. Rather than dress him like a ridiculous cartoon character, which would only bring more attention to him, I gave him one of my old Pharcyde T-shirts. Kanish was kind enough to loan him a pair of jeans. Frankly, the ensemble was slightly shocking. I don't believe I've ever seen Aardy in jeans, let alone a collarless shirt.

We left the house at midnight. The Bentley led the way, followed by the Sikhs in the Stingray and two other Sikhs in the BMW. The formation was anything but inconspicuous.

Driving through Torrance was a shit show as per usual. I swear that the traffic lights throughout the city are timed in such a way that everyone is forced to waste as much gas as possible. Of course, that might have something to do with all the big oil refineries operating there. It's in Torrance's interest to waste gas. Unfortunately, MC Skanky O lives in the dead center of the expansive city. As a result, there was really no avoiding it.

Sevaka made the final turn onto a residential street just off Western. Skanky was on the sidewalk in front of his apartment complex. He was all decked out in a freshly pressed T-shirt—featuring a large silk-screened marijuana leaf—low-riding khaki shorts, which extended to his knees; and an Adidas baseball cap with a perfectly straight brim. It looked as though it had just come off the line, and it may well have. His entire ensemble still had the tags attached.

"Yo, yo, yo, what up wit da sled, yo? Holy fuck, you wasn't kidding, yo!"

Skanky O jumped in the front seat of the Bentley and extended a fist-bump toward Sevaka.

"What up, yo? I'm MC Skanky O. You da chaperone?"

"That's Sevaka," I said. "He doesn't take kindly to fist-bumps."

"Suh Wattevah! I'll just call you Yo, yo!"

Skanky immediately turned his attention to Kanish.

"You must be the boss man, cuz you in da back. You da rich one. Yeah, I can smell dat shit, yo. Put it heah. Don't leave me hangin', yo!"

Skanky bumped fists with Kanish, and then he dropped his voice to a more serious tone.

"What up, daddy," he said to Aardy.

Skanky launched into all sorts of nonsense about some other rapper who wanted to kill him. Apparently, he made a YouTube video in which he accused a big-time Gangstah rapper of ripping him off. As a result, Skanky had spent the past week bunkered at his buddy's place in Idyllwild. At first his whole act is quite entertaining. After a while, it becomes a bit much, and I really can only take him in short doses. We'd barely gotten out of Torrance and we were already well past the first dose.

Skanky directed us to a seemingly abandoned building somewhere in Compton. Two behemoth black men sat in lawn chairs in front of the dimly lit structure. There were no other people. There was no activity. Just two bouncer types lounging on an inner city street in the wee hours of the morning.

"Where the fuck is everyone?" I asked.

"Prolly inside," Skanky replied.

"What time did this event start?"

"I don't know, yo. Ten? Eleven? Dey reserve a spot for me, yo. Dis is my place. I go last around heah."

"You're fucking kidding me! The whole point was for us to check out rappers!"

"Aw, naw, naw. You said you wanted to see a show, yo. Dis is it. Right heah. You only need to spy on one rapper, cuz you already wit him."

Motherfucker! Dude just loves to waste my fucking time.

Skanky O jumped out of the Bentley, as did we.

"Twenty bucks each," said the bouncer on the right.

Skanky looked expectantly toward me, and I to Aardy, who pulled out two crisp $100 bills and handed them to the immense man.

"That should cover everyone, plus a tip," Aardy said.

"You can't leave those cars there," the bouncer on the left ordered. "It brings too much attention."

I couldn't imagine how parked cars, even expensive ones, could bring more attention than two gigantic human gargoyles in the middle of a sidewalk in Compton. Just the same, the Bentley, the Beemer, and the Stingray did look a bit out of place in the Hood. So, after a quick strategy session, we all agreed that two of the Sikhs and Sevaka should wait for us in the cars around the block.

"And what's in the backpack?" the bouncer asked one of the Sikhs.

It was a good question. I'd never seen any of the Sikhs carrying a backpack, and couldn't understand what on earth he might be carrying in one. I'd already made it quite clear that they weren't to be carrying any firearms into the Hood, and I couldn't for the life of me understand what he might need to bring with him inside the club. The Sikh handed over a bag, which the bouncer sifted through. I, of course, tried to catch a glimpse inside the bag, but the way the bouncer stared me down, it was almost as if he didn't think it was any of my business.

Once cleared, we entered the ancient building and followed the muffled booms of 808 kick drums. The halls were insufficiently lit, the walls made of plaster, entire patches of which were now nothing more than exposed strapping. The three of us made our way single file through the creepy narrow hall. The farther we walked, the louder the music. We climbed down a rather steep set of stairs to yet another door where a bouncer stood sentry. He stamped each of our hands with a number—420.

"What up, Skanky," the sentry said. "You better get in dare. You about up."

The music jumped dramatically in volume and clarity the moment the ultra-heavy metal door swung open. The walls inside the chamber were made of crudely laid brick slathered over in many thick layers of paint, the latest coat in red. The ceiling was low, seven feet at most, and the place was filled with the haze of pungent smoke, the kind that comes from a hundred people passing around large blunts of Medicine in a small unventilated room. As one might expect at an underground hip-hop club in Compton, the crowd was entirely black. In fact, Aardy and I were the only white people in the place, Kanish and the Sikhs the only Indians, and Skanky O the only one with any obvious Asian features.

Being the only white guy in an inner city hip-hop club in and of itself isn't a problem. It's when you're the only white guy in a room full of Gangstahs that you have to worry, but then, that's true regardless of their ethnicity. Pissed-off Gangstahs will kill you regardless, which is why I brought the Sikhs—just in case we found ourselves in a room full of Gangstahs. Of course, the Sikhs, too, were getting the once-over, but that's what happens when you run around the US in an orange turban. People view you with suspicion. I'm not saying it's right. I'm just saying it happens.

The crowd didn't seem overly hostile, but that didn't stop us from getting some rather long looks. I'm sure that many in the crowd were merely curious as to how a couple of white dudes and three Indians found themselves in an underground bar with a Blasian freestyler from Torrance. But with the stage awaiting the next performer, there was no doubt that we were now the center of attention. And while I wouldn't necessarily say we were unwelcome, we most assuredly didn't fit in.

On the back wall of the cramped room was a makeshift bar with a modest choice of liquor—vodka, gin, and whiskey—and a keg of beer; what brands, I couldn't say. There were no labels on the bottles, and this crowd seemed more interested in the weed. In the corner was a pint-sized stage with nothing more than a microphone, a three-legged stool to lay it on, and a black-carpeted floor monitor. In the back of the room was a sound man, cordoned off in his booth. Kanish excused himself to get us all some drinks.

"I'm up next," MC Skanky O announced to me.

"But I thought you go last," I replied in surprise.

"And last is next, yo. You only need to see one rapper, yo! You lookin' at him. Awright, I gotta get up dare."

As pissed as I was that Skanky fucked us from hearing other rappers, I had more pressing issues at that particular moment. We needed to win over this crowd.

"Hold on a second. I need you to do me a favor first."

"What you need?" Skanky asked.

"When you go up there, announce Produsah in da house for me, willya?"

"Word. Ya feeling the minority heat, yo? Not so comfy is it? But I gotcha back, yo."

The music faded out and the hosting MC jumped up on the stage and picked up the mic to make the final introduction.

"All right, all right!" the host yelled into the mic. "Let's heah it fah MC Skanky O!"

The crowd expressed their approval, some with enthusiasm, others with ambivalence. I got the sense that Skanky was liked but not adored. Of course, this was a competition, one that he apparently won on regular occasion. As a result, there were clearly peeps rooting against him.

"Yo, yo, yo, yo, yo! Got some big-time Produsahs in da house, yo!" Skanky yelled into the mic as he pointed directly toward Aardy and me. "Dey produced the Pharcyde and shit, and dey heah to see MC Skanky O lay down some flow, Yo! Let's heah it!"

I was glad that Skanky mentioned the Pharcyde, as it gave us instant legitimacy with the crowd, and the announcement most certainly helped to shift the tide of any possible animus. Unfortunately, I was now being mobbed by an entire room of rappers in need of a Produsah. I swear to you, at one point I had two MCs flowing on either side of me, and in all the commotion I managed to completely miss out on MC Skanky O's freestyle. To make matters worse, I'd lost Kanish, which wouldn't have been a big deal if his Sikh bodyguard hadn't been standing right next to me. The Sikh, who was clearly well versed in the universal language of panic, tapped me on the shoulder and pointed toward the stage.

"We have a late entry, peeps! Let's give it up for MC McKay!"

I wouldn't have believed it if I hadn't seen it for myself. Kanish was now on the stage wearing an oversized white T-shirt, a straight-brimmed hat turned sideways, untied bright-white kicks, and gold clip-on teeth. So, that's what was in the knapsack! That little fucker.

One of the unfortunate limitations of documenting this kind of story is that I must relay things to you from memory. Where I can, I try to deliver past conversations verbatim, but sometimes I merely provide you the gist of a conversation. Such is the nature of the medium. And while I'm certainly not past punching things up a bit when necessary, believe me when I tell you, I cannot do justice to the flow this kid laid on that audience. Had I not been so shocked, I might have thought to record the performance with my phone. And while it would have been nice to share it with you verbatim, his rhymes really don't tell the whole story. It was his performance that was so stunning. Kanish was not only dynamic and engaging, he delivered a hilariously well constructed freestyle about an Indian rapper looking to take over the entire Industry. He even managed to get "ogle my Mogul" in there. Suffice to say, the kid could lay down a flow the likes of which I haven't heard in quite some time.

Let me put it another way: Kanish, or I should say MC McKay, took home first place in a stunner. MC Skanky O came in second.

It was a bitter ride home for Skanky O. The $200 in weekly prize money was something he relied upon, and frankly, I was feeling bad about that. Once again, the Billionheir walks away with the prize. Isn't that always the way? Were he not my very own Billionheir, I might find it an unsettling theme.

Sevaka pulled up in front of Skanky's apartment complex. Aardy, being the swell guy that he is, pulled out $500 cash and handed it to Skanky O.

"That's payment for your services. You've helped us out a great deal tonight, and I won't take no for an answer."

There would be no no's from Skanky O, as he snatched up the cash and bid us farewell. He was happy. As was I. For there was no doubt about it, not for anyone at that club, certainly not for anyone in the Bentley—Kanish was a star.

He's also compulsively secretive.

"Dude. What the hell? Why the fuck didn't you just tell us you could rap?" I asked.

"You did not ask me," Kanish replied.

Aardy clearly had no interest in prosecuting Kanish for his covert ways, and rather than allow me to continue, he interjected his thoughts on the matter.

"Kanish," Aardy began. "you realize there is no question here, right? You must rap the Douchebag Song."

"Yes, yes. I've known that for days," Kanish replied with a smile.

"Then why didn't you say something?" I whinged.

Kanish cracked a tiny smile.

"I might best answer you, my Guru, in the form of a lesson."

"Sure," I said resignedly.

"A spacious ground is the right place to demonstrate one's skill in wrestling."

It most certainly is.

Mixerman

CHAPTER FIFTEEN

THE ENTITLED ONE

Suppose someone like Beyoncé is in need of a song to release. We've already established (a few chapters back), that she can "cowrite" with a Songwriter Producer. But this isn't always a viable option. If she's on tour, she may not have time to sit down and write with Producers. At which point, she'll seek submissions from Publishing companies who have a whole roster of Songwriter Producers looking to score a Beyoncé song. And seeing as Beyoncé is currently one of the hottest singers on the planet, I can assure you all of the submissions, every one of them, will be hot off the presses and written specifically for Beyoncé to sing.

As you can imagine, when someone like Beyoncé needs a new song, she's going to get hundreds of submissions, all of them from professional Songwriter Producers signed with Publishers. Her managers might even, on some occasions, be inclined to include an all-call by placing a small classified ad in a trade rag like the *Hollywood Reporter* or perhaps *Billboard*. On those occasions, you, I, or anyone can submit a song for consideration. Clearly, it's a long shot.

You see, once the submission deadline is reached, the song demos are prioritized. At the top of the pile are demos from the hottest Songwriter Producers with the most recent string of hits. Next come the tracks delivered by the once-hot Songwriter Producers, followed by the up-and-coming Songwriters. Given the seeding process of song demo submissions, the current and hottest Songwriters have a massive advantage.

The procedure is simple. Beyoncé and/or her managers listen to the demos, one at a time, starting with the hottest Songwriters, and continue through the pile until she finds her perfect song. Once that happens, the search is over. The rest of the songs are thrown out, never to be heard again.

As you can imagine, the chances that Beyoncé will make it through all of the professional Songwriter submissions, followed by the up-and-comers, and on to the all-call submissions is highly unlikely. So why do they have all-call submissions? Frankly, I'm not sure they do anymore. Someone as big as Beyoncé probably doesn't get through more than ten tracks. She's getting submissions from the hottest Songwriters in the world.

At the end of the day, Songwriting is a business, and there is a great deal of competition. Any advantage, no matter how small, can make a difference. Given this, a smart professional Songwriter will first perform a detailed analysis of Beyoncé's catalog in order to determine her tendencies in regard to subject matter, key, tempo, melody, harmony, rhythm, and even arrangements. A professional Songwriter will then hire a demo singer who sounds a little like Beyoncé, but is not quite as good. The goal is to deliver a song that Beyoncé hears as her own. In other words, to write a Beyoncé song.

Now, sometimes a song is written with no particular singer in mind. The Douchebag Ditty would be a good example of that. Clearly there was no point in pitching the Douchebag Song to Beyoncé. Even if we could get an audience with her, our meeting wouldn't last long. Beyoncé tends to sing about love. The Douchebag Song is about hate. This was no Beyoncé song.

At first blush, I thought approaching the Pharcyde made some sense. Not only does the Pharcyde have something to say, the Ditty's hook seemed to align with their humorous style. But as I've given it more consideration, I've had questions. For starters, is *Douchebag* a word that the Pharcyde would use?

As I've expressed before, I'm not sure it makes a whole hell of a lot of sense for middle-aged rappers with roots in the inner city to be complaining about Douchebags driving Priuses. It's just not a theme that rings all that true. At least not until cops start driving Priuses, which would be somewhat amusing, because I don't think they'd ever catch anyone.

But when you think about it, a Billionheir would seem an equally unlikely messenger of the Ditty. And just for the record, the Douchebag Song has nothing to do with criticizing environmentalists. That's not the message at all. I'm just pissed off at all the Billionaire Douchebags who feign oblivion as they gum up the works for their own selfish purposes. Admittedly, that's not a great message coming from a Billionaire's Heir. Not that it matters. Most people don't pay attention to subtext. Oblivion abounds.

Sometimes I wonder just how many people actually think about lyrics. For instance, "Every Breath you Take," the mid-'80s hit song by the

Police, is about a stalker. Yet somehow, this song is often featured at wedding receptions.

It just goes to show you, the feeling of the music is far more powerful than what you say. Musically speaking, "Every Breath You Take" feels like a love song. Which it is. From the perspective of the stalker. It's actually kind of creepy when you actually think about the lyric.

Every breath you take
Every move you make
I'll be watching you.

Because that's what normal relationships are about. Watching your partner's every move?

It's kind of like when you call someone a Douchebag with a smile. The meaning is the same—it just appears less hostile, given the friendly delivery. The point is that most people will take away the wrong message from the Douchebag Song, so it's really not a problem for Kanish to be the messenger, despite being a Billionheir. If we make the Song fun to sing, no one will ever notice the darker message of the Song, or the blatant hypocrisy in the person performing it.

Kanish was in the back of the garage working on the Douchebag lyric as Aardy and I set up some lounge chairs in the driveway. It was far too beautiful an afternoon to be holed up in the garage as Kanish looped the same four bars ad nauseam.

With our makeshift driveway lounge in full effect, Aardy pulled out a bottle of Illuminati vodka from his bag. Admittedly, it was a vodka I'd never heard of before, and for good reason—it's Canadian. It's also a relative newcomer to the ever-growing vodka scene, and it's not even imported into the US, making it my current favorite premium vodka, as it's impossible to get. It also made for the most divine vodka martinis I've had in quite some time. And that's saying something, as I happen to be an unapologetic vodka snob.

Aardy and I were enjoying our afternoon Illuminati martinis in the driveway when, much to our surprise, the Rev pulled up. In a Rolls-Royce, no less! What the fuck?

In the back of the Rolls was a young man, Indian, clad in pure white. The Rev jumped out of the car to greet us. The kid remained in the back.

"Holy shit!" the Rev announced. "Quentin Tarantino was right—you *are* in the sticks!"

He was referring to a scene in *Pulp Fiction* in which the Cleaner, played by Harvey Keitel, disses Redondo Beach by calling it the sticks. Of course, Quentin is right about that. Even with a population above 67,000, this was surely the sticks. I swear they roll up the streets by ten around here.

"Nice ride," I said. "Where's your driver?"

"I don't like sitting in the backseat while someone else drives. I like to be in control of my own destiny, you know what I mean?"

"I do. I think your fare is waiting for you to open his door."

The young man in the back of the car sat motionless and petulant. Ooh, boy. The Rev may have gotten a bad seed.

"What the hell?" Rev muttered. "Mukesh!"

Kanish was so deep in thought, he didn't even realize the Rev had arrived. That is, until he heard his best buddy's name yelled out.

"Mukesh?"

Kanish bolted from the garage to the car and opened the door for his friend, who inexplicably shut it again and began speaking sternly in Hindi through the open window. Kanish reached in and smacked his friend on the head, and then opened the door so as to physically pull this white-clad Mukesh person from the car. Both of them were chattering excitedly in Hindi, which ceased abruptly upon the two of them reaching our position.

"This is Mukesh, everyone," Kanish announced. "We were dorm mates at Eton."

"Hello," Mukesh said unenthusiastically with a wave.

"Come, come, Mukesh!" Kanish said as he herded his friend. "Have you been to the ocean yet? We will be back!"

"Look at that," the Rev said almost sentimentally as he watched the two Billionheirs frolicking toward the beach. "Thick as thieves. I bet there's no secrets between those two."

As much as I enjoy impromptu visits, the goal for today was to get the rhyme written for the Douchebag Song. Still, the creative process is not one that can always be scheduled. If Kanish preferred to gallivant with his friend, then so be it. The writing brain does not confine itself to a timeline, and your subconscious will work on a creation as you go about your day. In fact, I would argue it's critical to engage in some level of procrastination.

Not only does that give the brain time to sort, it also allows for seemingly random events to have some influence on the process. Besides, we had time.

Rev and Aardy shot the shit for a bit. I had introduced them several years back, and they've been golfing buddies ever since. Aardy, who was already dressed the part, invited the Rev to play a round, which he turned down outright. This was not on the agenda, and the Rev immediately focused his attention toward the open garage.

"So! This is your room! And you have a Slate MTX, too! I was thinking about getting one of these. Can I try it?"

Without prompting, the Rev opened Logic and began moving faders on the touch screen.

"Holy shit! This is so much better than a mouse! Look at this, I can bring the fader up and down with my hand."

"Check out the knobs," I encouraged.

"Oh, shit! They're rotary. Son of a bitch! Did your Billionaire's Heir get you this?"

"Of course not." I chuckled.

Annapurna brought down a large plate of bite-sized sandwiches (all of them with the crust cut off), which the three of us began to devour.

"You have a chef, too? Damn. I gotta talk to this kid. He's a bit douchey. Your Billionheir is so . . ."

"Gregarious?" I said.

"Yeah. He's gregarious. Mine is . . ."

"A Douchebag."

"You really have a way with words!" the Rev complimented.

The Rev sparked up a cigarette in the driveway, and Aardy arranged the lounge chairs so we could all talk.

"Gentlemen," Aardy began. "I don't think there's any need to be protectionist here. Everyone knows everyone, you know?"

"Exactly," the Rev replied. "The kid wanted to see his friend, so that's the main reason for the visit. But I've been thinking about all this shit, and I want to apologize to you, Zerman. You asked me to keep the whole Billionheir thing to myself, and I fucked up and told Willy about it, and that was dumb. I was wrong and you were right. If you want to keep this whole Billionheir crap quiet, then I'm all for it. You gotta accept my apology, brother."

Sure! Now that you have your very own Billionheir, now you want to keep it quiet!

"I really appreciate that Rev," I replied. "Of course I accept your apology. Thank you."

"Aw, I knew you couldn't stay sore at me. Shit. Neither one of us would have a Distribution deal with Willy if I hadn't opened my big fat mouth. So it's not all bad, right?"

Motherfucker!

"You have a deal with Willy? As a Producer?"

"Fuck that! Everyone and their brother is a record Producer these days. As a Mogul!"

"As a Mogul? But there's no such job position as a Mogul!" I said indignantly.

"Sure there is! You and I are now Moguls, my friend. There's no way around that. Willy has blessed us both with this. Don't question it!"

I don't know what pissed me off more. The Rev telling Willy about my Billionheir, or Willy dishing out Mogul status to other Producers. Aardy, who had been quiet to this point, interjected a thought.

"So, let me guess," Aardy said. "You're cowriting a song with your Billionheir, and you get an eight-figure Label deal if the track is a big hit?"

"Yeah. Hey. Whoa. Wow! You guys too? Well, that's pretty nuts."

Who knew that mentoring Billionheirs could be so universally lucrative?

The boys had returned from their walk, and I was certain Kanish was going to suggest we play the Douchebag track for his friend. This would have been nothing short of awkward, because there was no fucking way I was playing this track for what it now turns out is our competition. Much to my surprise, Kanish chose to beg off.

"Thank you vehdy much for bringing Mukesh for a visit, Rev. I vehdy much appreciate the gesture, but I'm afraid my Producer wants me to deliver a vocal today."

"We should get out of your hair then," the Rev replied.

We all said our goodbyes as Mukesh stood expectantly at the back of the Rolls-Royce.

"I'm not opening the fucking door for you!" the Rev admonished. "That's not my gig, kid."

Mukesh begrudgingly opened his own door and the Rev drove off. Kanish took a seat in the driveway lounge.

"I'm afraid I have some vehdy distressing news." Kanish winced.

"Let me guess: the Rev and Mukesh got the same deal as us," I replied.

"To be Moguls, no less! And Mukesh is going to perform the rap!"

"Really? They're doing a rap song too? What the hell does the Rev know about hip-hop?"

"You know what this means, right, boys?" Aardy interjected.

"The race is on."

"The race? What is this race you speak of?" Kanish asked quizzically.

"Well, it's like this," Aardy started. "Willy isn't going to be handing out two eight-figure deals. Either we get the deal or they do. That means . . ."

"We need to hit first," Kanish reasoned.

Clearly, if the Rev was producing a hip-hop track with an Indian Billionheir Artist, and we were producing a hip-hop track with an Indian Billionheir Artist, finishing first could be the difference between eight figures and none. There are only so many radio slots, and putting out two songs from new Artists, both Indian, and both rappers, could potentially kill everyone's chances. Without a hit song, there is no Label deal. And since Willy would likely only push one of our songs to radio, we had to beat Rev to the punch.

"I noticed you didn't offer to play your friend the track," I said to Kanish.

"Certainly not. Why would I share our unfinished work with my competition? Do you think that I brought Mukesh here so that he could become a Music Mogul before me?"

"Good point. So, how are we doing on these Douchebag verses then, Kanish?"

"I am vehdy much ready to record."

After a few minor tweaks to the lyric, we began to record the vocal to the Douchebag Song in earnest. Kanish did a great job. He performed like a pro. He took direction. He delivered passionate performances. He was able to make changes on the spot. The beat was working. Kanish was working. Everything was working.

Kanish took a final drag from the late-night Fatty. The three of us were all well past the high fives and accolades that come from capturing a money vocal.

"What is the lesson today?" Kanish asked.

As cutthroat as things have become, and despite being in a race against the Rev to deliver a hit record, I would not allow our newfound competition to Manifest into any kind of animus. Deep down, I've been greatly annoyed with the Rev for betraying my trust, but as he pointed out, if he hadn't, we wouldn't be in these rather exciting circumstances in the first place.

"To understand everything is to forgive everything," I replied.

Mixerman

CHAPTER SIXTEEN

OPERATION DISTRACT-A-BILLIONHEIR

Saying there's no money in Music would be like saying there's no money in the US. There is, it's just all crammed up at the top.

In the US, 5 percent of the adult population controls 62 percent of the wealth. The next 15 percent control 31 percent, leaving the bottom 80 percent of the population with the remaining 7 percent of the wealth. That's right. According to Wikipedia, the bottom 80 percent in this country hold 7 percent of the assets.

It would be difficult to figure out statistically how that compares to the Music Business. But if I had to make a guess—and it's probably a pretty good one—I would say that the top 1 percent controls 90 percent of the revenue generated in the Music Business. In other words, as obscene as income equality has gotten in the US economy, it's nothing compared to how revenues are distributed in the Music Business.

Now, consider these concurrent realities:

Trade schools spit out thousands upon thousands of future Producers on a monthly basis into an already über-competitive job market of a contracting industry chock-full of Producers and engineers with scads of RIAA Gold and Platinum awards.

Torrent sites based in Russia and China collect a fee in exchange for unfettered access to millions of illegally stored intellectual products. The Creators of that property get nothing out of that. Not a penny. And this isn't a small problem, either. We're all getting crushed by it. Best as I can tell, my books are downloaded from torrent sites at a rate of eight to one against sales. I can make that determination based on the download tallies that these sorts of sites keep. That's right, the Torrent sites flaunt the popularity of a Creator's work, thereby guaranteeing more illegal downloads.

Big Tech Streaming—and that includes video-sharing sites—essentially colludes with Major Labels to pilfer money from a generation of

Songwriters and Producers. The Majors have the catalog that Big Tech needs access to, and so it's the Majors that get the Tiger's Share of the revenue generated, much of it delivered in the form of advances rather than as payments for works streamed. This leaves some question as to whether the Labels are even bothering to distribute that money to their Artists in a fair and equitable manner. Actually, there's no question. They don't and aren't.

Welcome to the clusterfuck that is the Music Business.

To make matters worse, now Artists have to be experts in everything that goes into making and selling records, including search-engine optimization (SEO), website design, and Internet marketing, which doesn't leave much time for creating. There used to be enough money to go around in this business such that everyone could do one job and do it well. There was the Artist, who would write and perform the music. The manager, who would take care of the business so the Artist could stay focused on creating music. The Producer, who would help the Artist arrange the track and deliver a great performance. The recordist, who captured the moment. The Mixer, who came in and balanced the arrangement. The mastering engineer, who prepared the track for delivery to the consumer. The Mook Record Exec, who brought the Artist weed and pretended like he knew something about music. The Mogul, who ran the Label that hired a whole team of people to market and promote the Artist. Everyone had their own unique and important full-time job.

Now look at us. It's just as Aardy pointed out the first day. We are operating as the Artists, the Songwriters, the Producers, the Recordists, the Mixers, the Mooks, and the Moguls. And it would make sense for us to perform all those jobs, but I might point out, we also have a Distribution deal that came with a $50K advance!

How the hell did that happen?

As you can imagine, when you perform that many jobs, things have a tendency to slow down. Sometimes they even come to a grinding halt. That would be the case here, as I was getting nowhere with the mix. Dejected, I planted my forehead against the glass of the Raven MTX.

"Talk to me," Aardy encouraged.

"Something's just not right," I groaned.

"I figured that around day two of this madness. It's now day five and you still don't have a mix."

Just to give you some perspective, a mix doesn't take five days. A mix, which results from the process of balancing all of the parts in an arrangement, takes a day, if not half of one. Granted, if things get particularly hairball, then a mix can take up to three days. They don't ever take five. Even a twelve-minute-long track, which seemingly takes forever to mix, doesn't take five days. And seeing as the run time on the Douchebag Song is three minutes and thirty seconds, there was absolutely no earthly reason why I should still be mixing this track, other than the fact that I still wasn't happy with it.

Aardy had demonstrated remarkable patience these past five days, as had Kanish. But then, Aardy wasn't producing this record. His job was to shut the fuck up until such time as I needed him. Kanish wasn't even around and for good reason. He was on a critically important mission. We call it Operation Distract-a-Billionheir.

The plan was simple. The mix was taking longer than expected, and we needed time. We couldn't possibly risk the Rev and Mukesh releasing their song before us. The best way to prevent that was to leave the Rev without a performer, and so Aardy asked Kanish to take his friend for a multi-day tour of Los Angeles. I mean, you can't record a vocal if your Artist won't go the studio, right?

Look, if you find that plan despicable, I have three words for you. *Eight fucking figures.* Okay? So anyone calling out my morals can fuck off. Music can be a blood sport. Especially today.

Ahem.

As you can surely tell, I was beginning to feel the pressure. We had one shot at this, and frankly, I've been all fucked up because I must somehow negotiate my decisions from the perspective of Mook, Producer, and Artist all at the same time, an impossibility if there ever was one.

"Aardy." I sighed in exasperation, my head still down. "What about the video?"

"That would require a mix."

"Yes. I understand that, but I'm not having a mix issue. I'm having a Production issue. It's also a Mook issue."

"How can it be both?"

"How can it not be both?"

"You don't have a Mook on this project."

"I'm the Mook. By default. I'm virtually auditioning for the role."

"Well, I'd say you're failing miserably at it."

Aardy isn't really the hand-holding type. He tells me like it is, which is why we work together. Unfortunately, I was in a delicate state, and that particular reply wasn't helping matters. Neither was an incoming Skype from Paneer. Fuck! Normally, I'd have declined the call, but it's not like I was being productive.

"Hello Paneer," I said coldly.

"I would vehdy much like a report on your progress. My patience grows weary."

I'm not sure how patience grows weary, but the sentiment was clear. I needed to send him something to listen to; otherwise everything could get really fucked up, and fast. It's one thing for Kanish to be cut off from his Trust, which he has ways around. I was far more concerned with Kanish being recalled back to India.

"I think you're going to be pleasantly surprised," I said. "We're just putting the finishing touches on a song now. Shall I send it to you?"

"What is this Song you speak of? What is my son's role in it?"

"Talking about music in the abstract is a waste of time, Paneer."

"You are a cheeky and difficult man. Send it to me presently, then," Paneer scolded as he hung up the Skype.

I immediately prepared my current mix for transfer to Paneer.

"You're nuts," Aardy said.

"I have to send him something, and that's all we have."

"You're opening a can of worms. What if he gives you notes?"

"Notes! That's absurd. He's not qualified to offer us notes!"

"Neither are Mooks. Why not just send him a track you mixed last year?"

"Dude. What year is it? I can't send him something that he could just Shazam. The guy's a tech magnate. I'm better off just letting him hear his son's talent for himself."

I put the mix up on my Dropbox, messaged Paneer with the link, and ten minutes later we were back on the Skype.

"What is this that you have sent me?"

"I told you. It's a track that Kanish and I are producing together."

"Kanish is the one making that chattering?"

"It's called rapping. And yes, that's Kanish. He's quite talented, you know. You should be proud of him."

"Don't be absurd. It is not my son's obvious talent that concerns me. Let me tell you, it is this arrangement of yours. It is all wrong. What kind of hack Producer are you after all?"

"Yes. Thank you, Paneer. The track isn't even finished yet."

"You are vedhy right about that! Where the hell is the motherfucker sitar?"

The sitar?

The sitar?

The sitar!

THE SITAR!!!!

Of course!

The motherfucker sitar!

"That's it! Paneer! You're the best!"

"What is it that I have done to make you so happy? This concerns me."

"A motherfucker sitar! That's exactly what this track needs! Thank you!"

"This answer does not satisfy me!"

One of the negative effects of never being satisfied is that those around you stop trying. So I hung up the Skype. At that moment, convincing Paneer to give Kanish access to his trust fund again was not my most pressing matter. If all went according to plan, Kanish would no longer require Paneer's money. The best gift I could offer Kanish was to help him acquire his independence. We were well on our way.

"I would call those notes," Aardy gibed. "I take it you now want to add a sitar."

"And Indian percussion, among other things," I replied. "I've been getting so bogged down negotiating everything with myself that I totally missed the obvious. We need to tie in the Indian element."

"I thought that's what the Bollywood strings were for."

"They're too subtle. We need to make this track even more Indian."

"I think that's a good idea. Do you know a sitar player?"

I really only know one sitar player, and that's Bob Coke.

I've worked with Bob on more than one project. I met him in the mid-'90s when I was mixing Ben Harper's *Fight for Your Mind* album. He was a co-Producer on that album. I also recorded him playing sitar for the French Artist Piers Faccini. Bob was the perfect candidate to play sitar on the Douchebag Song. Unfortunately, his outgoing voicemail message was explicit: "Thanks for calling. I'm in India and will be unreachable for the unforeseeable future."

Kanish and Mukesh returned from one of their many Distract-a-Billionheir jaunts. Mukesh was once again wearing all-white muslin loungewear. As cozy as his outfit appeared, I'm not sure I'd be comfortable walking around society draped in stark-white pajamas. But then, I'm not a Billionheir.

Sevaka began to pull out many large bags full of overpriced Universal Studios apparel. Then he began to pull out cartons of Woodcock Reserve wine.

"The wine! We totally forgot about the wine!" I exclaimed.

"Wine?" Aardy said as he perked right up.

There was a time when I was into wine. I'll still drink a glass occasionally with dinner if it's served, but these days expensive bottles of wine are wasted on me. Just the same, I was thankful that the weather wasn't overly warm lately, as we would have surely managed to cork the whole lot. Aardy immediately opened a 1992 Woodcock cabernet.

"Do you know how much all this wine is worth?" Aardy asked, still rummaging through the boxes.

"No idea," I said. "Well, some idea. They're expensive. But beyond that, no idea."

"Some of these bottles have to be worth close to a thousand dollars."

Mukesh excused himself to go to the loo. Kanish waited patiently until Mukesh was fully out of earshot before inquiring as to our progress.

"Is the mix done now?" Kanish whispered.

"I've had a revelation."

"I should take that as a no?"

"I want to tie in your roots."

"Tie in my roots? I should have dreadlocks?"

"Not your hair, your culture. I want to add a sitar part."

"You took five days to decide that we need a sitar part?"

"Spoken like a true Mook," I said.

"You're calling me a Mook?"

"When you act like one I am."

Mook Record Execs are notorious for cutting down the creative process with their negativity. When I was producing Australian phenom Pete Murray's album back in 2006, I had a Mook question me as to why I was recording the "big single" for the fourth time. This was a classic case of the Label insisting on a song that didn't really fit the Artist, tasking me with figuring out how the hell to make it work for him. As it turns out, I did. It was the biggest hit of his career, but that might have something to do with the fact that I kept going back and recutting the track until it was right.

Kanish was mildly amused at my rather surly response. As it was, I wasn't happy that it took me five days to figure out I needed a fucking sitar. It was bad enough that his father was the one to point it out. I most certainly didn't need Kanish giving me shit about it.

"My apologies," Kanish offered. "I think sitar is a fantastic idea. I only tease you because I have a solution to our problem."

"Our problem?"

"You need a sitar player, do you not?"

"We do. You know a sitar player?"

"It just so happens that my friend Mukesh is an excellent sitar player."

I was just about to shoot the idea down outright, but then Mukesh appeared before I could.

"Sitar? I have been playing the sitar since I was a child," Mukesh proclaimed.

"Yeah, well, unfortunately, I don't have a sitar." I sighed.

"But Ben Harper has vehdy many sitars at his store. He is your friend, is he not?"

Mukesh was referring to the Folk Music Center, which is owned by Ben Harper, and which has been in his family for some generations now. The center is located in Claremont, a charming artsy town nestled in the foothills of the Angeles National Forest. I typically shop there around the holidays to pick up unique musical instruments as gifts. I've been eyeing the sitars there for years, but could never justify the expense. For starters, I don't play sitar, and I rarely ever have the need for one. As appreciative as I was to Mukesh for the help, the issue here wasn't actually finding a sitar. This is Los Angeles—you can find anything here. The problem was the proposed sitar player. I didn't even want Mukesh to hear the track, let alone play on it.

"I think that's a great idea, boys," Aardy said. "Why don't you have Sevaka drive you to the Folk Center and pick up a sitar?"

The boys summoned Sevaka, hopped in the Bentley, and took off for Claremont. I addressed my concerns to Aardy.

"Dude. I don't want Mukesh to play on this," I whined.

"Because he's going to hear the track and steal it before we even release it?"

"Mock me if you like. There's something deeply evil about that kid. I don't trust people who wear all white. It's like he's making a conscious decision to literally hide his true colors," I reasoned.

I wasn't basing my distrust exclusively on his fashion choices. Mukesh was the very definition of an entitled Billionheir, and he's a bit of a Douchebag to boot. Had Mukesh shown up on my doorstep for a mentorship, this adventure probably wouldn't have lasted more than a day.

"Look at it this way," Aardy said. "You could have a sitar on this track by tonight. And then you're done."

Aardy was right as usual, of course. I took some time to add Indian percussion parts to the production.

Kanish and Mukesh returned with a gorgeous sitar and a whole shitload of Indian percussion instruments, none of which we needed at this point. Just the same, I was happy to add them to my percussion collection.

For those of you unfamiliar, a sitar is a large guitar-like instrument with strings that lay across a fret board. Below the frets, there are a slew of thin-gauge strings that run the length of the neck, and which resonate in a drone-like manner based on the sound emitted by the upper strings. Given its size, the instrument is typically played in a seated position.

Introducing a sitar into popular Western music is certainly not without precedent. The Kinks used sitar on "See My Friends." But it was George Harrison and the Beatles who first featured the instrument on their track "Norwegian Wood (This Bird Has Flown)." George Harrison was so fascinated by the instrument that he sought out Ravi Shankar from India to teach him how to play it. They collaborated on some records, too. Interestingly enough, Ravi Shankar fathered early-aughts pop star Norah Jones.

Mukesh, as it turned out, was a decent sitar player but a terrible listener, and I basically had to spoon-feed him the part and then put him in loop record in the hopes that he might play something useful. As much as I would have loved to use my position to beat the kid up a little—to knock the little shit down a peg or two—I was actually my usual encouraging self. Besides, he was doing us a favor, even if I was against his involvement.

Upon wrapping up our two-hour sitar session, I opened up the garage to get some fresh air. Mukesh and Kanish ran upstairs for some refreshments, and like clockwork the Rev pulled up in his Rolls. What the hell was he doing here?

"Hey, Zerman! You know, it's the goddamnedest thing. It turns out I can't record a motherfucking vocal without my Artist!" the Rev said as he lit up a butt. "I thought I'd come down and pick up Mukesh myself. You know, if I didn't know any better, I'd think you were trying to keep him away from me. Where is the little shit, anyway?"

Admittedly, Operation Distract-a-Billionheir was only supposed to buy us a day or two. Rev isn't an idiot. Clearly we'd pushed the plan beyond its breaking point. Further problematic was the fact that Rev was about to cut vocals. That could only mean one thing. We were nearly out of time.

"Who's playing the sitar?" the Rev inquired as he pointed to the beautiful instrument perched against the wall.

"Mukesh performed for us," Aardy replied.

"He plays sitar?" Rev said with a rub of his chin. "Say, could I borrow that sitar for a few days?"

Motherfucker! The Rev was going to put sitar on his production too! Aardy, who remained calm, chimed in.

"Sure, you can borrow it," Aardy replied. "It belongs to your Artist."

"Ain't that a son of a bitch! My Artist has a motherfucking sitar."

The Rev seemed intent on completing his own mission called Operation Give-Me-Back-My-Billionheir-So-I-Can-Put-a-Motherfucker-Sitar-on-My-Production-Too. He loaded up Mukesh and the sitar into his Rolls-Royce, and with a tip of his hat, he bid us all a friendly farewell.

"All right, lets get this track done," I announced.

"I think you're done," Aardy said.

"What do you mean, I'm done?"

"I mean you're done. You're way too deep. Let the kid have a crack at it. You need some distance."

Aardy was right, and I knew it. I was completely oversaturated with the track, and given the chance, I would likely spend five more days fucking with it. The only thing that was going to help was for me to get away from it. Besides, if Kanish and I were to be partners, then I had to relinquish some control. I can't do it all, no matter how hard I try.

We left the kid to his devices and had Sevaka drive us up to Manhattan Beach for a steak dinner and one of the $1,000 bottles of Woodcock Reserve. Sadly, the bottle was corked. Pure vinegar. I guess we shouldn't have left them in the trunk of the car.

Aardy and I returned home two hours later, filled to the gills, only to find Kanish relaxing on the back couch.

"Hey! What the hell is this! There's no resting!" I said sarcastically.

"I would vehdy much like to play you magic now."

"You would, huh?" I replied dubiously.

I strolled up to the Raven, pressed play, and took a seat in my mix chair.

Behold! The track was a celebration! It drew me in, it made me move, and, most important of all, I couldn't stop singing. Aardy kept yelling at me to stop, but then I'd forget and start rapping and singing again.

"You got it, Kanish! That's the mix!" I exclaimed.

"Yes, yes, yes! This is so fantastic! Let's put it out there!"

"Perhaps," Aardy interjected, "we should play it for Willy first, gentlemen."

"Ah yes, yes, yes. A vehdy good idea," Kanish replied.

"Give me your phone, please, Zerman."

I handed Aardy my phone, and he immediately texted Willy the news on my behalf.

"What the hell did you do to the mix?" I asked Kanish.

"Aside from adding a sitar, I have done nothing to the mix."

"Are you trying to tell me that all you did was chop up the sitar and balance it in the mix?"

"That is correct."

"You didn't even use the Indian percussion?"

"I did not."

"Motherfucker," I said.

Oh, don't be surprised. There comes a point in a mix and a production when one tiny little change in balance perspective can make the difference between absolute magic and pure shit. As it turns out, all this track needed for the past five days was a sitar.

Aardy held up the phone. A new text had come in.

"Willy says come by at noon."

"That's fantastic!" Kanish beamed as he sparked up our usual late-night Fatty in celebration. "I suppose that means it is time for today's lesson. Hit me with it!"

My phone buzzed again. It was a continuation text from Willy, which Aardy read to us both.

"He says to bring the Pharcyde."

"You still want today's lesson?" I asked.

"Now more than ever," Kanish lamented.

"Man with no time and too many hats needs more heads."

Mixerman

CHAPTER SEVENTEEN

SHELL GAME

Don't ask me how one forgets a detail as crucial as telling the guy who gave you $50K to make a Pharcyde record that you're no longer making a Pharcyde record.

In my defense, Willy did tell us that we had "full creative autonomy," and I've known him long enough to say with absolute certitude that he meant it. Still, that didn't help me to sleep any better last night.

Informing Willy would be simple. I'd just blurt it out. I'd say, "The Pharcyde are out." Just like that. Then I'd explain the rationale of why that was, which would be as as easy as saying, "The messenger doesn't fit the message." There was no reason to hem and haw about it. Or to parse it. That wasn't going to change the news. Why fuck around? Really, how I delivered the bad news to Willy was the easy part. It was the where and when of breaking it that was proving difficult.

After considering our options, we all agreed that it would be best to text Willy in the morning in a vague sort of manner, letting him know that the Pharcyde couldn't make it.

Mixerman: *Currently unable to locate the Pharcyde.*
Kanish, Aardvark, and I attending.

Seeing as Willy had never met Aardy, he would have no idea what *Aardvark* meant in this context. The way I figured it, he wouldn't question it, and as it turns out, I was right. Willy never did respond to the text.

Sevaka pulled into the carpool lane on the 405. The three of us were in the backseat of the Bentley, with Aardy in the middle.

"Let's talk about the video, boys," Aardy began. "Starting with the budget."

"Shouldn't we start with a concept first?" I questioned.

"I already have the concept."

"You do? And what's that, exactly?" I asked.

Admittedly, the video is almost more important than the song these days. I don't really know why. I mean, I grew up with videos just like everyone else. I've just never understood watching music. Personally, I much prefer the art of setting music to film, than creating a film for the music. Like I need your fucking storyline to decipher the song? And half the time the video doesn't relate to the lyric anyway, which is total crap.

"I've been researching this on the Internet," Aardy began. "There is one thing that goes viral more often than anything else."

"And what's that?" I asked.

"Kittens."

"Kittens?"

"Kittens."

Kanish flashed me a confused look and then began to openly question Aardy's sanity.

"I am vehdy sorry, but you have lost me, my friend," Kanish said.

"Kittens! The clip for the Douchebag Song should feature lots of cute little kittens."

"And what in Buddha's name are the kittens doing?"

"They could be doing all sorts of things," Aardy replied.

"Like what?"

"You know. Cute-little-kitten things. That's what people love."

"Are they driving Priuses?"

"Maybe."

I'd had just about enough of this.

"Dude!" I shouted. "This is what you want to propose to Willy? A kitten video?"

As much as I think videos are bullshit, I wasn't going to be the one to put that theory to the test. Regardless of my feelings on the subject, a video is most certainly a requirement, and if you're going to produce a clip, it would be best not to thumb your nose at the audience in the process. As if kittens have anything to do with Douchebags, or even Priuses, for that matter. Kanish seemed keen on alternatives.

"And what of Plan B?" Kanish asked.

"Bollywood!" I snapped. "Let's do a full-scale Bollywood production!"

"That makes no sense!" Aardy scoffed. "A Bollywood production about Douchebags in Priuses?

"And how the fuck do kittens make any sense!" I yelled incredulously.

"Because kittens are popular!"

"Oh, and Bollywood isn't? There's like over a billion Indians, and every one of them lives for Bollywood."

"Not quite everyone," Kanish interjected.

Aardy was quick to point out that India wasn't our target market, and I was just as quick to concede. We probably should have discussed all of this sooner, but we did just finish the track last night, after all. So, it's not like Willy would expect us to have a video concept locked in. Besides, the budget itself was the more pressing issue.

"Okay, fine. Forget Bollywood," I said. "How much do you figure we need to make a clip?"

"We only need fifty dollars to make a kitten video," Aardy replied.

"Aardy. Seriously, dude."

"Fine. A quarter mil."

"That's what I was figuring."

Frankly, that was probably $200,000 more than we should actually spend on a clip. And although Willy would pay the initial costs to produce it, we would ultimately have to pay back half of that budget. This would leave us on the hook for $125K, to be recouped out of our royalties. The way I figured it, without a solid concept, we should significantly pad our budget. Aardy and Kanish agreed.

Sevaka pulled up to Mel Odious Sound and parked directly behind Rev's Rolls-Royce, which was sporting more than a few parking tickets. I had half a mind to call the city and see if they might put a parking boot on his front wheel—if only for the picture. C'mon! A Rolls-Royce with a bright-yellow boot on its wheel? That's pure Internet meme gold.

Willy was waiting for us in Studio W. I introduced Aardy, and as they kibitzed, I sat down in front of the expansive recording desk and loaded the track onto the computer. If we were going to listen to the track on the Bigs in a proper studio, then it didn't make a whole lot of sense to play the track through the bullshit converters on my phone. That's fine for consumers. It's not fine for the guy who's funding our record.

"It's too bad the Pharcyde couldn't make it," Willy said.

"Yeah. About that," I replied. "The Pharcyde are out."

Aardy grimaced, as did Kanish, at the boldness of the delivery. I don't know why. I announced precisely how I'd do it. And in my experience, you don't pull lightly at a Band-Aid; it's best to just rip the fucking thing off. Besides, I was moments away from playing Willy the track. The cat was nearly out of the bag, as it were. It was best to just inform him of the change without apology.

I mean, why should I be apologetic about bringing something great to Willy? Granted, I probably should have given Willy more warning. I could have called him the day after we'd recorded Kanish's vocal. But you know what? Then he'd want to hear a rough. And I didn't want to send Willy a rough, because we were assured creative autonomy. Sending him a rough mix goes against the whole principle of "creative autonomy." Besides, I wanted Willy to get the full impact of a finished track.

"The Pharcyde are out? What happened?" Willy asked.

"Eh. The message doesn't fit them. Priuses in the Hood seemed problematic."

"I see. Well, that makes sense. So who is delivering the message then?"

"Funny thing, that. We went out to a hip hop battle and young Kanish here won the big prize. If I hadn't seen it myself, I wouldn't have believed it, but the kid's the real deal."

"Rap me something," Willy said to Kanish.

Kanish instantly stood up and launched into a somewhat animated freestyle about Willy and blunts and videos and Bentleys and whatever else was on the top of his head. His rhymes were exquisite and he never missed a beat. Willy was in awe, as he should have been. The kid can flow.

"Wow. You *are* the real deal," Willy said to Kanish. "Let's hear this Song, then!"

Willy listened as he always does. Stoically. Eyes closed on the back of the couch. Aardy, Kanish, and I stood on the side of the room so that we could observe his reaction. Unfortunately, Willy doesn't tend to move as he listens, which is torture for me. The Song was nearly through the first verse, and Willy had yet to offer us any indication whatsoever of what he thought. Then the first chorus hit.

> *Just another Douchebag,*
> *Another Douchebag,*
> *Another Douchebag driving in your Prius,*
> *You know you sees us!*

How you gonna beat us when your're driving in a Prius?
You slow down—

And then it happened. We got the validation we were seeking. Willy cracked a smile.

He loved it!

Yes, I realize that proclamation may seem premature. And clearly, I write this knowing full well what happened next. So I'm not really going out on a limb here. You'll just have to trust me when I tell you that I have never before this day, not even once out of many opportunities, seen Willy smile while listening to a mix. Not even a little.

"Wow!" Willy said the moment the Song was finished. "I just love that track. And the rap! My word. Great idea bringing in Kanish. And great call on the sitar. Whose idea was that?"

I didn't dare tell him that the idea for the sitar came from Kanish's father. I suppose his question was rhetorical, because Willy stood up and pointed toward the recording room.

"Let's convene to my office," Willy said.

We followed Willy to the beanbags, and we were all sure to jump just a little higher in the air before plopping down into them this time. These were high-quality suede beanbags with exquisite stitching. They could take my two-hundred-pound flop without bursting. Willy pulled some Stellas out of the SkyMall fridge, popped their tops with a lighter and handed one to each of us.

"Cheers," Willy said as we all touched bottle necks and took a swig. "What's your stage name?"

"MC McKay?" Kanish asked trepidatiously.

"I'm quite sure we can do better than that. And yours, Mixerman?"

"Mine?" I chuckled momentarily until I realized he was serious. "Why do I need a stage name?" I asked innocently.

"You can't rightly have a hip-hop act without a DJ. And I'd much rather market a hip-hop group than an Artist."

"But I'm not a DJ."

"You are now, old boy," Willy replied with a chuckle. "Oh, come on, now. This is only for marketing purposes. We'll find some young kid to play the part of Mixerman, of course."

"Really?" I said in surprise. "How young?"

The concept most certainly piqued my interest. I could squeak out another forty years in this business if I could reinvent myself in my twenties.

"Try this on for size," Willy said as he gestured dramatically with his hands like he was spelling out words on a marquee high into the air. "DJ Mixerman and MC Knish Knosh."

"Ooh," Aardy gushed. "I like MC Knish Knosh!"

Everyone agreed that MC Knish Knosh was money. DJ Mixerman, on the other hand, wasn't working, mostly because some dickhead in Europe pinched the name Mixerman some years back, and slapped "DJ" in front of it. As it turns out, he doesn't get much play on the Internet, but then, you have to be pretty dumb to steal a popular name these days. I mean, I absolutely crush him on every search engine on earth; as a result, it seems his career is languishing. As much as I'd really like to teach him a lesson and take the DJ moniker too, I do believe he's sullied the brand. I much preferred to distinguish myself, and DJ Mixerman wasn't cutting it.

"You know," I said, "since everyone seems to be a Producer these days—I think I'd rather be known as DJ Producer Mixerman. How 'bout that?"

"I like it," Willy replied. "But how about we freshen it up a little and make it . . . DJ Produsah Mixerman."

"Produsah?"

"That's right. DJ Produsah Mixerman. It's got a nice ring to it, yes?"

"Well, I think that's just great!" Aardy exclaimed. "DJ Produsah Mixerman and MC Knish Knosh Too."

"That's fantastic!" Kanish burst out.

It was a ridiculously long name, and after all that I had half a mind to go back to plain old Mixerman, but we'd made such strides in the negotiation, I couldn't bring myself to gum up the works. Besides, now that I've gotten used to it, I kinda like it. Particularly the Produsah part of it. *Producer* is so prim and proper and professional sounding. Produsah makes me sound more like a hack. And these days hack status has clear benefits. I'd even go so far as to say that the term *Produsah* has a certain hack cachet to it.

"I guess I can live with DJ Produsah Mixerman," I acquiesced.

"Excellent," Willy replied. "So, here's what I want you guys to do. Make a video. Come up with a concept that will generate some Views, and then market it virally as a hip-hop track by DJ Produsah Mixerman and Knish Knosh Too."

"And what about radio?" I asked.

"Radio and Spotify come after you manage to blow up the Internet with this song. That's the plan, anyway."

Wait! What? I was stunned. What just happened? That wasn't the plan. The plan was for Willy to get us on radio, and then we would blow up the Internet. Not the other way around. How could this be? I mean, if the track and the video go viral on the Internet on the strength of our efforts, we would get radio airplay, regardless. And we most certainly didn't need Willy's Label to get our track onto Spotify. There are Indie Distribution avenues for that. Anyone can get their song on Streaming. So what the fuck does Willy bring to the table?

"Does a quarter million work for the clip?" Willy asked.

Oh yeah. That.

"I believe this will be perfectly acceptable," Kanish replied.

"Excellent. Leave me your bank details, Mixerman. I'll have cash deposited later today. The contracts should be ready for your lawyer to redline later this week. Do you guys have a concept for the clip yet?"

Aardy opened his mouth as if to speak. Kanish left nothing to chance.

"We're still working on it," Kanish interjected.

"Work fast."

Willy adjourned the meeting and ushered us to the studio exit before offering one last bit of advice.

"You only get one shot at this, boys. Be clever," Willy concluded as he shut the door.

Before I could even say, "What the fuck just happened in there?" I was accosted by the Rev, who was looking unusually frazzled.

"Zerman!" Rev said. "We need to talk. Alone."

"I'll meet you outside, guys," I said.

Kanish and Aardy excused themselves. The Rev stared them down the hall and out the door. I'm not sure I understood the purpose of the secrecy. It wasn't like I would hide any of our conversation from my partners, but the man looked nearly possessed, and I thought it best not to test him.

"The El Capitan has a Billionheir!" he whispered.

"What! Where the fuck did the El Capitan get a Billionheir?" I bemoaned.

"India. Isn't that where everyone gets them?"

"No shit, Rev. How did he come to get his very own Billionheir?"

"Well, you know how these things happen."

"No, I really don't," I replied in irritation. "And if I did, I wouldn't be asking the fucking question, that's for sure."

"You don't gotta be sore. I mean, you know, I was having dinner with the El Capitan, and I don't know, I might have been a few scotches in . . ."

"You told him! Dude! You promised that you'd keep this shit on the down low!"

"I know! I know! But I told him about it before I got my own fucking Billionheir! How was I supposed to know there were so many Billionheirs looking for Internships?"

"You're killing me, Rev."

"I talked to him, all right? Everything's gonna be fine. The El Capitan isn't gonna tell anyone."

"And what about GQ? The two of them eat breakfast together practically every day."

"Funny you should mention that," the Rev replied.

Funny I should mention that? *Funny I should mention that!*

"What the fuck does that mean?"

The Rev fidgeted uncomfortably as he stared down the hall, avoiding eye contact with me at all costs.

"Motherfucker!" I exclaimed as the Rev cringed. "GQ got a Billionheir too!"

"Not yet! It's on the way!"

"*It's* on the way? What do you mean, *it's*?"

"I mean he's—*he's*. GQ's Billionheir is on his way! Okay?"

I dropped my head into my hands in exasperation and spun myself a circle. I wish I could say this was all for dramatic effect. For some reason, spinning in circles calms me.

One of the Interns was now rubbernecking from the reception area. I'd managed to make a scene, and the spectacle needed to end presently. There was no reason to continue beating the Rev up over this shit. All I could do now was attempt to stop the bleeding.

"We gotta take this upstairs," I hissed.

The Rev and I hastened through the Hard Rock Cafe–like hall of Gold and Platinum records, up the grandiose stairway, and straight into his lair.

"I really think you're overreacting," the Rev said as he immediately shut the door behind us.

"Okay Rev. You're right. But tell me this. Are these Billionaires' Heirs going to be Interns?"

"I doubt it," the Rev replied.

"Then what are they going to be?"

"You know." The Rev said pointing back and forth between us. "The same as what we've got going."

"Wait. Why did you just nod your head toward the door?"

"'Cause, you know, that's where Willy is."

"Where Willy is?

Oh my god!

"Does the El Capitan have a deal with Willy too?"

"Don't be silly!" Rev exclaimed.

I breathed an enormous sigh of relief.

"The El Capitan and GQ signed with Marv Ellis over at Armageddon Records."

For those of you who haven't read *The Daily Adventures of Mixerman*, Marv Ellis is one of the original Music Moguls. A Mogul's Mogul, as it were, and where it comes to Moguldom, compared to Marv, Willy was small potatoes. The two Moguls were also the best of friends, which makes one wonder, or at least it made *me* wonder—were they somehow in cahoots?

I was feeling somewhat dejected over the news, and nothing good was going to come out of beating Rev up any longer over it. The damage was done, and I was deeply regretting ever having flaunted my Billionheir.

"All right, Rev. Well, thanks for telling me."

"You're not sore, are you?" The Rev cringed.

Well, my ass is a little sore where you keep fucking me, but other than that!

"It'll be fine," I said diplomatically.

Aardy and Kanish were waiting patiently for me in the Bentley. I slid in next to them.

"What was that about?" Aardy asked immediately.

"Two more Billionheirs are in town."

"What!" Kanish and Aardy yelled in alarm simultaneously.

"Who are their Produsahs?" Aardy asked.

"The El Capitan and GQ," I replied.

"You must tell me," Kanish insisted. "Who are the Billionaires' Heirs? I know them all."

"That's what you're going to have to find out, my friend."

As shocked as we were by Willy's admission that our marketing plan relies almost exclusively on the viral sharing of our video, we were now completely distracted by the arrival of two more Billionaires' Heirs. What's more, we were talking about Billionaires' Heirs in front of Kanish as if he weren't one of them.

We made one final attempt to brainstorm clip ideas, but there was no recovering from this hellacious day. We would have to regroup tomorrow, after some much-needed sleep.

"This is all shit," I said, pointing to our brainstorming wall filled with lists of video concepts.

Whether it was shit or whether it wasn't made no difference. I was done.

"Good night, guys."

"And what of my lesson?" Kanish asked.

"A Billionheir in hand is worth more than two in the bush," I replied.

"This makes no sense, as you are fond to say. What does it mean?"

"It means we're still good."

For the now, anyway.

Mixerman

CHAPTER EIGHTEEN

THE FUTILISM OF FEUDALISM

When it comes to the creation of art, there is nothing quite as useful as money.

There is an inherent irony—a disconnect, even—that goes along with being an Artist in a Capitalist world. On the one hand, the Arts are the life-blood of an intelligent society. Art is how we describe ourselves, and it helps to spark societal conversations necessary for improvement, if not for survival. I would go so far as to say that pop art is the ultimate reflection of society.

Don't think about that too much. It's too painful.

On the other hand, it seems no one wants to pay for their art anymore. The increasing attitude is that art belongs to the commons—although I doubt it's that well thought out—and many view the purchase of art as nothing short of obscene. Why buy a book? That's what Torrents are for. Why buy music? That's what Streaming is for.

And while it's true that downloading a book from a Torrent site is theft perpetrated by the consumer, and Streaming is Big Tech legally taking advantage of technological loopholes caused by stagnant laws and even more stagnant lawmakers, the results are the same: Artists don't get paid.

Unfortunately, this produces a great many "starving Artists," which tends to propagate the meme that it is through an Artist's suffering that she bears her art. Which is true. But there are a great many ways to suffer that don't necessarily involve being poor. Rich people suffer too.

It's not poverty that drives one as an Artist. I mean, would Picasso—who had a Middle-Class upbringing, and who was arguably the most successful visual Artist in history—have made a better Artist were he poor? And wouldn't a comfortably wealthy and world-famous Picasso be precluded from continued success? And how would we explain Seward Johnson, one of the Heirs to the Johnson & Johnson fortune, whose unique brass sculptures can be found adorning yards all over central New Jersey? Of course, his art is generally panned as kitsch, but that shouldn't diminish my point—that is to say, you don't have to be poor to reflect the world from an unusual angle.

I've always wondered how great life must be for those who win the MacArthur Genius Grant—officially called the MacArthur Fellowship. The grant of $625,000 paid out in $125,000 installments over the course of five years is awarded to people in a wide variety of fields, mostly within the Arts and Sciences. According to the MacArthur Foundation's Wiki page, "the fellowship is not a reward for past accomplishment, but rather an investment in a person's originality, insight, and potential."

How the fuck do you invest in someone for their potential without proof of concept through past accomplishment? That makes no sense. It's *Rrritarded*, even. There has to be something worthy of notice. I mean, is the foundation just going to hand the award out to some random person with a nice smile? Here. Congratulations, Walmart shopper! You won a MacArthur Genius Grant today!

The most intriguing part about this fellowship is that the nominations for the award are made by a top-secret board, which includes an unspecified number of members. They're like the Illuminati of the grant-giving world, and thereby nearly impossible to lobby. I suppose the best one could do is make a public spectacle of himself in the hopes of getting their secret attention. As you can imagine, I'm manifestly beneath such things.

Ahem.

Still, these were not times for grant envy. As nice as it would be to see $125K in my bank account, it would only be half as nice as the quarter mil deposited by Willy Show this morning. MacArthur MacSchmarthur! This was no handout. This was big business.

Of course, my Douchebag banker was desperately trying to get ahold of me. He made all sorts of offers designed to pay me a little money so that the bank could make a lot of money without any risk. Such are the perks of being too big to fail, I suppose. And as nice as it was—as secure as I felt seeing that quarter million in my bank account—it wasn't my personal money, even if it was in my personal account. Those funds were designated for my business and were nothing but a down payment on a massive prize should we prove successful. In all honesty, I was starting to get a bit overwhelmed.

You see, it is now painfully apparent to me that we are in way over our heads. I say this because Willy Show has made it quite clear that we are being left to our own devices until we prove that the Douchebag Song can garner a reaction. Unfortunately, we have no infrastructure with which to push the Song. Technically, we still don't even have a business yet, although Aardy did file the paperwork to incorporate. We chose the name C@taclysmic Group Inc., which had much to do with Aardy's relentless sharing of kitten videos. At all times, kittens were on the mind. Besides, C@taclysmic Group Inc. just seemed perfectly appropriate given that our Distributor is Easter Island Records. What could be more C@taclysmic than extinction?

Further problematic is the fact that we still haven't received the contract from Willy, and while it's not unusual to negotiate the fine details of an agreement like this well after work has begun, the terms—as I understood them—seemed to be morphing, much like in a game of Calvinball, in which the rules are made up as you play the game. This is precisely why we put agreements in writing, to lock in the terms. Inexplicably, Kanish and I were now somehow completely responsible for unlocking radio through a viral Internet campaign. And here I'd thought this was going to be a two-pronged attack.

Then there's the video, for which we had no director, nor the time to hire one. Aardy, Kanish, and I were all in agreement. We couldn't take the chance. It was critical that we beat Rev out of the gate, but were we really the ones to make a video? What happens if it turns out that we suck at conceptualizing and directing our own music videos? Would that kill our chances to blow up the track? Can a song spread virally without a video? I don't know the answer to any of that, yet here I am making decisions as if I do.

It gets worse. We have no idea of the demographic that would be attracted to this song. We haven't filed with a Performance Rights Organization like ASCAP or BMI who would collect Performance Royalties for us. Before yesterday, we didn't even have stage names. Hell, we technically didn't even know who the Artist was until Willy dubbed us DJ Produsah Mixerman and Knish Knosh Too.

At this point, I must acknowledge that we literally have no fucking plan whatsoever. We're just making this shit up as we go along. But then, that's no different than before—it's just that now we have what seems like a sizable chunk of money to burn in the process. And I do mean burn, because a quarter mil isn't nearly enough to accomplish our goals. Volatile human viral reactions require an enormous injection of cash and manpower at just the right moment, and if we've learned anything throughout this journey, it's that it takes $7 million and a full staff at Universal in order to blow up a song by a proven commodity. Which begs the question, how much does it take to blow up an unproven one?

We have no support whatsoever from our Distributor. We've never spoken to any staff at Easter Island Records. We've never been to Label headquarters. Our only relationship is with Willy—who we always meet alone at Mel Odious Sound. And thus far, all that he's really offered us is a little play money. That alone wasn't going to break us. We needed significantly more resources for the task at hand.

I can assure you it's a bit unsettling to realize that you've somehow managed to metaphorically hike miles into a deep dark cavern, only to get precisely halfway through before you run out of light. But let's face it, aren't we all kind of in that situation? Aren't we all just groping around in the dark right now? Everything has changed so rapidly in this business—in life, really—that the old way of doing things rarely seems to apply. Except for one thing. Money. Money is still king, and it's worse now than it ever has been.

Say what you want about how great the Internet is, say what you like about how it's changed the way we consume entertainment and how it's opened the doors to entrepreneurship. Argue all that you might that anyone can now break through from any position, so long as they have a great product. Tell me all day every day how anyone can be discovered on the Internet. The reality is, you need more money than ever before in order to break into the collective consciousness of society. And while that may happen out of nowhere from time to time, the odds of achieving widespread artistic success without substantial backing is about as likely as winning the lottery. Yes, people all over the US win the lottery every day. The odds of doing so are still astronomical.

Yes, our task was simple in its impossibility. We had to reach large swath of listeners with the Douchebag Song in order to spark a viral reaction, and we didn't have enough resources to reach a tipping point. To make matters worse, we had but one shot at it. This was the longest of long shots.

Fortunately, despite my own doubts, Kanish was undeterred.

"Forgive me, but it is time to now stop fucking around," Kanish announced as he tossed four darts toward the board, all of which crashed spectacularly midair before careening to the floor.

"You both are vehdy, vehdy wonderful at what you do, but I do not believe that either of you are to be Moguls. It is clear to me that Willy has left us to man this ship ourselves, and so it is now time for us to shuffle the buffet tables."

I didn't have the heart to tell Kanish that the ship sinks after the shuffling of the buffet tables. The deck chairs too. As hurtful as it was for Kanish to crush my dreams of Moguldom, it was really only a matter of time before he figured out the truth of the matter, and that time was now. Indeed, Aardy and I were not to be Moguls.

"I have come to the conclusion," Kanish continued, "that we need a marketing plan for the Douchebag Song. I have some tricks up my sleeve, let me tell you. But our first goal is to put out a video that will bring to us some attention, is it not? I believe I know precisely how to do that."

Aardy shot me a look, as if to say, *Who the fuck is this?* I wasn't sure myself, but I liked him vehdy, vehdy much.

"As Mixerman is fond of saying," Kanish continued, "the Douchebag Song is an Everyman song. The party nature of the group chorus is inviting to all who hate Douchebags. And we do all hate Douchebags, especially when they are driving slow in a Prius."

"There's no arguing with that," I agreed.

"I ask you this. If the Everyman will sing this Song, then why shouldn't the Everyman make our videos, too?"

Yes, of course! Why shouldn't the Everyman make our videos too?

Kanish was describing the business model of Big Tech. Get the user base to create content, which generates eyeballs, which advertisers pay to reach. In exchange, Big Tech shares just enough of the ad revenue with their largest content providers to make it appear as though it's a viable business model for the rest of us. This is nothing new, mind you. It's really just a modern spin on Feudalism—the Lord of the Manor exploits us lowly Serfs to work the land in exchange for our own meager sustenance.

It sounds so terrible when I put it that way, doesn't it?

Kanish was right. It makes no sense to create our own video when we could get all sorts of submissions for no money down. This would reserve that quarter mil for much more important expenses, like promotion. As Kanish pointed out, we would only need one good clip. What better way to find it than to take advantage of desperate would-be Directors looking for a break?

Hey, as fucked up as it may be that many of us are now living in a modern version of Feudalism, we do have to operate within the structure that exists—fair or not, and it's never fair. I mean, look at me. I sell more books than 98 percent of the authors out there, yet I'm posting this story for free. Granted, that's partly because of my agreement with Paneer, but I can assure you that I would have done so anyway. We're all getting so crushed by rampant Copyright Infringement, there's almost no choice. The only way to actually make any money is to reach millions of readers, and that requires some modicum of fame. As far as I can tell, there really is only one viable business model anymore: Get famous. Capitalize.

"Here is my proposal to you both," Kanish said as he laid his darts on the Raven. "There are many, many young video Directors in need of much notoriety. I would suggest we put the Song to a clip that simply says 'Your Video Here,' in bold letters. It seems to me vehdy, vehdy foolish to make our own video when we could get ten for free by the end of next week."

Certainly, most of those videos would be atrocious, but we only needed one of them to go viral. The problem is that the most atrocious video could be the one that takes off. Still, we'd take what we could get. Viral is viral. We have but one goal—to generate $5 million in revenue before any of the others. What with Produsahs the El Capitan and GQ due to get their very own Billionheirs, we would soon have plenty of competition.

"Now," Kanish said as he took a swig from his beer, "we should discuss our next order of business. Our Billionaires' Heir infestation."

I must admit, I have not been as careful with my words as I probably should have been around Kanish. I accidentally let the term *Billionaire's Heir* slip a few days back, and much to my surprise, Kanish glommed onto the term as if it weren't almost slur-like.

"I spoke with Mukesh earlier today," Kanish continued. "As I surmised, I do indeed personally know the Billionaire's Heir arrivals. Whether we are all friends or not is debatable, but all four of us are certainly quite friendly. As it turns out, it is Mukesh who has been spreading word of all the available Producer Internships in this city."

The way he'd said it, I was half wondering if he'd come across a Craigslist ad:

Producer seeking Billionheir to make sweet music. Apply within.

"Now, I'm afraid I also have some vehdy, vehdy bad news," Kanish said as he lit up a Fatty. "It seems there are more Billionheirs on the way."

The moment we got to four Billionheirs, I knew it was only a matter of time before there would be more. It seems everyone wants to Produce music these days, and the Billionheirs are the only ones who can actually afford to do so. It was predictable that the Billionheirs would arrive in droves. Still, I wasn't happy about it.

"How many more Billionheirs are on their way?" I quipped. "And who are their owners?"

"I'm not sure that's nearly as interesting as the nature of the Billionheirs," Kanish replied.

"The nature of the Billionheirs? What the fuck does that mean?"

"It means they are not Indian Nationals. One of these Billionaires' Heirs is English, one German, and another American," Kanish said as he handed me the Fatty. "It has become a problem of international proportions."

Damn. A Limey, a Kraut, and a Cowboy were coming to town.

"Let me see if I have this straight," Aardy piped from the back couch. "As far as we know, there are four Indian Billionheirs teamed up with four Produsahs and two Moguls. Correct?"

"Present company included, yes," Kanish replied.

"And now there are three more Billionheirs coming into town from Western countries, each of whom will have their own Produsahs as well?"

"It vehdy much seems to be the way."

"Do you know what Produsahs?"

"I do not as of yet."

"Do these new Billionheir-Produsah teams have Distribution?" Aardy asked.

"Indeed they do. Two of them with Willy Show. One with Marv Ellis."

"And you waited all day to tell us this!" I barked.

"This is my way," Kanish replied.

It *was* his way, too. And it kind of drives me more than a little crazy. Kanish just springs shit on me, and thus far it's been really good shit—so how can I be mad at him for it? But couldn't he give me just a little bit of a heads-up? Must everything be fully on a need-to-know basis? I don't even understand how he does it. Seriously. How the fuck does this kid keep this sort of information to himself? I'd be busting!

"Kanish," I said, "you know how your Dad cut you off?"

"How could I forget? What a ridiculous question," Kanish replied, sounding more like his father at that particular moment.

"What are the chances that all seven of the other Billionheirs are also cut off from their fortunes?"

"This concerns you, does it?"

"Well, I shouldn't have to tell you, my friend, but despite our massive head start, we might be at a significant disadvantage on the funding side of this race. And I may not be Mogul material, but I do know that large sums of money could mean the difference between winning and losing even larger sums of money, regardless of who comes out with the best song and video first."

"Yes. I am well aware of this, and I would suggest that you worry no longer, my friend. I have a plan."

"Any chance you might share that plan?" I asked innocently.

"It would be best if I did not," Kanish concluded mysteriously.

As I wrap up this particular chapter of our story, and I reflect upon all that we've been through thus far, I can't help but smile. The moment Kanish Kanish acquired his rightful position as leader of this operation, he had taken his first major step toward Moguldom. I don't think I could be any prouder of him. For Kanish now understood the obvious: that I—his Guru—was well out of my element. That I could only lead him so far down the path of Moguldom, and that wasn't very far at all. And for the first time since we began this journey, we were finally all in our proper positions. Aardy as advisor. Kanish as Mogul. Mixerman as Produsah.

It was nearly midnight, and I was now the newly crowned Redondo Beach Open Beaver Champion. I somehow eked one out in a squeaker.

"Do not even consider retiring before delivering my lesson," Kanish insisted as I packed up the darts for the night.

"The Jackal and the Hyena live best safely behind the Bengal Tiger," I mused.

Mixerman

CHAPTER NINETEEN

MAKING MOUNTAINS OUT OF MOGULHILLS

It has been a week since my last entry. In that time, we have received our Corporate seal from the State of California, which Aardy used to established our bank account. It's official. C@taclysmic Group Inc. is open for business.

As of this morning, our "Your Video Here" experiment has been Viewed just over 3,500 times. I shouldn't have to tell you that's an abysmal performance. In our defense, we've had a bit of trouble getting the word out. And although Aardy and I have visited all sorts of Internet forums that cater to would-be music video Directors, our posts have been treated as nothing more than spam. Sadly, the tolerance for shameless self-promotion is at an all-time low these days.

For all we knew, there could be hundreds of kids out there furiously editing together their version of the Douchebag video. There could also be none. Which was kind of pissing me off.

I just have to say, it's so fucked up that record Labels will spend as little as they possibly can on the recording only to turn around and spend an obscene sum on a video. I realize videos are often far more expensive to produce than recordings, but I'm not sure I really understand why. It took just as long to create the Douchebag Song as it would take to film and edit a clip. Besides, in most cases it's the song that sells. Not the video.

It's the song that will stand the test of time. It's the song that will be recorded over and over again by new Artists across the decades, perhaps even through the centuries. The video itself has a definitive shelf life. I mean, how many videos of classic '80s pop songs do we watch at this point and time? None. Yet many of the great songs from that era are Spun all the time.

A song can have a shelf life too, particularly if it's kitschy or has some kind of reference that will date it. And while railing against Douchebags who purposely prevent the rest of us from progressing is a sentiment as old as mankind, it's the Prius reference that will one day date our song. We can't rightly expect that a Prius will even exist a century from now. Not only will we have fully cashed in on the Song by then, we'll be dead, to boot. So, really, who the fuck cares?

The total production cost of the Douchebag Song itself was zero. This is the advantage of having both the gear and the recording know-how—our only real investment was our time. Still, if I were to put a number on it, I'd have to place the production costs at around $2,500. That would make the proposed video budget a hundred times the total cost of the record itself.

Does that make a whole lot of sense? The song is supposed to be the hero here.

Look, I get why a Major Label would sink money into a video. Between Vevo and YouTube, the "Blurred Lines" video has been Viewed over 500 million times. The clip, which features three exceptionally handsome and relatively young men with three smoking-hot babes is also designed to sell sex appeal. A video is critical for marketing a pop song. But then, so are large buckets of cash. Which makes you wonder, is a clip for everyone?

Between terrestrial radio, satellite radio, clubs, Streaming sites, and local playlists, there is no doubt that a song reaches far more listeners than a clip. When a radio station Spins a Top 40 track all day long, they are often reaching millions of listeners on each and every Spin. Multiply that times the hundreds of radio stations Spinning the "Blurred Lines" record ad nauseam for the better part of three months, and there's absolutely no way that the Views reach more listeners than the Spins. How, then, does anyone justify spending money on a video?

Oh! You can't possibly break a song without a video! It's impossible!

Sadly, at this point that's probably true. Until it's not. In the meantime, we all get to make a video to justify the record. How is an Independent Artist supposed to compete with Major Labels in this regard? More importantly, why would one try? Doesn't producing a clip require a special talent? Do we for one moment believe that every brilliant musician is equally adept at conceptualizing a clip? And if an Artist can't even afford to hire a Produsah for the record, then how the hell will that Independent Artist afford a Director and his crew? Surely, the thinking is that the clip is far more likely to go viral on the Internet than the track itself. But is there really any evidence of this?

Aardy, who is generally far more patient than I, was no longer willing to wait for clips to come in from strangers. He decided to place an ad on Craigslist titled "Cash for Kitten Videos $100." Within the hour he had ten full minutes of clips featuring cute furry little Kittens doing cute furry little Kitten things. No wonder Kittens are so popular!

As for Kanish, he went to the Silicon Valley the other day to deal with some "vehdy important business" at the Code Shack. This, of course, left us without a driver or a chef, which I can assure you is nothing short of inconvenient. As a consequence, we've been holed up in the garage playing countless games of Beaver and eating takeout.

By the time noon rolled around, Aardy was putting the finishing touches on his Kitten Video masterpiece as I pondered a change to my mix room, now known as C@taclysmic Group Inc. Headquarters.

"Is there a particular reason we have the Raven in the mix position, when we could be using it as a forty-six-inch viewing screen?" I asked. "Seeing as we're in video mode now."

"You think we should turn it around and move it to the back?" Aardy inquired.

"That would certainly be more conducive for viewing videos."

Aardy and I disconnected the Slate Raven MTX, carefully moved the beast to the back of the room, and placed my two mix chairs in the front, just below the brightly lit dartboard. No sooner had I finished reconnecting everything when the Skype began to ring. It was Paneer.

"Huh, this will be good for Skype calls, too," I said to myself.

I pointed the webcam toward the front of the room, answered the Skype, and ran to my position under the dartboard.

"Why do you look so far away!" Paneer demanded, his ugly mug filling the large screen like a weather balloon. "And what is this? A dartboard? Is this what you do all day? Play darts?"

At times it was, but I wasn't going to tell him that. Nor was I going to bother explaining how important downtime is when you're trying to create. It's the time that you spend not thinking about your creative work that allows your brain to Manifest its most amazing connections. Which got me wondering, does Paneer ever take time off?

"Paneer, have you ever, like, gone to the beach?"

"Certainly not! Much like this conversation thus far, that would be nothing more than a waste of my time."

"You should try it. Maybe pick up surfing or something. It's never too late to learn new things, you know."

"I do not know! Where is my son right now? I have been unable to reach him."

"I'm not running a babysitting service here, Paneer. I have no idea where he's off to," I lied.

"I am starting to wonder if you know anything at all! A few thousand Views? This is vehdy, vehdy bad!"

Ever since I shared the Song with Paneer, he has been closely monitoring our progress. And while it may seem like I'd made a tactical error in allowing him to hear the track in the first place, that would belie the fact that he would just figure out some other way to make my life miserable. This is what Billionaires do best, don't you know? That said, I've found an exceptionally effective way to chase him away.

"Hey, while I've got you on the Skype, Paneer, let's talk about my next installment. I'm starting to run out of money," I said.

"You will see money when I see results! Good day!"

I'm not sure how my fee had become results based, but if it got Paneer off the Skype, that alone had great value.

Regardless of how unpleasant the conversation proved to be, the conference did manage to reveal a major flaw in our new communication system. The conference chairs were too far away from the camera. So we rigged a USB extender and attached the webcam to a mic stand such that Aardy and I were perfectly framed. Just in time for another Skype, too. It was the Rev.

"Hey, boys! Where's Kanish?" the Rev asked.

"He's out of town taking care of some business," I replied.

"Huh. So is Mukesh," the Rev replied pensively.

"Mukesh is out of town? Where did he go?"

"I'm not sure. Listen, just forget about that for a sec. I'm calling you because the newest crop of Billionheirs have landed and I know where."

"If you're talking about GQ and the El Capitan, they've had their Billionheirs for days now."

"That's old news. I'm talking about the other three Billionheirs."

"Do you mean the Limey, the Kraut, and the Cowboy?" I asked.

"I just call them Five, Six, and Seven, but hey, it all works. The point is, they've landed, and I know where."

"I'm confused. Didn't they land in LA?"

"Of course they landed in LA! I'm talking about . . . you know . . . *where* they landed. As in, with whom!"

I looked around to see if there was someone else in the room. There wasn't. Why the hell was Rev talking in code?

"And with whom did they land?" I asked casually.

"That would be the Empress, the Crusher, and the Saint."

"The Saint? But he lives in New York."

"And now he's camped out at the Beverly Hills Hotel. Wouldn't you be? Oh shit. I got another Skype coming in. I'll talk to you guys later."

All three Produsahs have had fabulously successful careers in this business. Saint has his name on over 300 million records over the course of four decades, including albums that he made with Mick Jagger, Whitney Houston, and U2, just to name a few. The Crusher and the Empress are easily credited on another 300 million records between them. And although their royalties surely weren't what they once were, I was having a hard time believing any of them really needed a Billionheir.

Silly me. Who doesn't need a Billionheir?

Aardy prepared his Kitten Video for the big reveal on the Raven screen. Unfortunately, it would have to wait. GQ was now ringing the Skype.

"What up!" GQ said upon his appearance on the screen, the magnificence of which was sullied by a bit of food caught in his thick red beard.

I began to rub my chin in the hopes that he might mimic the motion and whisk away the particle. It didn't work.

"You've got some schmaltz in your beard," I said.

GQ put his face closer to the camera to reveal the precise nature of the glistening matter. It was a half-chewed bit of mac and cheese, although it could have just as easily been a wayward maggot. Whatever it was, he plucked it from his beard and put it directly into his mouth. Despite his name, there was nothing GQ about GQ. He looked more like a bearded schlub in surfing attire—but then, most successful Produsahs do.

"I saw your video, you know." GQ smirked.

He didn't really need to say anything more than that. That was code for, *Do you guys know what the fuck you're doing?*

"It's all good," I replied. "We actually just got our first submission before you called."

"Yeah, mine!" Aardy said as he plopped himself down in the conference chair next to mine.

"Hey Aardy!" GQ boomed. "I didn't know you were in town!"

Aardy catered a party at my house a number of years back, and as a result, many of my industry friends are also his. To this day, my friend EveAnna Manley talks fondly about the pork loin he served. She's not the only one.

"Oh wow, man," GQ moaned, rubbing his beard again. "Just seeing you makes me hungry for pork loin. Anyway, I'm reaching out cuz I want you guys to make an appearance in my video."

"When are you filming?" Aardy asked.

"Whenever my DJ Produsah gets back from his trip."

"DJ Produsah!" I exclaimed. "Your Billionheir is a DJ Produsah? How the fuck did you come up with that?"

"I think Marv suggested it."

"Motherfucker!" I screamed. That's what I am! I'm DJ Produsah Mixerman!"

"Whoa . . . you're a DJ Produsah too? How crazy is that? Is that like synchronicity?"

"Hold on a moment," Aardy interjected. "If your Billionheir is a DJ Produsah, what does that make you?"

"I'm the MC. Which makes no fucking sense. Holy shit, look at me. But my stupid DJ Produsah Billionheir insists that dad bods are, like, hot right now. Can either one of you tell me how the fuck I could have a dad bod if I've never even had a kid?"

"That you know about," Aardy pointed out.

This was all rather shocking news. Not the dad-bod part. The MC part. GQ was most certainly not MC material. And as pissed as I was that Marv Ellis—Willy's best friend and president of Armageddon Records— was passing around my DJ Produsah title like a Sunday-morning Fatty, there was a more pressing issue at hand. GQ's Billionheir was on some sort of trip.

"Excuse me, GQ," I started. "But how long has your Billionheir been out of town?"

"I don't know. He left as soon as I finished recording my rap. What was that? Like three days ago or something?"

"Do you know where he is?" Aardy asked.

"He said something about Northern Cal, but I don't know. He doesn't tell me much. The El Capitan's Billionheir is up there too."

"All four of our Billionheirs are in Northern Cal? That's weird."

"Yours too? That *is* weird. Maybe they're the fucking Illuminati." GQ chuckled as he held up his buzzing phone. "I need to take this call. We'll be filming in Culver City. I'll let you know. Out."

The fact that the Heirs were all out of town and in the same general area left little doubt—they were all together. As to the Illuminati—don't even get me started on that bullshit. GQ never met a conspiracy theory that he didn't like. Still, something was going on.

Rather than play guessing games, I texted Kanish. I swear I hadn't barely hit send before Kanish was ringing us on the Skype.

"It took you four days to finally miss me?" Kanish said wryly before continuing. "Do we have any video submissions yet?"

"Aardy made a Kitten Video. Other than that, no," I replied.

"My Kitten Video is all we're going to need," Aardy said confidently.

"Ah, this is vehdy good news." Kanish beamed.

Kanish looked to be sitting in some sort of starkly decorated office, the coldness of which seemed oddly familiar.

"Are you at the Code Shack?" I asked.

"Much to my displeasure, I am. I would like you to please upload this Kitten Video to the C@taclysmic YouTube channel. Skype me when the video is fully Published."

Before I could even broach the subject of the other Billionheirs, Kanish hung up the Skype.

Aardy immediately uploaded the Kitten Video from his computer, I took a moment to watch the clip of cute furry little Kittens doing cute furry little Kitten things on the big screen. As sick as I was of hearing the Douchebag Song, as much as I never wanted to hear the stupid Song again, the Kittens were so damned hysterical in their cuteness, it almost made the track sound—dare I say it—fresh. And although conceptually none of it made any sense—I found myself unable to look away. In fact, I watched the damn thing five times in a row.

The moment the clip finished processing, Kanish was already calling us back on the Skype. How did he do that?

"Okay, I see the clip," Kanish replied. He then looked up and spoke a one-word command in Hindi, which was repeated verbatim over an intercom.

"Vehdy good. Now, without refreshing, how many Views do you currently show?"

Aardy and I found this question rather confusing. We just loaded the fucking thing, and I had been Viewing it locally. The answer was none.

"Um . . . none," Aardy confirmed.

"Now refresh," Kanish commanded.

Aardy refreshed the page.

"Over a thousand! What the fuck?"

"Fantastic! I need you both to fly up here right away. There is a private plane waiting for you at LAX. Sevaka will pick you up when you arrive at the San Jose Airport. I will text you all the details."

"Still a thousand," Aardy announced as he refreshed again.

"Yes, yes, yes. Refresh every few minutes. In the meantime, what are you waiting for? Time is vehdy much of the essential."

Aardy, being a mountaineer, always kept his belongings in one bag, and he was ready to walk out the door the moment we hung up the Skype. I, on the other hand, was not so organized, and went into a mad scramble to collect my things. It took me the better part of half an hour just to find my wallet, and I was absolutely certain we were going to miss our flight. But then, I've never had the pilot meet me in the terminal before. Nor have I ever been escorted through expedited security and then out the doors directly to the tarmac. So, this is what it's like to be a baller.

As you might expect, private jets do indeed come with free Wi-Fi, and Aardy and I certainly got our money's worth out of that. I swear we refreshed that video page a hundred times for the fifty minutes we were in the air, each refresh registering yet another impressive whack of Views. By the time we were in the Bentley, Aardy's Kitten Video had reached just under 30,000 Views.

Sevaka drove us through the Silicon Valley as we transitioned from a vibrant sprawling community to a vast wasteland of venture capitalism gone bad. This was Aardy's first experience through the disturbing Lynch-like scene.

"You're right. This is more than a little creepy," Aardy commented.

Sevaka made the turn into the expansive silver, faded parking lot. The Bentley pulsed as we made our way across the crumbling pavement and around to the back. The same five American cars were parked along the rear of the building. There were no other Bentleys to be found. Where were the other Billionheirs?

Kanish bolted out of the door to greet us, happy as the day I met him. I didn't even have an opportunity to open my own car door.

"C'mon, c'mon!" Kanish prodded as he physically pulled me from the car. "Are you ready to have some fun?"

I took that as a rhetorical question, since he was literally dragging me into the Code Shack with Aardy tagging close behind. Besides, there was nothing fun about the Code Shack.

"Holy fuck," Aardy muttered in disbelief upon entering the warehouse.

"Is it not just as I described it?" I replied.

Aardy answered in prose:

> *"Indian Coders in perfect rows*
> *Sit at tiny little desks, where a computer goes*
> *Each of them works like a busy bee*
> *One row then another, as far as the eye can see."*

Aardy and I share Ditties on a nearly daily basis, and as you can tell, this particular one stuck with him. How could it not? There was one thing the poem didn't account for, however. The Coders were now wearing headphones. But why?

"I am certain you have many questions," Kanish began. "I might suggest I begin with some answers. I have been vehdy uncomfortable at the prospect of leaving things to chance where our success is concerned."

How Billionaire-like.

I immediately approached the nearest Coder and flipped his screen toward me, which kinda freaked him. There on the screen was Aardy's adorable Kitten Video. I looked toward the scared little man and pointed at my ears, then to his headphones. The Coder looked at Kanish for approval and then lifted his phones. The moment he did, I could hear it for myself— he was listening to Douchebag Song.

"As you can see," Kanish began, "I have pulled all of my Coders off of their contracted work so that they can repeatedly stream the Kitten Video. This in turn should give us the boost that we require."

"That's pretty brilliant, Kanish," I said. "But you realize they don't actually have to listen to the Song, right? And they certainly don't have to play the whole video for it to count."

"Yes, yes. I am well aware of all of this. But we must create an illusion," Kanish said, as he began walking down the center aisle of the Coders. "We have set up the network such that each terminal is spoofing a unique US Internet address. This way, we disguise our centralized location from Google. I have no doubt that Google believes their proprietary rights are more important than our own, and so we must protect against any sort of SEO retaliation."

"Or lawsuits," I countered.

"And in order to prevent such nasty business as lawsuits, we have also implemented a number of measures that will make the Views more random in nature. A small percentage of our Coders listen to part of the Song before relinquishing their IP address. Others listen to the entire track before they renew their IP address. The Coders even approach YouTube from random websites. In fact, Mukesh—"

"Mukesh! So you *have* been with the other Billionheirs!"

"Indeed I have. And they are on their way back to LA as we speak. If I might continue. Mukesh developed an algorithm at Oxford that allows us to mimic viral behavior. Rather than automate the algorithm, we shall implement it as a script, which our Coders will act out. This way we guarantee Google sees a normal viral reaction."

"It's a little late for that at thirty thousand Views in just under three hours, don't you think?" Aardy interjected.

"We will be generating millions upon millions of Views. My chief tech assures me that we are below the threshold of raising any red flags. And now that we have verified our system is working, we can bring the others into the fold."

"The others? What others?" I questioned.

"The other Billionheirs, of course."

"But . . . aren't the other Billionheirs our competition?"

"Producers compete, my friend. Billionheirs Share. Follow me."

I was thankful he didn't try to say "Billionaires' Heirs' Share," which is a mouthful even if your first language is English.

Kanish led us down the seemingly endless aisle, past the many corn rows of Coders to a solid metal door with a keypad entry. In the room, there was nothing more than a chair, a desk, and a computer. The walls of the room were equally as barren as the neighborhood outside. Kanish turned the laptop toward us and refreshed the open YouTube page to reveal just over 40,000s Views. He then spoke into his phone.

"Go," he said before returning his attention to us. "I own two Code Shacks in the US, as do each of the other Indian Heirs. Most people get watches when they graduate university. Billionheirs get highly profitable Code Shacks, wouldn't you know? You may refresh."

Over 48,000 Views.

"And again."

Over 52,000 Views.

"By our calculations, we should be able to generate several million Views per day without Google ever figuring out that the Views are coming from just six main locations. The splatter pattern of Views is modeled to appear like an organic reaction. And since real humans are clicking on the links and listening to the tracks, there is absolutely nothing illegal about it."

That was debatable.

"Look, Kanish. Views are all well and good, but without Sharing, we got nothing. And I doubt your Coders have many American Facebook friends between them. Ultimately, we need some sort of organic viral spark."

"Yes," Kanish said as he shut his MacBook and placed it in his bag. "The Sharing problem shall be rectified. Hopefully by tomorrow. It's time for us to go now. I hate this fucking place vehdy, vehdy much."

"Me too," I concurred.

Sevaka drove the three of us to the airport. We took the same jet back that brought us to San Jose, and Aardy drove us home from the airport. I was silent for most of the trip, as there was quite a bit on my mind. Aardy and Kanish, on the other hand, chattered the entire time as if nothing at all untoward was going on.

"I don't know, guys," I said as I unfolded myself out of the BMW and into my driveway. "This kind of feels like collusion to me."

"Collusion?" Kanish objected. "We are Corporations subcontracting with other Corporations. If that is collusion, then there can be no commerce."

"There's nothing to worry about," Aardy concurred. "We'll reach out to our lawyer tomorrow, and we'll have some contracts drawn up between the Corporations. C@taclysmic can pay the Code Shacks for services rendered; then everything is aboveboard."

Although my two partners in crime were likely right, at that particular moment, I wasn't feeling all that great about it.

I opened up the garage to reveal our newly configured communications center.

"Ah, I vehdy much love what you have done to the place!" Kanish beamed. "Now, please! I have greatly missed my Fatties and my lessons, both, these past four days."

I selected one of the many prerolled Dispensary Fatties I keep on hand, sparked it up, and passed it to Kanish.

"These three have crooked ways," I said. "Mavens, Mountains, and Moguls."

Mixerman

CHAPTER TWENTY

KAISAPAISA

The big problem with morals is, even the most obvious moral positions are in the eye of the beholder, require nuance, and are often clouded by rationalization.

Thou shalt not kill another person. That seems reasonably moral.

What about a mercy killing in order to prevent months of excruciating and unbearable pain? Is that immoral? Or how about the State killing a convicted serial killer caught red-handed in the act? There's no chance it wasn't him. Is that immoral? What about killing someone in self-defense? What about in war? Regardless of how you might answer any of those questions, I think it's clear that killing another person is not a purely binary question of morality.

Thou shalt not steal. Also reasonable, until we start to define "steal."

When Barclays, Citicorp, JPMorgan Chase, and the Royal Bank of Scotland colluded to fix currency markets in the early 2010s—was that stealing? They were Manifesting an advantage that would help them to enrich themselves at the expense of everyone else, so I would say yes. All four banks pled guilty to felony collusion—a rarity for Corporations. They also paid out $5 billion in fines between them—a stunning number until you realize JPMorgan Chase alone hauled in well over $25 billion in pretax income last year. And the year before that. And before that. And you get the picture. Oh, and despite the felony conviction, not one person went to jail for it.

When Duke Energy was caught on video dumping millions of gallons of their toxic coal ash waste into North Carolina waterways used to supply drinking water to several communities, was that stealing? Toxic coal ash waste brings with it negative health issues for humans and fish alike. Hence the term *toxic*. Is that not stealing sustenance from the millions who rely on clean waterways? Some among us seem to forget that we live in the environment.

What about fracking companies that ruin the water supply? Is that stealing? Fracking negatively affects local home prices. It adversely affects people's health and destroys their way of life. Then, of course, there are the the earthquakes that happen with mysterious regularity near fracking sites. Fracking companies argue there is no proof that the alarming wave of frequent earthquakes in Oklahoma and Texas have anything to do with their fracking. Same with the new and improved flammable water coming out of local spigots. Coincidence! There's no scientific proof! Whatever, who listens to the Scientists, anyway? Certainly not the climate deniers.

When British Petroleum devastated the gulf by discharging millions of gallons of toxic crude oil into our most important US fisheries, was that stealing? They deprived an entire industry of its livelihood. They robbed the whole region of tourism dollars for years. They robbed us all of safe shrimp. That's not stealing?

To make matters worse, oil companies have developed technologies that allow them to drill in impossible places, yet they're still using outdated and ineffectual technology for when things go wrong. Of course, not only do we allow it, our policies absolutely encourage it! Sure, Shell! Go drill in the treacherous waters of the Arctic. What could possibly go wrong on your third failed attempt?

Consider this hypothetical for a moment. Suppose a representative of El Destructo Inc. offered you a million dollars to dig up your backyard with the understanding that this would essentially ruin the way of life for the ten thousand others in your town? Not enough money? What about $10 million? Maybe that's still not enough money. How about a billion? Is there a price that would make you say, "Fuck it," as you take the money and run? And if you're thinking you'd take the billion and buy out the town, even at a billion you don't have enough money to make the entire town whole as you make the decision to uproot them. A billion dollars is a staggering amount of money for one person. It's shit the moment we start dealing in even modestly large numbers of persons.

Now, what if there was some question as to the level of destruction? What if El Destructo Inc. could show you all sorts of studies and provide numerous, seemingly credible testimonials demonstrating limited environmental impact? Keeping in mind that people live in that environment, would you take the billion then? What if the CEO of El Destructo confided in you that the studies and the testimonials were all lies? Could you sell the town out for a billion then? I know I couldn't.

When a Corporation is caught stealing the way of life from millions of us, through an intentional act of malfeasance that has been proven to negatively impact vast swaths of people—they get fined. Yet when a young inner-city kid is caught peddling marijuana on the streets, a drug that has been proven safer than alcohol—he goes to jail, is labeled a felon, and will have to personally deal with the consequences of that for the rest of his life.

When a Westerner frustrated with the organ-donation system visits Bangladesh to purchase a kidney for pennies on the dollar from a person even more desperate, is that stealing? The waiting list for a kidney here in the US is around five years. So what kind of sucker would spend hundreds of thousands of dollars and endure five years of dialysis twice a day when you could get a kidney in just a few weeks for well under $6,000?

If you flinched at my use of the word *sucker* there, good. I find it equally as morally reprehensible as you do. But then, I don't need a kidney. Hopefully, neither do you.

What if I go to a garage sale in an Upper-Class neighborhood, and find an ELA M 251 microphone worth approximately $24,000 tagged for $5, and then negotiate the price to $1, is that wrong? Hard to say. But it's certainly not as wrong as the thousands of people who go to Bangladesh every year to negotiate a better price for a kidney. I mean, how rich is that? The people with working kidneys are so destitute, the guy who is going to die without one of them is somehow in the better negotiating position.

Which brings us to my own moral dilemma. Was C@taclysmic's decision to generate Views, and thereby the appearance of widespread interest in our video, unethical? I've already demonstrated just how debatable ethics can be. And since C@taclysmic is a Corporation, the only pertinent question becomes—is it legal? That's why we have lawyers.

Since the monetization was turned off on our C@taclysmic YouTube channel, you couldn't rightly say we were stealing from Google. Stealing what? And what advantage are we Manifesting, exactly? All we're doing is generating the appearance of popularity. What the fuck do SEO companies do? They help you appear more popular than you actually are so that you can become even more popular. That's the whole online game right there. To optimize the numbers to your advantage all so you can get a higher ranking on Google.

All we're really doing is hiring real people to generate real Views, and spoofing the IP locations of those Views to avoid Google penalizing us for our efforts. I mean, why should we have to reveal the exact location of our listeners to Google? By law, we have a duty to our C@taclysmic stockholders to protect our Corporate secrets. It just seems to me, the precise nature and location of our customers would be a rather important secret to keep.

Frankly, we had more to fear from Google than from the Department of Justice. Google could erase us from existence. They could also sue the bejesus out of us, and so we gave our new attorney a retainer of $20K to put all the necessary protections into place. He assured us that we would be "squeaky clean," and he used that precise terminology, like we were in the mob or something. That made me feel more than a little icky. But then, the Music Business is the ickiest business around.

To date, I haven't had to deal with this rather gross side of the business—the side where a Corporation will skirt laws, if not outright break them, in order to Manifest an advantage. Like in the late '50s, when DJs were getting paid "listening fees" by record Label Promoters, ostensibly to evaluate the commercial viability of their records. Which was total crap. The promoters were paying DJs to play their record, which translated directly into Spins. It's called Payola, and Congress outlawed the practice in 1960. That didn't stop it from happening again. Repeatedly.

Over the years, record companies have used various loopholes in the law to come up with technically legal ways of delivering bribes for Spins. Eventually, Congress would catch up, figure out what was going on, and close the loopholes. Then the process would start again. Collusion and kickbacks have been a staple of this business since the invention of the piano roll in the late 1800s.

Icky or not, if our competitors are willing to take every advantage they can, then certainly C@taclysmic must be as well. If we don't, we won't survive. After all, we are currently going head-to-head against six other Heirs, and we're expecting more. Yes, two Russian and two Chinese Billionheirs have arrived in LA to team up with four more Produsahs. This brought the total number of Billionheirs in town to eleven. The Music Business was downright infested with Billionheirs.

I'm happy to report that by morning, our Kitten Video had been Viewed just over a million times. Furthermore, the Views generated from the eight Code Shacks were now showing up on search engines, and this was translating into a relatively small volume of Sharing—nothing viral in nature. The fact of the matter is, if we shut off the Code Shacks, we cut off the Views, and that just wouldn't do. We were in grave need of Shares.

Aardy and I were seated in the back of the Bentley, Kanish in the front, buried in his phone. We were on our way to Culver City dressed in costumes delivered early that morning by the Pimps & Ho's Wardrobe Company.

"I didn't realize pimps wore mouth guards," Aardy said facetiously as he pulled out his diamond-encrusted clip-on teeth.

"You don't have to wear it all day, dude. Put it in your pocket," I replied. "And take off your skullcap. You look more like a gypsy than a pimp."

"What's this Halloween shit show called, anyway?" Aardy whined.

"You lost me," I replied.

"The song! What's the name of the song?"

"I believe it is called 'Cash Money,'" Kanish interjected as he dropped his phone to address us. "In other news, I have just received word from Lakshmi. We are set to meet with her this afternoon to work out our Sharing issue."

"Which one is Lakshmi?" I asked.

"Lakshmi is the Limey," Kanish replied. "She is with the Empress."

"Great. What's the plan?"

"Lakshmi owns a vehdy large Telemarketing firm with locations all around the US. She has devised a way to generate Shares."

Sevaka announced us at the studio gate as DJ Produsah Mixerman and Knish Knosh Too, secured our three ALL-ACCESS guest badges and drove us to the last building on the lot. There were fifty punters forming a line along the side of the soundstage, all of them wearing badges labeled EXTRA. Sevaka pulled the Bentley into the adjacent lot and parked it right next to a Lamborghini with a personalized plate: MAHVLUS.

"Whoa! Marv Ellis is here," I said.

"This is fantastic!" Kanish yelled.

"You mean 'Marvelous,'" I said.

"Yes, yes, yes! I mean Mahvelous! Mahvelous! Just like in your first book."

The fact that Marv Ellis was here to personally oversee GQ's video shoot was a good indication of just how important this project was to him. While it's not unheard of for a Label President to be personally involved with his Artists, I seriously doubt Marv ever attends video shoots. I mean, Marv Ellis is the biggest Mogul around.

Kanish, Aardy, and I made our way past the extras waiting in line, and upon revealing our badges to security were granted access to the soundstage. The massive room was painted all black and was large enough to house a basketball court. There were lights hanging from scaffolding, cameras on tracks, and all the people that run those sorts of things. Even with all the markings of a film shoot, the place looked more like a party, what with waiters running through the crowd of onlookers carrying trays of champagne and appetizers.

At the end of the room was the brightly lit set of an ultra-posh bathroom, featuring an oversized golden claw-foot bathtub. The walls and the floor of the set were covered in mosaic tiles of gold and silver leaf, interspersed with color for contrast. Directly behind the tub was a green-and-gold-tiled inlay spelling out the words CASH MONEY in block letters. The entire scene looked like a Klimt painting gone bad.

There were three camera stations in front of the stage, and a plush red velvet throne, which I had to assume was the director's chair. Despite the party atmosphere, gaffers and crew continued their preparations, as makeup Artists put the finishing touches on Indian Princess ho's in six-inch stiletto heels and wrapped in American flag sarongs.

Marv Ellis was fully dapper-sleazy, what with his bright-white suit over a deep-purple shirt. He kept it half unbuttoned so as to expose the thick gold chains nestled in the mat of hair on his chest. This was a costume, of course. He was playing the part of an old mack daddy. He fit the role perfectly.

"Mixerman!" Marv yelled from across the room as he approached.

I don't know what it is about this guy, but anytime Marv Ellis calls out my name, I swear it feels as though he's hitting on me. It doesn't help that he's so touchy-feely, either. Dude likes to grab my shoulders like he's going to carry me home with him. Not that he could. He's a full foot shorter than me.

"Mahvelous! Mahvelous to see you!" Marv gushed. "Willy tells me your video is starting to catch a spark!"

The fact that Willy was even aware of our video was news to me. And I wasn't sure that Views without Shares counted as a spark, but I certainly wasn't going to argue the point. This was precisely the perception we were seeking to proliferate.

"Quiet on the set!" the Haired Director announced over his bullhorn. "Can I please have some quiet? Thank you. The girl in the red dress. Yes, you. Shhhh. Okay. Extras are not needed for this scene, so we need everyone to stay behind the yellow tape, please. You, sir. If you could move back. A little farther. Behind the tape. Thank you. Let's have the talent in their positions, please. Girls?"

The eight Indian Princess ho's in American flag Sarongs clip-clopped their way onto the bathroom set. Kanish and Aardy made their way over to my location near the throne.

"Paging GQ. Paging GQ," Haired Director squelched.

A young Asian man sporting a bright-yellow Sherwani jacket over white muslin pajamas pushed his way through the crowd straight toward the Haired Director, who immediately relinquished his bullhorn.

"Who is that?" I whispered to Kanish.

"That is GQ's Billionheir, of course."

"But I thought GQ's Heir was from India."

"You do realize we have other ethnicities in India, do you not?"

"Good point."

"His name is Kaisapaisa," Kanish continued. "It roughly means Cash Money, wouldn't you know?"

"I'd like to meet the Billionaire who named his kid Cash Money," I replied.

"I do not believe that you would."

"I suppose I wouldn't."

Kaisapaisa looked a bit awkward as he called out to a closed door across the room.

"Gee Cuehoooooooo!" Kaisapaisa sang over the bullhorn. "It's time to come out and show us why you're going to be a star! Your fans await you!"

Kaisa spoke in a perfect West Hollywood effeminate accent and brandished his flamboyance like a weapon, which he was now pointing toward the Green Room door.

"Where's his accent?" I asked Kanish.

"He pretty much grew up in Los Angeles."

"So, he's an Asian from India who grew up in America. That's not difficult to follow. Has he told his father that he's gay?" I asked.

"He would never," Kanish replied.

The Green Room door whipped open with a crash to reveal GQ wearing a leopard-skin sarong the size of a parachute—a requirement, if he was to be fully covered. To make matters worse, it was wrapped around his body like a toga, and I wasn't the only one to notice. Inexplicably, Kaisapaisa reverted to an Indian accent.

"Agh! Your sarong ees sarong!" Kaisapaisa screeched as he marched toward GQ.

The entire crowd began to percolate in murmur.

Sarong, Sarong?   Sarong is Sarong?   Sarong ees Sarong?   Sarong Sarong Sarong
    Sarong?   Sarong is Sarong?   Sarong Sarong?   Sarong is Sarong?
Sarong   Sarong   Sarong   Sarong?   Sarong, Sarong?   Sarong
Sarong, Sarong   Sarong   Sarong   Sarong Sarong Sarong   Sarong
Sarong? Sarong?   Sarong   Sarong ees Sarong?   Sarong?

There was seemingly no end to the whispers of Sarongs.

"Did he just say, 'Sarong is Sarong'?" I asked Kanish. "That makes no sense."

Whereas the crowd was murmuring, I'd somehow managed to blurt it out at full volume, perhaps even a bit louder than that. And although I'm pretty sure he was going to address the crowd anyway, he now had a fall guy—me. Kaisapaisa stopped dead in his tracks and turned to face me, bullhorn at the ready.

"I said! Your Sarong is so wrong!"

"Oh!" I exclaimed. "Your Sarong is *so wrong*!"

The murmurs turned to mutterings.

Sarong is so wrong!   Sarong is so wrong?   Sarong, Sarong   So wrong!   Sarong
Sarong? Sarong, so wrong!   So wrong   So wrong Sarong   Sarong?   Sarong
is so wrong!   Sarong, Sarong, so wrong!   Sarong?   Sarong so wrong   Sarong
Sarong   Sarong ees so wrong   Sarong Sarong?   Sarong is so wrong!

Everyone was in agreement. GQ's Sarong was indeed *so wrong*.

Kaisapaisa disappeared into the dressing room with GQ, and returned to the set a few minutes later. This time the Sarong was wrapped around GQ's waist, which unfortunately left his rotund belly fully exposed. The whole Sarong thing was not a good look for GQ.

GQ scanned the crowd with trepidation and then carefully stepped into the gargantuan tub. Kaisapaisa snapped his fingers and two Sikhs, similar to our own, scurried out of the Green Room with oversized army-style duffles, which they carried directly to the stage. The Sikhs unzipped the large bags and dumped out what had to be thousands of crisp new $20 bills into the tub, and all over GQ's mostly naked body.

"Slate, please," Kaisapaisa called out.

"Cash Money, the American Dream scene. Take one," the Haired Director announced with a thwack.

"Cue up the music," Kaisa announced over the bullhorn. "And . . . action."

The track had all the markings of dubstep, with its heavy syncopated Gangstah beat and pulsing low end. It was dirty and deep, and few in the audience could resist the urge to nod their heads in affirmation to the infectious beat. I liked it.

The eight Indian girls in American flag Sarongs were arranged symmetrically around the tub as they fawned over GQ and massaged handfuls of money over his red-haired chest like it was suds.

"That's it!" Kaisa announced. "Rub it all over him, girls. Rub him like the sexy beast that he is!"

Sexy beast would not be the term that I would use to describe GQ, or just about any of my Produsah brethren. You can't swing an oversized burrito without hitting a portly white Producer in this business. But then, Producers work behind the scenes and don't need to be beautiful. MC Produsahs, on the other hand, are supposed to be front and center. Not to be too distasteful about it, but I'd much rather have been watching the beautifully cut, camera-loving queen in a yellow Sherwani jacket than a schlub in a tub, if you know what I mean. What the fuck were they thinking?

The girls continued to scour GQ with the $20 bills and it looked painful even before his eyes began to well with tears. Of course, it's possible he was just moved by the raw emotion of the music. It most certainly wasn't coming from the lyrics. There weren't any.

"Okay, we're coming up to the Sitars!" Kaisapaisa called from his throne.

Motherfucking Sitars. They would have been better off pinching our Kitten Video concept rather than stealing our Sitars. The whole thing was difficult to watch.

"Get ready . . ." Kaisa announced. "And . . . on my mark . . ."

Cash money
Cash, cash money
Gimme, gimme, gimme
Gimme, gimme, gimme

"Not yet, not yet," Kaisapaisa warned.

Cash money
Cash, cash money
Gimme, gimme, gimme
So wrong, so wrong, so wrong

"Now!" Kaisa shrieked.

There must have been one big-ass fan underneath that monstrosity of a tub. The moment Kaisapaisa yelled "now," it was literally raining twenties. Every last one of those fucking bills flew up at least twenty-five feet, and were now floating down among the crowd. As you might imagine, the crowd erupted, and several hundred extras began to hysterically chase and grab at $20 bills as if this was some sort of reality show.

GQ was out of the tub faster than he could say, "Holy shit, that's my video budget right there," and he even began wrestling over money with his guests. Kaisapaisa was screaming in Hindi to the Sikhs, who really couldn't do much about any of it. The scene was chaotic. It was mayhem.

Kanish tapped me on the shoulder and motioned for Aardy and me to follow him. We were both more than happy to get the fuck out of there.

We escaped to the parking lot, where we were met by Lakshmi, the attractive Limey Heir. She, too, was of Indian descent, dressed in Western garb, but spoke in a perfect British accent. With seemingly nowhere else to go, the four of us climbed into the Bentley to have a meeting. Kanish introduced us all. Lakshmi got right down to business.

"I've made all the arrangements," Lakshmi said. "My Telemarketing firms can provide you with Shares from our ten thousand American employees. We will stagger the Shares over the course of the day. That should be enough to properly produce a viral reaction. We have already implemented your IP spoofing, and I have forwarded the Shares algorithm to all of the call centers."

"Fantastic!" Kanish exclaimed with delight.

"And what happens when people start squawking?" I asked.

"My employees don't squawk," Lakshmi scolded.

"Sure they do."

"Do you wish to engage my Telemarketing Corporation in a contract, or do you not? This is not a favor, you realize."

"How much are we paying for this, exactly?" I asked.

"The same rate that everyone else pays for our services!" Lakshmi scolded.

Lakshmi began cackling in Hindi to Kanish, who just sat there and took the lashing. Thankfully, a text came in.

Willy Show: *Meet me in the dressing room.*

"Bummer. We have a meeting with Willy," I said.

Things had calmed down considerably since we left. The remaining crowd was being patted down by bouncers. Many of the visitors seemed to have escaped out the multiple emergency exits, and it was unlikely that they would be stopped at the gate.

Willy was calmly smoking a Fatty on the couch in the back of the dressing room.

"Did Marv leave?" Willy asked.

"I would imagine," I replied.

"Your Kitten Video . . ." Willy said as he paused to take drag from a Fatty.

Usually, I have some idea of what to expect when walking into a meeting such as this. But in all honesty, I've been a bit off balance ever since Willy unilaterally changed the initial terms of our deal. Then, of course, there's the fact that we accepted a $250,000 budget for a video that cost all of a buck-two-eighty to make, if that. I had no idea whether the next words out of Willy's mouth were going to be "what the fuck," or "good idea." Then Willy exhaled.

"Your video has completely taken off. And the only reason I know that—clever boys that you are—is because someone Shared it with me on Facebook about an hour ago. The numbers are stupendous."

Kanish, Aardy, and I instantly pulled out our phones to View the C@taclysmic YouTube page.

"Imagine my surprise when I saw a Kitten Video of the Douchebag Song," Willy said as he passed the Fatty to Aardy. "Kittens. They're so cute. You can't help but watch them. Well done."

"Over fifty thousand Shares and four million Views!" Kanish exclaimed.

But how? The Telemarketers hadn't even begun to Share.

"So here's the plan," Willy continued. "Given these numbers, we'll immediately push the Douchebag Song to radio and submit it to Spotify and Pandora. I'd be willing to bet terrestrial radio is already Spinning it. You're trending. Of course, we should probably call the Guinness Book."

"Did we break a record?" I asked.

"Why, yes. That had to be the most expensive homemade Kitten Video ever produced."

Aardy began to Hammina Hammina as he waved the Fatty in dismay, but Willy stopped him short.

"I'm fucking with you. We'll be moving forward with the full Label deal. I'm convinced."

"This is fantastic news!" Kanish said.

"Hold on a second," I said. "What does 'I'm convinced' mean exactly?"

Kanish seemed simultaneously alarmed and relieved at the bluntness of my question. The kid is shrewd and wise beyond his years, of this there is no doubt. But he's still young and excitable and was not so skilled at hearing the fine print. The phrase "I'm convinced" left too much wiggle room. As it stood, I was still a bit miffed at Willy for his bait and switch on the original terms. Obviously, I'm not going to blow up the entire deal because he was a little less than scrupulous. That would just be stupid. I'd never work if I treated half-truths and exaggerations as blatant lies. That didn't mean I was going to give him the opportunity to do it again.

Aardy, I could tell, wasn't embarrassed by my pushback in the least. And while in most instances, I would much prefer for my manager to question the meaning of Willy's caveat, I wanted to send a message of my own. It was partly personal in nature—I'm not happy with the way things went down.

"Yes, I suppose I deserve that. You have your bank account set up for C@taclysmic Group Inc.?"

"As it happens," Aardy said, "we're fully open for business."

"Excellent. How about I put ten million in your account tomorrow as a good-faith payment on what will amount to a $90 million Label deal? Would that suffice?"

Convinced indeed!

There are rarely moments in life when someone says something so outrageous to you that you can only smile, as if you're absolutely paralyzed. Other than perhaps your lips, which begin to quiver as if you're trying to form words, but for whatever reason no sound comes out. And then you look around at your friends and partners, who are equally as stunned. It's like you're bees who just got blasted with smoke. No. It's like you're Kittens picked up by the scruff of the neck, frozen in submission. This would be one of those times.

"I'll take that as a yes," Willy cajoled.

"Yes! Yes! Yes!" Kanish yelled as he began pogoing around the room.

I guess this is just what Kanish did when he was happy. He turned into a human pogo stick.

"Okay! Okay, excited one." Willy chuckled. "I need a photo for promotional purposes. Hurry up, then."

"But we're wearing pimp outfits," Kanish said.

"You're in the Music Business now, son. Get used to it."

Willy pulled out his selfie stick and snapped a shot. No need for a professional photographer when a selfie will do.

Our VIP badges were enough to get us off the soundstage with nothing more than a quick pat-down. We all had wads of cash in our pockets—as usual—but none of us ever carried anything but hundies, which cleared us outright. Twenties are for suckers.

Kanish, Aardy, and I made our way to the parking lot, where we found GQ leaning against the Bentley smoking a butt, which I accepted from him. What the hell, I could buy a new lung soon.

"Can you believe that shit, man?" GQ complained. "I didn't even want to do that fucking scene. I mean, who wants to see my fat ass in a tub? Look at me!"

GQ lifted up his shirt to reveal his impressive belly covered with tiny little paper cuts, many of them bleeding.

"Why did you agree to be the front man in all of this?" I asked.

"I don't fucking know. He's a Billionheir, I figured he knew what he was doing, man."

"But you're the one with success in Music, not him."

"I know, I know! But he's overbearing, man. And he had it in his head that I should be the MC. It's so fucked up. And now a huge portion of our budget has walked out the fucking door. And Marv walked out too. And he didn't look happy. This is such a fucking fiasco."

"So what are you going to do now?" I asked as I passed back the butt.

"I guess we're going to have to figure out how much money we have left and come up with a new plan."

A $20 bill came flitting toward us like a tumbleweed. GQ held his cigarette away from his body in his left hand as he awkwardly chased the twenty around the lot. He finally managed to pin it against a car with his right hand.

"Got it!"

"Thank goodness for that," Kanish said sarcastically.

GQ put the twenty into his pocket, snuffed his cigarette on his shoe, and stuck the extinguished butt into his pack of smokes. He then walked right up to Kanish, looked him up and down, and announced in no uncertain terms: "I'm no fucking litterer!" Then he stormed off.

The three of us remained mostly silent for the drive home. We were all quite baked from Willy's Fatty, and still in shock that C@taclysmic Group Inc. was going to be funded for 90 million motherfucking dollars. Ten million of which would be in our account tomorrow.

Are you shitting me?

I asked Sevaka to turn the radio to KIIS FM in hopes that we might hear the Douchebag Song. We didn't.

At first, Beaver seemed the best distraction from our success, but we grew bored of it quickly. The three of us would just chill out with some Medicine until we were ready to retire—even if there would be little sleep. As usual, the moment I threatened to go upstairs, Kanish demanded his lesson. I was well prepared to deliver it.

"To walk straight on a crooked path is pure folly."

Mixerman

CHAPTER TWENTY-ONE

THE LAUGHING KITTENS

"**M**ixerman!" Kanish wailed from below my bedroom window.
"What the fuck?" I mumbled from under my pillow.

"In the garage! Hurry, hurry, hurry!"

Something was wrong.

I threw on my bathrobe, ripped open my bedroom door, and flew down the stairs, out the front door, down the sidewalk, under the arboretum, and into the wide-open garage we now call Headquarters. Aardy was on the back couch casually eating breakfast. Kanish was facing the monitors, sporting an impossibly wide smile. He was listening to the Douchebag Song, of all things.

"What!" I exclaimed in full pant.

"Wait for it," Aardy replied.

The final Sitar strum was followed by the exquisitely honeyed voice of DJ Dahling.

@DJDahling: "You gotta love that Sitar, sistah!"

"We are on the radio!" Kanish announced pridefully.

@DJDahling: "For anyone living under a frickin' rock, that was the soundtrack to that adorable Kitten Video that's trending on Facebook. It's called the Douchebag Song by the impressive duo DJ Produsah Mixerman and MC Knish Knosh Too! And I just love the mystery surrounding these two. No one has ever heard of them. A very smart play."

There is nothing quite like the first time you hear a song that you produced on the radio. I remember it like it was yesterday. I was absolutely horrified at how crappy my mix of The Brand New Heavies' "Dream on Dreamer" sounded on the radio. It was excessively bright, ultra distorted, and sounded completely different from what I had delivered. Then I heard the same mix on another station. This time the track sounded dark and ultra distorted. As it turns out, there was no problem with the mix. It's just the nature of radio.

Of course, Streaming MP3s is equally as atrocious. And as far as I'm concerned, satellite radio sounds the worst of all the mass-delivery mediums. Pick your poison. At the moment, that was terrestrial radio. Otherwise known as the goal.

@DJDahling: "Let's take some calls."

@GentCaller: "Hello?"

@DJDahling: "Talk to me, Sherman Oaks. You're on the air."

@GentCaller: "I am? Can you play the Douchebag Song again?"

@DJDahling: "Right? They remind me of the Pharcyde. How about you?"

@GentCaller: "The who?"

@DJDahling: "Oh wow. The Who is not the right answer, dudester. Let's take another call. You're on with DJ Dahling. Kiss me!"

@LadyCaller: "Hey, Dahling. Can you play that other Kitten Video?"

@DJDahling: "The other Kitten Video?"

@LadyCaller: "It had something to do with laughing?"

@DJDahling: "You don't mean the one with the laughing Kittens, do you?"

@LadyCaller: "That's the one!"

@DJDahling: "I'm not familiar with it."

@LadyCaller: "Really?"

@DJDahling: "What am I, living under a rock? [*Cue music*] There are no laughing Kittens on radio, I'm afraid, but there are plenty of Sitars! [*Beat enters*] This is 'Laugh!' by DJ Produsah Rev and the Mukesh Machine. Laughing is such a great sentiment! We all need to laugh more. Kiss me!"

"They made a Kitten Video," I lamented.

"On my way to YouTube now!" Aardy declared.

"It wasn't enough to lift the Sitar? They had to steal our Kittens concept too?"

I was beginning to wonder whether we were listening to an instrumental track, since there didn't seem to be anything much going on in the verse other than a tamboura drone and a looped Sitar part. Then came the chorus.

Take as much as you possibly can.
Waste what you do not need.
Laugh in the the faces of those who have none,
Ha ha ha ha—
You see?

"Is it just me?" I asked, "or is that lyric slightly disturbing?"

"Either that or absurdly hilarious," Aardy said as he plugged his laptop into the Raven and killed the radio feed. "You need to see this video."

There were Kittens, all right. Lots and lots of cute furry Kittens fighting over some yarn, which is always entertaining, but hardly revolutionary where Kitten clips are concerned. That is, until the chorus came in. This was the big payoff as the furballs all lined up in a row, which was impressive in its own right. But the real miracle here was—and I realize this may sound crazy—the Kittens were laughing. Yes, the Rev's clip featured laughing Kittens, and the three of us were in absolute stitches it was so fucking amusing. I mean, how does one get Kittens to laugh like that?

"How many Views?" I asked as I wiped away tears of laughter.

"That's the thing," Aardy replied. "There aren't that many Views or Shares yet. Certainly not compared to what we have going on."

"There would be a vehdy good reason for that," Kanish replied. "Mukesh has not yet requested Code Shack intervention."

"So, how the hell did they get on radio?" Aardy wondered aloud.

"Motherfucker!" I yelled. "Willy got a twofer."

"A twofer?" Kanish questioned.

"Two-fer-one. Terrestrial radio has only so many slots on their play-list, and they tend to limit how many they'll provide any given Major Label at a time. They try to spread the wealth so they can maximize kick-backs, but if a Label sends them a track that garners no reaction, they lose their slot. So Willy probably picked up an opening on the strength of our track."

"I see," Kanish said. "So Willy gets two for one? Which you call a twofer?"

"Exactly."

The moment "*Laugh!*" ended the Skype began to ring. It was the Rev, and despite how annoyed I was at him for lifting our Kitten concept, I promptly accepted the incoming call. The Rev and Mukesh appeared on the Raven screen. Kanish and I took our places under the dartboard.

"Nice robe," the Rev chided.

"Nice Kittens," I parried. "You realize our tracks were played back to back on KIIS FM in Los Angeles just now?"

"No shit! That's why we're Skyping you! Waddya think of it? Did you catch the video yet?"

"Dude! That shit is hysterical. How the hell did you get those Kittens to laugh?"

"That's the secret sauce right there, my friend. Those laughing Kittens are what locked in our Distribution deal with Willy Show!"

"Your what?"

"He couldn't stop laughing when we showed it to him."

"Specifically, how big a deal did Willy offer you?"

"The same as you."

"That's not even close to specific."

"Why do I need to be specific? Don't you know what your deal is with Willy?"

"You're the one insisting we have the *same* deal," I pointed out.

Mukesh grew impatient with our silly little dance.

"Why must you American Producers always compete against each other? Willy offered us a $10 million Distribution deal as a good-faith payment on a $90 million deal, just as he did for you. Do you not think that we Billionheirs talk? Do you forget that we are all working together now? Do you not recall that you have Corporate obligations to assist us in our quest to be Number One? What precisely is the point of withholding information from us?"

Kanish hissed at Mukesh in Hindi, which drew a rather heated response back from Mukesh.

"Speak American!" I insisted.

"It is time to implement the Code Shacks for '*Laugh!*'" Mukesh concluded. "I cannot say it more simply than that!"

On the one hand, Mukesh made a good point. The other Billionheirs helped us with their Code Shacks and Telemarketers, and we were obliged to provide the same service for them. On the other hand, his thirst for Number One seemed at odds with the whole Share-and-Share-alike concept. It was the very definition of competition.

"Forgive me," Kanish replied. "We are indeed working together, and I have Shared with Mukesh the details of our deal, just as he has Shared with me. Moving forward, I believe that it would make vehdy much sense to engage the Coders and Telemarketers with Phase Two of our operation."

"And what's Phase Two?" I asked.

"Phase Two requires the calling of radio request lines."

"You don't think that thousands of Coders with Hindi accents calling up radio request lines is going to seem a bit suspicious?"

Aardy got up from the couch, walked toward the webcam, leaned in briefly to reveal himself, then held his laptop up, as if any of us could see what was on his screen.

"I have a solution to that!" Aardy announced.

"I'm not in my twenties anymore," the Rev complained. "What the fuck are you showing us?"

"This is an online request form," Aardy replied. "Most radio stations have them these days, so you don't need to call in. Let's just get the Coders to fill in request forms as they simultaneously generate Views. Some refer to this as multitasking."

We could double the Coders' workload without raising their pay. Bonus! We were really getting the hang of this Corporation thing.

"That's a good idea," I said. "But it's going to seem suspicious if there aren't call-ins, too."

"Agreed," Aardy replied. "Let's have the American-born Telemarketers make the call-in requests. I assume Telemarketers still use phones?"

"Of course they do!" the Rev exclaimed. "That sounds like the plan to me. The Coders generate the Views and online radio Requests. The Telemarketers handle the Shares and the call-in Requests. You guys get the Coders going. Mukesh here will reach out to Lakshmi to schedule the Telemarketers, and we'll be on our way to the promised land. We'll talk soon, boys!" And with that, the Rev hung up the Skype.

As much as I wished to dissect the meaning of Rev's identically high-valued Label Distribution deal, that would have to wait. Another Skype call had come in, this time from GQ and Kaisapaisa. GQ's face was covered in tiny little splotches of what I can only assume was antibiotic gel. Kaisapaisa sat close beside him in a bright-purple velvet jacket with matching fez. He would have looked absolutely smashing were it not for his bright red swollen eyes. Kaisapaisa had obviously been crying.

"We've been dropped!" Kaisapaisa blurted the moment the two appeared on the Raven MTX.

"Dropped!" I barked. "But why?"

"Marv doesn't think my GQ should be the face of us!"

"Well, Kaisa—"

"Oh, what! Don't tell me you feel the same way!" Kaisa sobbed as he buried his face into a matching purple hanky.

This was a little awkward, because clearly it made no fucking sense whatsoever for GQ, a veritable poster child for poor lovable schlubs the world over, to be the front man of a pop duo. But then, how could I say that without insulting them? When in doubt, ask a question.

"Well, how do you feel about it, GQ?"

"I don't think it makes a whole lotta sense for me to be front and center," GQ stated bluntly.

"But I programmed the beat!" Kaisa protested. "Doesn't that make me the DJ Produsah? And if I'm the DJ Produsah, doesn't GQ have to be the MC?"

"Kaisapaisa, it's your art," I encouraged. "There is no formula."

"But you can't have two DJ Produsahs together. How would that work? You need a DJ Produsah and an MC in order to create a hit. And GQ is so manly. It just seemed so right. It seemed so smart to make the manly man the MC. And . . . and . . ."

Kaisapaisa dropped his hanky and leaned forward to give us a better view of his hysteria.

"AND IT WAS THE WRONG DECIS-UH-UH-UH-UN!"

GQ looked somewhat shell-shocked and did not avert his forward gaze even as Kaisa was falling apart on his shoulder. Kanish Kanish was equally astonished and clearly didn't know how to handle this sort of meltdown. Of course, Kanish hadn't spent the last two decades working with Artists. I mean, Produsahs.

"Okay, Kaisa, I need you to chill out for a little bit, and let me ask GQ some questions, okay? We might be able to help you."

That statement triggered head snaps from both Aardy and Kanish. Kaisapaisa crossed his legs and bit down on his lip.

"All right. GQ, what happened?" I inquired.

"You know. It was like one minute we had a quarter million and no video; the next minute we didn't have a quarter million and still had no video."

"What! You lost all of that cash?"

"We recovered most of it. But Marv returned last night and took it all fucking back."

"And you gave it to him? He can't just take it back."

"He can't? Well, he did. And then he dropped us. Just like that," GQ said with a snap.

"I don't understand. Why not buy out your contract from Marv and put the record out yourselves?"

Kaisapaisa removed his hand from his mouth and put it on GQ's leg.

"Am I allowed to speak now? Or am I still on a chill-out?"

GQ turned his head methodically toward Kaisapaisa and stared him down.

"I didn't tell you not to speak," GQ grumbled.

"Well, someone in a highly unfashionable robe did, and I didn't hear you defending me."

"Say whatever the hell you want, man. Holy fuck!"

"You don't need to take that tone with me."

Kanish gave Kaisapaisa a much-needed Hindi scolding, but it may have been a bit strong given Kaisapaisa's state. The reprimand sparked a clear and present lower-lip tremble, followed by the rapid-fire gibberish of a Hindi confession, straight into uncontrollable sobs.

"What did he say?" I asked.

"He's completely cut off at the moment, and his father will most certainly order him back to India without the Number One song."

"Or a Grammy!" Kaisapaisa bawled. "That's never going to happen without Distribution! I grew up in America! I can't go back to India! I'd rather be . . . I'd rather be . . . I can't even say it!"

"Poor," GQ finished, launching Kaisapaisa into hysteria again.

"Hold on!" I yelled. "Just wait right there please, both of you. We'll be right back."

I stood up and made my way over to the laptop to put the Skype on hold. Aardy, who was camped out on the couch in the back of the garage, was so alarmed, he stood up himself.

"You're not seriously thinking what I think you're thinking, are you?" Aardy asked.

"That we should pick them up? Hell yeah, that's what I'm thinking."

"This is not a charity!"

"Charity!"

"The song's a dog! Cash money? Gimme, gimme, gimme cash money? That's just terrible. The song has no chance of ever being Number One."

"I know! I know! But really, how much is it going to cost us to pick them up? I'll bet you anything that Marv gave them the same advance that Willy gave us. That means we can probably buy their contract for $50K. I mean, the track is fucking done already. All we need to do is make Kaisapaisa the MC, slap the track onto another Kitten Video, and it's ready for the Code Shack to generate Views."

"None of which changes the fact that it's a shit song," Aardy lamented.

"No . . ." Kanish interjected in an almost pensive manner. "I mean, yes, it is most certainly a shit song as you say, but tell me, what does it matter? We are the ones who generate the Views and the Shares, which translate into the Spins. We should test the effectiveness of our formula with 'Cash Money.'"

Ah, you got to love the ego. One hit song does not a formula make, and one Spin on the radio ain't even a whiff of a hit. Still, I understood what Kanish was driving at. He was clearly convinced that we could turn any old song into a hit just by manufacturing enough initial energy to proliferate a reaction. There is an entire faction of teenagers that believes that pop hits are Manifested through marketing. That any song, given enough capital, can be a hit. Of course, those teenagers become adults, at which point that line of thought becomes obvious bullshit.

The point of the Coders and the Telemarketers is not to turn a shit song into a hit song. It's to reach enough listeners for a great song to garner a reaction. Nothing more, nothing less. It doesn't matter how many Views or Shares we generate with Coders and Telemarketers. Ultimately, the Number One song would require an organic viral reaction. As much as we were gaming the system, we really weren't. All we were doing was putting ourselves in a position to capitalize.

That said, Kanish's little ego-driven theory seemed a worthwhile and relatively inexpensive experiment. I mean, if radio is going to jump on Rev's *"Laugh!"* track just because of some Sitars and Kittens, then there was no reason to believe that it couldn't happen with yet another track. Whether we thought "Cash Money" was "shit" or not was irrelevant. Once set to Kittens, "Cash Money" would carry all the markings of a hit.

Given the circumstances, $50K was a reasonably small gamble in the grand scheme of $90 million. And even if the total of our deal never cracked $10 million—a distinct possibility given the developments—the risk was minimal. Besides, we still had the Tiger's Share of our $250,000 video budget available to us. We could buy out GQ's contract immediately, given the option.

"I agree with you, Kanish," I said. "We should pick them up, fix the problems, and run them through the Viewing and Sharing mill. Besides, we kind of have an obligation to help them at this point."

"Yes, yes, yes. You are right, of course. Let us do this," Kanish announced.

"Great. You present the deal, then."

Kanish and I sat down in front of the camera. Aardy unpaused the Skype.

"I have a vehdy important question for you both," Kanish began. "How much did Marv advance you?"

"Fifty K total, most of which we still have. It doesn't cost me anything to program a track, you know?" GQ replied.

"Vehdy good. And how much cash did you happen to lose at the shoot?"

"About $20K."

"This is what we shall propose," Kanish began. "If Marv Ellis will allow you to purchase your way out of your contract, then C@taclysmic Group Inc. would be vehdy happy to Distribute you."

"Yeah?" GQ said suspiciously. "What kind of percentage are we talking?"

"The same deal. Fifty-fifty on all revenue streams."

"And the advance?"

"I would suggest that you keep your advance as it is, and we shall pay Marv the $70K it will cost to buy out your contract, but—"

"Deal!" Kaisapaisa screeched as he jumped out of his chair and skipped off the screen clapping in stiff hands.

"Oh, man!" GQ sighed in relief. "That's awesome, guys. Thank you!"

Aardy stuck his face right in the camera.

"There was a 'but'!" Aardy noted.

"A 'but'?" GQ replied.

"A 'but,'" Kanish parroted.

"What kind of a 'but'?"

"As I was saying," Kanish continued, "we shall pick up your Distribution, but you must agree to set your track to a Kitten Video, and Kaisapaisa shall be front and center as your MC. Does that sound good to you?"

"That sounds fucking great." GQ sighed as Kaisapaisa pranced in and out of the frame like a beauty pageant contestant. "You know, I have a version of the track with Kaisapaisa's demo vocals, which are actually pretty good. You want to hear that?"

"Most definitely!" Kanish replied. "Please send it presently."

"Will do. I'm calling Marv to see if we can strike this deal. We'll Skype you back."

Technically speaking, Marv did not have to release GQ and Kaisapaisa from their contract even after dropping them. Marv owned the Master because he paid for it with a $50K advance. But most Labels, in most circumstances, will let a dropped Artist buy back their Masters. On the rare occasion when a Label does refuse, it's usually personal. Should we as C@taclysmic approach Marv, he could very well attempt to charge us a premium, since he knows we should soon have at least $10 million in funding. If GQ and Kaisapaisa go to Marv directly, he would likely release them in exchange for his costs to date.

Kanish, Aardy, and I spent most of the afternoon discussing business, including our future Headquarters, which was a conversation I couldn't wrap my head around at all. What was wrong with my garage? It's comfortable, we can make and listen to music in it, we're all set up for Skype conference calls, and we can play Beaver while we think. The room was airy when we wanted it, and Womblike when we didn't. I could wear my pajamas all day. We were already in the ultimate office space, and Aardy wanted to trade it all for some fancy suite in a building full of fancy suites?

"Who runs a company worth a billion dollars out of their garage?" Aardy asked.

"How the fuck do you put us at a billion-dollar valuation? We have three employees."

I've watched a great many episodes of the hit show *Shark Tank*, in which contestants are given the opportunity to pitch an investment opportunity to five super -successful entrepreneurs. My favorite investors are Mark Cuban and Kevin O'Leary, neither of whom ever mince their words. Kevin O'Leary, also known as Mr. Wonderful, would be having conniption fits at the idea that we were worth ten times our initial cash investment— even after picking up a new asset. Besides, from what I could tell, Willy was now handing out Label Distribution deals like Tic Tacs at a garlic festival, and I didn't for a second believe he could fund two upstart Labels to the tune of $90 million each.

"Until we have the money in our account," I started, "and an actual fucking contract, in writing, we have no idea what we're worth. And speaking of money in our account . . . weren't we supposed to get our $10 million today?"

"I've been checking the account all morning," Aardy replied.

"We do not need to worry about any of that," Kanish replied. "I'm certain that Willy will match his word and provide us with the initial good-faith investment. I'm also certain that this does not change the stakes for any of us Billionheirs."

"And what stakes are those?" I asked.

"Kaisapaisa is not the only one who is in this country at the pleasure of his father. Failure is not an option for any of us," Kanish finished with a glance toward his phone. "Ah! Another Douchebag Spin! Let us listen!"

Kanish and Lakshmi had been texting each other back and forth all afternoon, and she was giving him a heads-up on what stations were playing the Douchebag Song when. "*Laugh!*" was getting nearly equal Spins, and more often than not was played back to back with the Douchebag Song.

Kanish was also in constant communication with the Code Shack Foreman, who was now acting as the point man for all the Views and Requests. As per the plan, the Coders began to focus their attention on Rev's track "*Laugh!,*" which was absolutely exploding on the Internet and had garnered more than three million Views in just a few hours time. Even with multiple Billionheir-owned Code Shacks at our disposal, we didn't have enough Coders for those kinds of numbers. That was mostly an organic viral reaction.

GQ sent us a link to a much-improved version of "Cash Money" with Kaisapaisa performing. The song was still a dog, but they would be far easier to market with Kaisapaisa as the frontman. Kanish Kanish returned to monitoring terrestrial radio station Streams of the Douchebag Song, which I was kind of sick of hearing, although I didn't dare stomp on the lad's enthusiasm. Thankfully, Skype interrupted the madness. It was Kaisapaisa and GQ again.

Kaisapaisa was all smiles, GQ still deadpan as ever.

"You have a deal," GQ said.

"And we have a Kitten Video ready to go-oh!" Kaisapaisa sang. "Shall we put it up?"

"You can put the clip up on our channel, if you like—Aardy will email you the credentials—but don't expect any Views, Shares, or Requests just yet. It's best if we have all the Code Shacks addressing one song at a time, and at the moment, they're hard at work blowing up '*Laugh!*'"

Aardy, Kanish, and I had already discussed this possibility, and we all agreed that it would be best if we waited a day before pulling the Coders off of the Rev's track, even if he really didn't need the boost. GQ and Kaisapaisa understood the logistics, and both accepted the terms.

By the end of the day, the Douchebag Song was in full rotation in most US cities. The plan was working. Surely we would have the Number One song in the country before the end of the week.

It was late, and the three of us were gathered in the driveway to partake of our usual late-night Medicinal Fatty. Kanish was now Streaming a Philly station, which Spun the Douchebag Song, as per usual, back to back with "*Laugh!*" Cue the fade.

@TheSmoovDJ: "Kittens and Sitars are hot! Are they not?"

The late-night DJ known as Smoov had the kind of mellifluous voice radio loves.

@TheSmoovDJ: "Now, is it just me, or is that '*Laugh!*' track just a little disturbing? You know what I'm sayin'? It reminds me of something my grandmother used to tell me. You can say the most outrageous things, so long as you do it with a smile and a 'Laugh!'"

"DJs spinning lessons," I mused.

"This is what DJs do best, don't you know?" Kanish replied.

Mixerman

CHAPTER TWENTY-TWO

THE EMPRESS

Even if you know nothing about the Music Business, you're probably at least familiar with *Billboard* magazine and its ubiquitous charts. Founded in 1894, it was originally a trade publication for the bill-posting industry, which certainly explains the name. Shortly after the turn of the century, *Billboard* moved into covering live entertainment such as circuses and carnivals, then adapted to the film industry. It wasn't until the jukebox became popular in the 1930s that *Billboard* began to rank songs based on their popularity. By the early 1960s, the magazine had completed its transformation to its current state as a weekly music trade publication.

Advertising in the magazine is not cheap, and around Grammy time, the Major Labels often purchase full-page "For Your Consideration" ads hyping their best contenders for NARAS member votes. NARAS stands for the National Academy of Recording Arts and Sciences, and its main purpose is to act as the governing body of the Grammys. Aside from that, it's difficult to say what the fuck they do. As you can probably tell, I'm no longer a member—standing notwithstanding.

Oddly, I can't seem to find a mission statement for NARAS, and they barely even seem to use the acronym anymore, opting for Grammy dot com instead. According to their Wiki page—which carries the Wiki warning *"This article contains content that is written like an advertisement,"*— NARAS is "a US organization of musicians, Producers, recording engineers and other recording professionals dedicated to improving the quality of life and cultural condition for music and its makers." If that's the goal, they have been nothing short of ineffectual, if not nonexistent. Perhaps both. Hey, they may do some good things, but I haven't seen any evidence of it, and perception is just as important as reality when an Award Show organization spells out such lofty goals as "improving quality of life." That's all just a bunch of bullshit. And really, how can we take seriously an Award Show that failed to properly recognize the Beatles when it actually mattered?

Back to *Billboard* magazine.

In the early aughts, around the height of the Music Business lunacy, it cost $50,000 for the full back-page ad spot. I'd have a difficult time believing it's anywhere close to that now. I wouldn't know. I don't have an advertising account with them, and I stopped even reading the magazine about twenty years ago. For a creative type such as myself, it's death to read. To make matters worse, for those periods that my work wasn't on the charts, I really didn't even want to open the fucking thing. At $20 a week, that's an expensive magazine to never open.

That said, when you're a Produsah, an MC Mogul, and a Distributor with a song that's sure to make the charts, Billboard is exactly the magazine that you want. And so you send your driver to pick one up for you at the local newsstand, which in this case was a full thirty minutes away. Newsstands aren't as common as they once were, it seems. I suppose that's why they put the charts online too.

There are all sorts of charts in *Billboard* for just about every genre you can think of including R&B/Hip-hop, Adult Contemporary, Country, Rock, Dance, Latin, Christian, Jazz. Frankly, all the various sub-genre charts are designed to make the current losers in this business feel good about themselves. When it comes right down to it, there's only one chart that matters, and that's the Hot 100.

The current *Billboard* rankings system incorporates digital downloads, radio airplay, and Internet Streaming. This boded well for the Douchebag Song, which was now well above 100 million Views and hundreds of thousands of Shares. Then there was radio. You can't listen to an R&B station in the US for much longer than twenty minutes without hearing the Douchebag Song. But would it be enough for Number One?

"Motherfucker!" Kanish yelled at the top of his lungs.

Apparently not.

"We are only Number Two on the Hot 100 chart!" Kanish whined. "Motherfucking motherfucker!"

"Why would you be upset about Number Two?" Aardy asked. "That's great news!"

"What's Number One?" I asked.

"What else?"

"'Cash Money'?" I said in jest.

"No, 'Cash Money' is Number Three."

"Number Three!" Aardy bellowed. "We have the Number Two and Three tracks in the country and you're upset about this?"

"Yes, yes, yes, I understand how wonderful it is to have picked up a record and then to have Manifested it to Number Three on the Hot 100 Charts in just two days. This does not change the fact that there is a song more popular than the Douchebag Song."

Motherfucker. "*Laugh!*" beat us.

I don't think that any song in history could have competed with the speed of our meteoric rise to the top, or near top, that is. We literally went from total obscurity to Number Two with a bullet in under a week—a previously impossible feat. Only problem is, Rev not only did it in a day less time, he took the top prize. Motherfucking motherfucker is right!

"I do not understand," Kanish said, nearly fuming, "how we could be losing to Rev's motherfucking song?"

"I hate to admit it," Aardy said, "but they do have the better Kitten Video. Apparently, people just adore those Laughing Kittens."

There may have been some truth to what Aardy was saying. "*Laugh!*" absolutely exploded on the first day because of radio, and was most certainly coattailing the success of our song. "*Laugh!*" did, however, have the better video, and that surely also played some role in its success. Frankly, I found the whole chant in the chorus of that song somewhat creepy. But then, somehow, when you put it to Laughing Kittens, the sentiment seems almost reasonable. But I can't for the life of me tell you how or why.

What was blowing my mind was the fact that "Cash Money" shot to Number Three, and in the least amount of time.

"I do not find this acceptable!" Kanish screamed like a petulant child.

"Easy there, Paneer," I said.

Paneer is my pet name for Kanish anytime he goes into that demanding posture of his—the one where the world must somehow conform to his will. And while it's a somewhat ugly little side to him, I don't denigrate it. I applaud it. But sometimes I want to disarm it, and the best way to do that was to call it Paneer.

"My apologies. You are correct. I was revealing my inner Paneer," Kanish said.

"Yes, you were. It's okay, buddy," I said proudly.

"We need a plan."

"I've got a good plan. Let's wait until next week and see whether we go up a notch with a bullet."

"Destiny is not a plan," Kanish replied.

Believe me, I get the disappointment. You don't want to say you have the Number Two and Three songs in the country. As impressive as that is, you want to tout the Number One song in the country, because really, only Number One counts. You know? No one ever goes for second place. So Kanish was right—we couldn't just rest on our laurels. To do nothing is an action, and as the stewards of the Corporation, we had a responsibility to our stockholders to do all that we could to maximize our profits. Racking up Views, Shares, Spins, and Streams is all well and good, but the Rev, he had people Talking. And when you get people Talking, you go to Number One. If we were to overtake the Rev, we would need people Talking too. And I knew just how to do it—controversy.

"Let's just troll all the Feminist groups," I said.

"Oh, that's too good. Too good!" Aardy gushed. "We go to Feminist sites and we rile them up about the video."

"I do not understand," Kanish replied.

"Rile them up," I said. "As in to aggravate. To wind up. To bother, annoy, or irritate."

"Don't forget inflame," Aardy replied.

"Yes, yes, yes. But why would we want to inflame them, as you say?" Kanish asked innocently.

"Gee, I don't know," I said in my most sarcastic voice. "How about this?"

I blasted the words into the air with my hands—like a headline.

"Pussies and Douchebags? Coincidence? Click the Link to Find Out!"

This was a classic news sensationalism ploy. You get people hooked into the story by posing a question so outrageous and inflammatory that your audience feels compelled to investigate further. Since the headline is posed as a question, there's no need for any real backup. There's no actual claim being made. Just a question posed. Of course, no one would pose such a question if it weren't true, would they? Yeah. They would. Because it's rarely true, and it's almost always followed by all sorts of theories, speculation, and conjecture, all designed to bias the viewer toward the original outrageous premise without actually taking a stand. Next time you read a headline posed as a question, keep that in mind.

Kanish was unsure of the Pussies and Douchebags headline, so I let him stew on it for a bit. Aardy, on the other hand, loved the idea, as I knew that he would, but then Aardy and I have a history of stirring up shit on the Internet. We've also managed to end some shit too, but that's a story for another time. I do, however, currently have one acoustician hack so upset with me, the little whiner actually has a hate page dedicated to me on the Net. He even distorted my picture that he pulled from my episode on *Pensado's Place*—a Web-based interview show for Producers. It's always a win when you can piss someone off such that they dedicate hours of their life documenting their hatred of you and doing all they can to maximize their SEO results. The best part? It sits there, like my own personal trophy, as if I'm somehow the one being judged by his display of obvious insanity. All I did was use the weight of his own words against him in our debate. I guess some people can't handle that.

Suffice to say, riling people up on the Internet was not foreign territory for us. It's what we do. Only problem was, neither of us tends to visit Feminist sites.

Now, while we probably could have gotten away with infiltrating the Feminist sites as anonymous newbies, it would be far more effective if there was a call to arms from within the ranks. Seeing as the Empress was the only female Produsah with a Billionheir, she seemed a good place to start. I got her on the Skype.

"You guys have to come up here," the Empress said the moment she popped up on my screen.

"Yeah, right."

"I'm totally fucking serious, right now. Stick your lazy asses into that Bentley or Rolls, whatever the fuck your ride is, and get up to my house right now. You know where I am. Oh. And take Fairfax or you'll miss it. You got me? Fairfax!"

As much as I didn't want to fight the traffic into Hollywood, I couldn't just say no, and then ask the Empress to do us a favor. Besides, that's why we have a driver.

It was bad enough we had to make the trek to the Sunset Strip in the middle of a Saturday; now we had to do it by way of Fairfax. To make matters worse, the one advantage to taking Fairfax over La Cienega is that you can stop at Canter's for a pastrami sandwich. Unfortunately, Annapurna, who never lets us go hungry, whipped up some sandwiches for the ride. Which were delicious, but not pastrami. By the time we were sucking tailpipe on Fairfax we weren't even hungry.

Of course, Canter's had nothing to do with why the Empress wanted us to take Fairfax. Really, she just wanted us to head west on Sunset Boulevard from there, and I'm glad we did, too. If I hadn't seen it for myself, I would never have believed it. There, on Sunset Boulevard, stood a Rushmore-sized vertical billboard of the Rev, sporting a forrest-green polo shirt, laughing joyously at nothing in particular. The top of his head even poked out of the frame of the billboard. It looked more like an ad for cigarettes. The copy read:

HEAR THE SONG THAT WILL MAKE YOU *LAUGH!*

#FORYOURCONSIDERATION
DJ REV—PRODUSAH OF THE YEAR

"Holy shit," I said. "The video is what makes people laugh. Not the fucking song!"

Sevaka pulled to the side of the road so that the three of us could get an extended view of the towering billboard. I'm not sure what the going rate is for a custom billboard on the most-traveled section of Sunset Boulevard, but I'm thinking it costs considerably more than the back page of *Billboard* magazine.

"What the fuck?" I said. "What the hell is he playing at?"

We all hopped back into the Bentley, and Sevaka whipped up the hill and then around the Empress's long driveway, which was perched just above the obnoxious billboard. She and Lakshmi spilled out of the house to greet us.

"Now you understand why I had you come up here?" the Empress said as she led us into the house. "You needed to see that shit for yourself! And he's got another one, too. On Santa Monica. I mean, of all the nerve—putting up 'For Your Consideration' ads in July! And who the hell puts up an ad begging NARAS for a Lifetime Achievement award? Has he given up?"

"His other ad is asking for Lifetime Achievement?"

"He listed his entire fucking discography. The man is out of control."

It was almost as if she hadn't noticed Aardy until that moment, as the attractive buxom salt-and-pepper brunette suddenly shrieked and placed him precariously in a bear hug.

"Hi, Aardy! Did you bring me some pork loin?" she continued as she pressed her bosom against him.

It takes a lot to make Aardy blush. Apparently that was enough.

The Empress walked us down the stairs to the lower level of her hillside home into a room full of Gold and Platinum records. A sliding glass door led to the patio with a magnificent view of the city basin, blocked partially by the back of Rev's obnoxious billboard. The hustle and bustle of city life could not be ignored given our proximity to Sunset Boulevard. The three of us took a seat in the oversized lounge chairs that surrounded a weatherworn teak coffee table with a chessboard inlay. The Empress brought out five Stellas and an ashtray. Kanish pulled out a Fatty and passed it immediately to the Empress as she took a seat.

"I am so fucking pissed about those billboards," the Empress complained as she sparked up the Fatty. "You know what this means, right? Now we're going to all have to buy billboards. I thought we were supposed to be working together here. It's that little cunt Mukesh!"

Lakshmi said something in Hindi, in a quiet manner, as if she didn't want us to make out the words. When Kanish didn't respond, she lost patience and barked some sort of command. That popped Kanish right out of his chair.

"Excuse us," Lakshmi announced sweetly as she rose from her chair. "I would vehdy much like to show Kanish the studio." The two quietly left us three Produsahs on the patio to speak freely.

As much as I wanted to ask the Empress if Lakshmi were stable, I wasn't sure that such a question was wise. We were just about to ask her help with the Feminists. Dissing her protégé in any way could piss the Empress off. I most certainly didn't want to inadvertently spark solidarity against us. As it turns out, that wasn't much of a concern.

"I probably shouldn't have called Mukesh a cunt like that in front of Lakshmi," the Empress started. "I don't know if you've noticed, but she is fucking crazy—like she just snaps out of nowhere. Which I might be afraid of if I wasn't off my rocker myself. Eh. We make it work, you know?— Anyway, Lakshmi has told me all about that Douchebag Mukesh. Did you know that he owns billboards all over Los Angeles? Did he think to Share his billboards with the others? No."

"Are you fucking serious?" I said. "He reprimanded us the other day for treating him like a competitor!"

"No shit. Doesn't that just take the cake! Those Billionheirs—they want to Share everything, until they don't. Once it no longer suits them, then all of a sudden, they're like, 'I got mine!'"

The Empress took a deep drag from the Fatty and held in the Medicinal bounty as she gazed out over the basin. She released and turned her attention to Aardy.

"It's so good to see you, Aardy!" the Empress fawned. "Sorry to make you guys come all the way up here, but everyone seems to work out of their house these days. I never get to see anyone anymore."

The Empress began to overtly twirl a long lock of her hair.

"It's nice to have Lakshmi around and everything—I love her to death—but sometimes you just need—"

"A man?" I interjected.

"Some dick," she replied without releasing Aardy from her piercing stare.

The Empress sucked on the Fatty seductively and blew the smoke directly into Aardy's face.

"So what do you need from me?" she asked Aardy, rapid eyeballing, high-voicing, and all. "You didn't come all the way up here because I asked you to, did you?"

The Empress and I have known each other for a great many years, yet you wouldn't know it, the way she was ignoring me. Rather than wait for her to start playing footsie with Aardy, I thought I'd move the conversation along a bit.

"Are you a Feminist?" I asked.

"Hah! Of course I'm a Feminist! What kind of an idiot would I be to not be a Feminist?"

Aardy raised his hand as if to say "I got this."

"Yes, well, Empress, I think that you could help us with our quest. We want you to troll the Feminist sites for us," Aardy said.

"Ha! I knew it! You guys thought the Feminists were going to get all pissed off because you put the Douchebag Song to little Pussies. Then the Rev comes out with his stupid fucking Laughing Kittens. How the hell did he get them to do that, anyway?"

"Hard to say. We're not in the video business," Aardy replied.

"That's where you're wrong. That's exactly the business you're in."

Lakshmi and Kanish returned and quietly joined us again on the patio. The Empress, who had been bogarting the Medicine, passed it to Kanish, who immediately passed it to Lakshmi, who took a drag upon it and then handed it right back to Kanish. In a surprising move, Lakshmi placed her hand on his knee.

"Kanish and I have spoken," Lakshmi said meekly in her British accent. "We'd be happy to help infuriate the Feminists."

"Speak for yourself, dear!" the Empress scolded. "You don't just accept gentlemen callers into your home and give them exactly what they want without making them work for it!"

Lakshmi immediately removed her hand from Kanish's knee. A bead of sweat ran down Kanish's cheek. It was seventy degrees out with no humidity and he was flush and sweating like a pig.

"Oh, good lord!" the Empress exclaimed. "No wonder I'm so fricking horny. You two just did it!"

"I'm sure that I do not know what you are saying to me. As I said, we'd be happy to infuriate the Feminists."

The Empress stared at Lakshmi, who stared blankly at the Empress before she overtly raised one eyebrow. A shiver came down the entire patio.

"Oh, fine," the Empress said resignedly. "You Billionaires' Heirs sure are all about the business. Here's the deal. Our video is ready for some manufactured Views, and that should be enough to blow us the fuck up. Ours is the only video of the bunch that makes any sense, after all!"

"What's the concept?"

"Power of the Pussy, baby!"

And then the Empress began to sing.

> *Power of the Pussy. Meow!*
> *You never want it bushy. Meow!*

"Your song is called 'Power of the Pussy'?"

"Meow!" the Empress purred as she mimicked the swipe of a cat claw.

"Kittens." I sighed. "You made another Kitten Video."

"Now there's a concept! Cute little Kittens doing cute Kitten things. Power of the Pussy. Meow!"

Kanish, who had been unusually silent and disengaged since our arrival, no longer seemed interested in the hypomanic display of Feminism before us.

"Here is what I should vehdy much like to propose," Kanish began as he wiped some sweat from his brow. "We will send word to the Code Shack to begin pumping up the Views for . . ."

"Power of the Pussy."

". . . your video. In the meantime, if you would be so kind as to agitate the Feminists."

"And why should I agitate the Feminists in exchange for something you already owe us? What do we get out of this, exactly?" the Empress asked.

"A smack on the tush?" I replied.

"How dare you!" Lakshmi scolded as she ejected violently from her chair.

"Oh, settle, Petal." The Empress howled with laughter. "You can't take anything he says seriously, and I'm not done toying with him."

Lakshmi thought about it for a moment, and then unceremoniously sat back down. The power struggle between these two women was fascinating to watch, and seemingly impossible to decipher.

"Look, Empress," I said. "In all seriousness, if you both get the Feminists Talking about our songs, and—I include your song in there—we'll surely knock the Rev off the top spot. A Number One record is more valuable than a Grammy, and a Grammy doesn't vault a song to Number One. You know? Our goals are aligned at the moment."

The Empress smiled broadly. It was the first bit of notice she'd given me, what with all the attention she'd lavished upon Aardvark. I didn't even know she was keen on him.

"Yeah. Sure. We can troll the Feminists," the Empress said with a wave of her hand. "They'll be firebombing your headquarters by morning."

"Just don't give them our address," I joked.

"Come on. I'll show you our clip."

Lakshmi and Kanish remained on the patio as the Empress led us to her studio to View the "Power of the Pussy" video on her big Slate Raven screen and listen to it through her even bigger speakers.

>*Power of the Pussy . . . meow!*
>*Power of the Pussy . . . meow!*

[Short Sitar break]
Power of the Pussy . . . meow!
Power of the Pussy . . . meow!

Lakshmi and the Empress had obviously put some effort into the clip, dressing Kittens up as "pink-collar workers," as it were. It was a Feminists' message if there ever was one. The Empress would be the perfect mole for riling up the Feminists.

"Nice Sitar," I said.

"Sitars are hot!" the Empress replied as she inexplicably stuck her nose into her armpit. "Oh, man. I have to take a shower."

The Empress stared at Aardy momentarily and then finished her thought with a smile.

"Why don't you join me, Aardy, and we can get all kinky on the clean. Know what I mean?"

"I'm sure that I do, but sadly we have to be getting off right about now," Aardy replied.

Upon our return, the patio was empty, and so Aardy and I made our way back up the stairs toward the front door. The Empress yelled up toward us.

"I'm coming to Redondo for more of that pork loin soon, Aardy!"

"Dude," I whispered. "Did you—?"

"Did I Share an extra serving of pork loin with her at your party? Don't be a pig."

"Holy shit. You did!"

I've known Aardy long enough to understand he doesn't kiss and tell. Still, a non-denial was as good as a confirmation.

Kanish and Lakshmi were having a conversation by the Bentley. I really couldn't understand anything they were saying other than one thing, and it made no sense. I swear that Lakshmi plainly said "AES." In my world, that stands for Audio Engineering Society, which is an organization that would interest wonky recording engineers. Not those who would be Moguls.

Lakshmi gave Kanish a quick hug, hopped out of the car, and ran back into the house.

"What was that all about?"

"It was nothing," Kanish replied.

"It was something."

"If you must know, she wanted to be sure that I remember to attend a meeting tomorrow."

"An AES meeting?"

"Something like that. I would vehdy much prefer to avoid talking about it."

"Be careful, kid. That girl is trouble."

Kanish seemed to be in a bad mood. I'm not sure what was bothering him exactly. Nor could I understand why anyone would have an impromptu Audio Engineering Society meeting with other Moguls. Whatever it was, he was all fucked up about it. Ah. Young love, I suppose.

It was dark by the time we arrived home. There was a package on the ground in front of C@taclysmic Headquarters. It was from our bank. Our Corporate checks had arrived, which reminded me.

"Aardy, when was the last time you looked at the bank account balance?" I asked as I opened the garage door.

"Yesterday. I thought you were checking it."

"I thought you were."

It had now been several days since Willy had promised to deposit our $10 million in good-faith money. Without it, we had no faith at all, and frankly, I was starting to think that maybe the money would never come.

I sat down on the couch in the back of the room, pulled out my phone, and absentmindedly scrolled through my emails. There was one from my bank.

"I have an email that says a deposit was made to our account," I announced excitedly.

"What!?"

The three of us scurried over to the Raven screen. Aardy immediately logged into our bank account.

Aardy placed two fingers on the 46-inch touch screen and dragged them away from each other in a diagonal direction so as to zoom in on our balance, which was now as large as the screen itself. It looked something like this:

$$\$10,169,342.97$$

"Holy fucking shit," Aardy exclaimed.

"Mother of god," I declared.

"This is fantastic!" Kanish celebrated.

A black Dodge Charger screeched and fishtailed around the corner. I got a brief glimpse of a hooded passenger, but my eye was almost immediately distracted by an object—a Molotov cocktail. It was flying gracefully through the air toward the open Stingray, and landed directly in the cockpit of the car with a rather impressive explosion.

"Douchebags!" a woman shouted as the Charger blasted past the house.

I grabbed the fire extinguisher from the garage and doused the flames.

"Oh! Oh! The smell!" Kanish exclaimed.

When you poke the hive to access the honey, take cover from the angry bees.

Mixerman

CHAPTER TWENTY-THREE

ILLUMINATI?

"Shut the garage!" I yelled. "Ugh! It stinks so fucking bad!"

Thankfully, this was by no measure a powerful bomb. It was, however, a loud one, as was the speeding Charger and its bellowing passenger. Neighbors streamed out from their houses to investigate the commotion, most of them in robes, given the time of night.

First on the scene were a pair of police cruisers, also Dodge Chargers, followed immediately by a ladder truck from Station One of the Redondo Beach Fire Department. The moment the firemen realized it was nothing more than a stink bomb, they left without incident. The police, on the other hand, wanted more information.

"So let me see if I got all of this straight. You were chatting in your driveway, and then a black Dodge Charger whips around the corner, at which point a female perpetrator tosses a stink bomb—which you thought was a Molotov cocktail—into your open Stingray."

"Correct."

"And you believe this was the work of Nazi Feminists?"

"Nazi Feminists? I believe they were just Feminists."

"And they did this because you pissed them off?"

"Because we riled them up."

An investigator was diligently sifting through the car to determine the true nature of the device. Obviously, this wasn't a Molotov cocktail, as I'd first reported, and clearly I was a few Fatties in. I was just about to go to bed, after all. The investigator seemed to be wrapping up his work when he paused momentarily to reach into the passenger side of the car in order to pull a coin-sized object out of it. The investigator held the shiny object at eye level and peered inquisitively at it as he carefully made his way to our position.

"Do any of you have a pet named Douchebag?" the investigator asked.

"Uh, no," I replied.

"Then I would say that someone doesn't like you guys very much," the investigator said as he presented what looked to be a custom-etched dog tag, the kind that you get from a machine at the pet store.

IF LOST CALL:

DOUCHEBAG

"Shouldn't you dust it for fingerprints?" I asked.

"There won't be any fingerprints. This was the work of Feminist vandals. Smart Feminist vandals," the investigator lectured. "It was a well-crafted device, one that was designed for maximum noise and minimal repercussions. I don't think it could have killed a small animal, let alone hurt a human . . . other than perhaps some ear damage. No. This was perpetrated by someone who really understands how to make a big stink and a lot of noise without getting caught."

"I see."

"And you'll never get the burnt-sulfur smell out of the interior of that Stingray. Such a shame."

"That's good to know, investigator. Thank you."

"Our job is done here, lieutenant."

The investigator left us to gather his investigative things.

"All right," the lieutenant concluded, "I have all of your information now. We'll let you know if we figure anything out."

I really didn't give a fuck about catching the Feminists who did this. Further, it was clear that the RBPD weren't going to bother looking for them. Not that I cared or blamed them—any of them. As sucky as it is to be stink-bombed, it was also a good sign. It meant that the Empress was doing an exceptional job at trolling the Feminists. We were supposed to rile them up. They weren't supposed to have my address.

Given the putrid smell, the three of us made our way to the back patio, a place that could not be reached by stink bombs ejected from speeding cars.

"What I'd like to know is, how the hell did they find the house?" I asked Kanish and Aardy.

Aardy averted his eyes downward toward the deck and began to slide his foot across the slats. I also couldn't help but notice that he overtly neglected to posit any theories.

"Aardy?"

"Well, it might have something to do with that fact that I listed your address when I filed for C@taclysmic Group Inc., and that might be public information."

"Motherfucker!" I exclaimed. "You couldn't have listed a PO box or something?"

"We don't have a PO box."

"And we can't afford one, right?"

"You might recall that I was the one who suggested we move the Headquarters from the house. You even asked me, and I quote: 'What's wrong with my garage?'"

"That was earlier today!"

A familiar voice came from behind me.

"What is wrong with your garage, indeed."

"Rajadut," I said in surprise. "I didn't realize we were expecting you."

"When there are police involved, I should be the first person you expect. I have spoken at length with the Captain of the Redondo Beach Police. Given the circumstances, I believe it would be best if you all stayed at the Crown Royale Hotel. The Penthouse suite is currently reserved in my name."

"It's the Crowne Plaza, Rajadut."

"Says you. This house is too vulnerable to the people who want Kanish dead."

"Dead!" No one wants Kanish dead, dude. They were just some prickly Feminists."

"Who blew up a bomb in Kanish's car."

"A stink bomb, and the cops don't even consider it dangerous."

"Three of the Sikhs shall stay here. The Dishwashing Sikh, as you erroneously refer to him, shall stand guard outside the Penthouse."

The three of us packed up our essentials and Sevaka drove us to the hotel. The Dishwashing Sikh stood casually just outside the side exit of the Crown Royale Hotel dressed covertly in surfer attire. Were it not for the orange turban, and were he not alone, he might have actually blended in. The Dishwashing Sikh escorted us up the concrete fire escape stairs to the second floor, down a long hall to the elevator. This was certainly a round-about way to get to our room, but Rajadut forbade us from using the hotel lobby. He had us so paranoid we didn't dare ignore him. The Sikh inserted an elevator key for floor P; upon arriving, the elevator opened directly into a magnificent suite.

The Penthouse suite was fancy, ostentatious, oversized, and had a spectacular view of the marina and ocean. It was as you would imagine a Penthouse to be, right down to the champagne and strawberries. There were three beds in two bedrooms and a pullout couch in the living room. It was the wee hours, and I immediately crashed, clothes and all, on top of one of the king-sized beds.

Senator Crou d'Etat and I faced each other. We were in the dining car of a moving train, the kind you might ride in another century. The Senator drank a Manhattan. I slurped a Sidecar, complete with sugar rim. It was delicious.

"Do you know where you're headed?" Senator Crou d'Etat asked.

"Hell?" I replied.

"If you were going to Hell, you wouldn't be traveling with me, my friend. They don't put people like me in Hell. I do too much good in the world."

"How is repeatedly shutting down the government good?" I asked.

"You don't want the government messing with your business, do you? Who are we to tell you what you can and can't do? So long as you're creating jobs, you should be able to do anything you like."

"Does that include poisoning children?"

"Poisoning their minds with your Socialist viewpoints you mean?"

"I'm hardly a Socialist."

"Oh, come on. I'm in your brain. You think I can't see what's going on in here? Deep down, you're a Marxist, yet you operate your business like a true blue-blooded Capitalist. No wonder you're so conflicted."

"That's absurd. I love Capitalism," I retorted. "It's the Corporatocracy that I object to."

"Or Oligarchy. You're the one here who has Manifested a multi-Corporate act of collusion, my friend."

"I did nothing of the sort."

"At the very least you stood by and watched it happen. Today you make a deal to get a few extra Views. Tomorrow, your Corporation is registered in the Bahamas so that you can stow your profits offshore and avoid paying taxes. All perfectly legal, of course. Well, not perfectly, but why close a loophole that serves my wealthy donors so well?"

I glanced out the window of the train. We were passing nuclear silos, clearly marked as such. Senator Crou d'Etat took a sip of his Manhattan, which was now pitch-black and milkshake thick, as was my Sidecar.

"Drink your crude," the Senator replied.

"Crude? Where are we?"

"We're in North Dakota. This is an oil train. Highly combustible."

"The North Dakota oil trains now pass by nuclear warheads?"

"Isn't that some shit? And they don't ever mention it on the *Nightly News*."

"But when these trains derail they blow up in spectacular fashion. Like, they have to evacuate towns and shit. Responders can't even get close enough to the cars to put out the fires. They burn for days."

"And your point?"

"Isn't that dangerous next to nuclear warheads like this?"

"It could be downright C@taclysmic, my friend. And all the media cares about is what outrageously brash thing us candidates for president are going to say next. Especially the Billion-hairs. It's wonderful."

"But if something happens, aren't you to blame?"

"My friend, you need to learn the art of the 'who knew?' This is my stop."

The Senator stood up and wriggled his arms into the straps of an over-stuffed backpack.

"You need to get yourself one of these. Otherwise, you're just a sucker. That's a word you like to use, right? *Sucker*? See you on the far side!"

The Senator opened the compartment door just as the train passed by a large open ravine. The moment he jumped, an enormous golden parachute unfurled and blossomed with air. The chute was broad, bright, and magnificent, and the Senator floated gracefully toward the ground below. The train began to derail. I woke up with a start. I was soaked.

"Hold on, Empress. Let me wake up his Highness," Aardy said. The smell of bacon and coffee was permeating the room. "Zerman! Wake the fuck up! It's past noon!"

I was a little groggy for a Skype call, but speaking to the Empress was a priority. Kanish and Aardy were already sitting in front of the laptop in a makeshift conference area. Lakshmi and the Empress were on the screen.

"Wake up, sleepyhead!" the Empress teased. "Kanish was telling us about your explosive run-in with the Feminists last night. That really stinks."

"Very funny," I quipped, as I was far too out of it to laugh at stupid puns. "I think we can cease the trolling now."

"Oh, we've ceased. But we can't undo the fury that we've unleashed. The Femis have gone red-meat bonkers over this."

"That's good news," I said as I poured myself a cup of coffee.

Lakshmi could be heard berating the Empress from a distance.

"Fuck. It's time to go. We'll see you in a few hours, then."

"We will?" I remarked. "Why is that?"

"Oh, don't you know? Our Heirs are having a little private shindig over at the AES Plant," the Empress informed.

"AES?"

"That's close, right?"

"It's three blocks away from our hotel," I replied.

"Great! I'll meet you at your suite. Us Produsahs can grab some drinks while they have their little Billionheir get-together. See you in a few!"

AES. So, that was what Lakshmi was referring to in her conversation with Kanish—the Power Plant in Redondo Beach. And while an electric plant may rightfully seem an odd place to have a meeting, AES does indeed rent out the site for events. I know. I've been to art shows on the industrial premises. But how would Lakshmi know this? And why would she choose that venue, of all places?

AES is a California Electric company. They currently own the large Power Plant facility that sits right in front of the harbor. Frankly, it's an eyesore, which the residents of Redondo Beach have loathed, probably since it was built to its present size in the 1940s. Of course, back then no one really lived by the beach. Still, that was a remarkably shortsighted decision by the city. I smell corruption.

The one saving grace of the blight we call the Power Plant is the massive concrete "whale wall." The life-sized whale mural painted in 1991 by world-renowned Artist Wyland is not only a landmark, it's also a source of pride for the city. If the plant ever gets torn down, you can be sure there will be a fight over that wall.

All of that said, as wonderful as the mural is, it really doesn't do much to spruce up the industrial monstrosity, which sits on thirty-eight acres of what has to be some of the most valuable real estate in Southern California. For decades now, the City has attempted to negotiate a deal to convert the oceanfront property into a mixed-use commercial and residential development. The citizens of Redondo Beach voted down such a proposal at the ballot box, not once, but twice, and for a very simple reason—we don't want fucking residential properties down there. You don't need a traffic study to realize there's only one viable way out of there. Of course, the geniuses at City Hall fucked up the traffic anyway, what with their new bike lane death trap in which cars are constantly intermingling with bikes. Don't get me started on that!

By law, the old ocean-water steam plants are to be phased out of California by 2020. That means AES must tear down the plant and either sell the land, develop it, or build a new plant. Given the value of the land, it doesn't make much sense to build a new plant, and so AES put forth a redevelopment plan on the ballot in March of 2015. Their threat was explicit. Either Redondo Beach citizens allow them to overbuild the property with a large swath of mixed-use residential and commercial property, or AES would build a new Power Plant, thus blocking the valuable view for another fifty years.

Fancy brochures arrived almost daily with testimonials from city politicians conned into touting how great life would be with even more housing in an already densely populated city. Given the sheer volume of the slickly produced material, it seemed as though there was a groundswell of support in favor of the proposal. I suppose that was the intended perception. Given the lackluster turnout, it almost worked. There were 5,213 votes for the proposal to redevelop the land; 5,614 against.

AES reportedly spent over $800,000 to get the measure passed in a special election. That's a voter acquisition cost of just over $150 per vote for a failed bid. The opposition to the proposal put up $16K and a prayer, for a voter acquisition cost of three Hail Marys and $2.85 per vote.

In most cities, that kind of spending power would win the day. Had voter turnout tripled, I contend the Measure would have been defeated by more than two to one. But how many decades can citizens fight for their community before they just say fuck it? The more time that passes, the more valuable the property, the more pressure there is to convert the land into residential properties. The politicians bought the AES threat hook, line, and sinker. I never believed it for a second.

It would be the very definition of *Rrritarded* to build another Power Plant on that property. Not only does its removal open up acres of prime oceanfront property, it also frees up the long swath of steep hillside greenbelt used to carry the towering high-voltage power lines out of the city. There have to be hundreds acres of prime real estate crawling up that hill, and it's currently used to grow potted plants under the constant radiation of high-tension power lines.

I had half a mind to write a letter to the editor of the *Beach Reporter* suggesting we build a football stadium on the land in the hopes of landing an NFL team. We'd call them the Redondo Beach Seamen. That's what I'd propose, anyway. Admittedly, there's not enough acreage for a proper NFL stadium, but if Trump can build a new golf hole on the top of Palos Verdes, what's to stop us from extending the usable land into the bay?

Of course, I can hear the naysayers now: *But what of parking?* Easy. You park the cars under the high-powered transmission lines, which you convert into chairlifts so as to carry the Redondo Beach Seamen fans to and from the stadium. I mean, if you want to put Redondo Beach on the map, that's how you do it.

Kanish was slumped in his chair and looked downright depressed. You'd think that the Empress had just revealed that our two Heirs were eloping or something.

"You're not getting married, are you, Kanish?" I asked.

"And why would I get married in a Power Plant?"

"I don't know. Why would you have a secret meeting in a Power Plant?"

"It is not secret. It is private. There is a difference."

One without a distinction, I felt, given our relationship, but if their meeting had nothing to do C@taclysmic Group Inc., then I suppose it really was none of my business. So I let it drop.

The early-summer breeze was beautifully crisp whipping off the ocean and into the Penthouse. The view was stunning as usual. The afternoon was drawing to a close, and Kanish put the finishing touches on his rooster comb, a hairstyle he liked to flip occasionally. I watched from the Penthouse balcony as the Empress and Lakshmi pulled up to the hotel in their stretch Mercedes limousine. This was expected. What wasn't so expected was the Bentley that followed it. Or the Rolls. Or the other Rolls, which was followed by a stretch Lincoln, and another stretch Mercedes, and even a stretch Hummer. Car after chauffeur-driven car passed directly in front of the hotel toward the Redondo Beach AES Power Plant. The Mogul Mobiles lined up on the newly minted bike lanes directly in front of the Power Plant to release their precious cargo.

"Kanish! Aardy!" I yelled.

"Kanish left already," Aardy replied.

Sure enough, just below me Kanish and Lakshmi were making their way down Harbor Drive toward the Power Plant.

"You better get out here, Aardy."

"What's up?" he asked as he stepped out onto the ledge. "Whoa!"

"What's the current Billionheir count?" I asked.

"Eleven," Aardy replied. "How many cars is that?"

The elevator doors opened, and the Sikh politely held them for the Empress. She made her way directly to our position on the patio.

"Are you seeing this shit?" the Empress spat. "They're like little Billionheir cockroaches."

"What do you think is going on?" I asked.

"I have no idea, but all those cars are lined up in front of the Power Plant right now. What dumb-ass designed those bike lanes like that? You can't even tell it's for bikes. Hi, Aardy!"

"Hello, Empress. How about we take a little walk down to the Power Plant and find out what's going on, shall we?" Aardy suggested.

"I thought you'd never ask," the Empress replied with batting eyes.

We continued to use our protocol of evasive tactics and took the elevator to the second floor, walking down the emergency stairs and out the side door. It took us all of ten minutes to make the beautiful walk down Harbor Drive, past the Wyland Whale Wall, beyond the structure to the parking lot entrance complete with sentry.

"Welcome to AES. More power to you," the sentry said as he pointed us toward the entrance. A man's ass was protruding from the doorway. And while I don't normally notice men's backsides, this particular ass seemed familiar.

"Rev?"

Rev nearly slammed the door on his own head, he was so startled.

"What! Oh! You don't sneak up on people like that!" the Rev scolded.

"Dude. What the fuck is going on in there?" I asked.

"That's what I'm trying to figure out."

"Well, let's just go in there!" the Empress insisted as she pushed her way past the Rev and through the door.

"I think they're holding GQ in there!" the Rev warned.

Despite the Rev's misgivings, we followed the Empress into the gigantic building and up a set of stairs to the enormous second-floor loft. Scores of twenty-somethings of various ethnicities were perfectly lined up on yoga mats in the grand industrial hall of concrete and steam pipes. There had to be at least thirty mats, each mat with an Heir, each Heir holding a perfect Hero's Pose. At the front of the group stood Lakshmi, frozen in Prayer Pose, dressed splendidly like a colorful princess, crown and all. It was like a Bikram yoga class without all the excessive heat. A symbol was projected in black light against the backdrop. It read:

HA

Princess Lakshmi came out of her Prayer Pose, turned gracefully and deliberately toward the symbol behind her, and issued her command.

"Begin!"

Still facing the mysterious sign, Lakshmi began to air-conduct.

Take!
As much as you possibly can.
Waste!
What you do not need.
Laugh!
In the faces of those who have none, ha, ha, ha, ha—

The Billionheirs craned their necks in perfect synchronized unison as if to act out the "ha's," and while the chant was the one from Rev's song "*Laugh!*," it didn't have the same cadence, nor did it rhyme.

"What happened to the 'you see'?" I wondered aloud.

"I added that part," the Rev answered. "Otherwise it doesn't rhyme."

"That was your big contribution?" I mocked dryly.

"It's Number One, isn't it?"

"For the now," I replied.

The chant continued.

Take!
As much as you possibly can.
Waste!
What you do not need.
Laugh!
In the faces of those who have none, ha, ha, ha, ha—

Over and over the group repeated the chant as Lakshmi conducted the ensemble in her most regal attire.

"They're laughing at us!" the Rev hissed.

"Come on. I've seen enough," I said in disgust.

I turned to take my leave only to find myself standing face to face with GQ. He was filming me with his iPhone.

"This is Mixerman . . ." GQ said. "The question on everyone's mind: Is he here to participate in this secret meeting? Or is he here to blow the lid off."

"Blow the lid off!" I exclaimed in surprise. "What the hell is wrong with you?"

"Just as I suspected. They always announce their intentions, don't they?"

GQ panned his phone toward the chanting Heirs, fully convinced that he was capturing something interesting.

"Holy shit!" I can't take any more of this!" GQ screamed. "It's the Illuminati!"

GQ ran with his phone held high toward Lakshmi and the mysterious HA symbol directly behind her.

"How dare you!" Lakshmi roared.

Surely she was speaking to GQ, but rather than face her wrath, I took off. As it turns out, so did the Empress, Aardy, and even GQ. None of us stopped until we'd reached the Whale Wall, where we literally ran into, of all people, Kanish.

"I've been looking all over for you," Kanish said.

"Dude! I thought you were in there!"

"I'm not interested in their little fraternity."

The cops were now arresting the drivers of the Mogul Mobiles parked in the bike lanes, and there were helicopters hovering over Harbor Boulevard. It was a shit show of epic proportions. The Empress grabbed an Uber and got the hell out of town. GQ was shaking like a leaf and speaking in gibberish. It took some doing, but we managed to convince him to come up to our room. We had to calm him down before he did something rash. Like Sharing that video.

It took the better part of an hour to chill GQ out from his delusional rants about the Illuminati operating out of a Power Plant in Redondo Beach. It all made far too much sense to him. Kanish summoned Kaisapaisa to the Penthouse, but GQ was still so out there that he even viewed his Billionheir partner with suspicion.

"How do I know you're not a part of the Illuminati, man."

"I don't even know what the Illuminati is!" Kaisapaisa protested.

Logic rarely has any place in matters of conspiracy madness, but the idea that Kaisapaisa was part of a multinational group of Billionaires controlling the world didn't pass the smell test, even for someone as paranoid as GQ. Besides, who wouldn't want a partner in the Illuminati? That just seems convenient.

It took some doing, but we managed to clear Kaisapaisa as an innocent bystander in the whole affair, same with Kanish, who wasn't even in the Power Plant at the time of the incident. Now we just had to figure out how to destroy that video.

Well! You didn't rightly think I was going to allow GQ to Share his video, do you? The last thing we needed was the media all fluffed up over the Illuminati. Only bad things would come of that.

Kaisapaisa, Kanish, and I joined GQ for a spell in the spa in the hopes of relaxing him. This would give Aardy enough time to delete the evidence from GQ's phone. After a good half-hour soak, we returned to the room. GQ was finally fully calmed down.

"Thanks for that, guys," GQ said as he picked up his phone. "I feel much better now."

That was about the point that the irony began.

"Agh! Agh! Agh! They deleted it! The video is gone!"

If GQ was unconsolable before at the prospect of the Illuminati, there would be no reaching him now.

"Oh my god! Oh my god! They are the Illuminati, and now they've stolen the proof!"

"You'd best take him home" I advised Kaisapaisa.

The moment the elevator doors had closed, even before the screams had fully faded away, I turned my attention to Kanish.

"Dude. What the fuck was that shit?"

"To what shit do you refer?"

"That whole meeting and chant."

"It's Lakshmi's church of sorts."

"It sounds more like a cult."

"Goodness, no. Really, she's just ridiculing Capitalism. She's a Marxist, don't you know?"

"A Marxist Billionheir? Well, now I've heard everything."

As interesting as I found the concept of a Marxist Billionheir, at that particular moment, I didn't care about the Illuminati, or Marxism, or anything other than an accurate Billionheir count.

"Kanish, how many fucking Billionheirs are here in Los Angeles now?"

"I can't say for sure, but there were over thirty at last count."

"But how! In that kind of time frame!" I protested.

"Word spreads fast when it comes to Mogul Manifestation, I suppose," Kanish replied. "And it's not like any of us are lacking resources. It takes less than a day to fly to Los Angeles."

It was all far worse that I'd even imagined. There were now thirty Billionheirs paired with thirty Producers turned DJ Produsahs, all of them pumping out Kitten Videos into the queue of an ever-expanding network of Code Shacks and Telemarketing firms. Kanish was having trouble putting a number on it, but it was clear to me that we had enough manpower to blow out tens of millions of Views and Shares like we were gods big-banging out universes into the multiverse.

We could even drop the pretense of Distribution at this point. Essentially, we controlled what was hot on the Internet. I shouldn't need to tell you this, but when you control what's hot on the Internet, you might as well control the world. We *were* the Illuminati.

The problem is, we were anything but in control. This had gotten bigger than all of us.

Aardy turned on the TV to the eleven o'clock news, which was now broadcasting overhead shots of the Power Plant. There were correspondents on the ground, and although there was some question as to why there were so many Mogul Mobiles in Redondo, the press seemed more intrigued by the stunningly stupid design of the bike lanes themselves. Go figure.

"Well, we really dodged a bullet there." Aardy sighed in apparent relief as he clicked off the TV. "The last thing we need is for that Illuminati shit to make the news. That chant in that Orwellian setting? That would get people Talking all right. Talking about the Rev's song *"Laugh!,"* that is. That won't do at all."

"It most certainly won't," I replied. "I'm going to bed."

"My lesson!" Kanish demanded.

"Sure, Kanish. It's a modern twist on George Orwell."

"Yes, yes, yes. What is it?"

"He who controls the Internet controls the future," I replied.

Mixerman

CHAPTER TWENTY-FOUR

#Oopsiedaisychain

#insomniahappens
#TVclicker

[*Click*]

Cable channel 604: July 2, 3:05 a.m. PST

@theAMJoe: "Let's get to headlines. Oh here's one! I know this is your favorite, Sally. Look at that. I have here a copy of the Daily Muse, and we have a picture of a cute little Kitten with the headline 'Douchebags and Pussies? Coincidence?'"

[*Laughter*]

#interjection

@mixerman: "Aardy! Kanish! Wake the fuck up! We made the news!"

@SidekickSally: "Stop! It's not funny. It's disgusting, actually. How could this be the Number One song in the country? What is wrong with people?"
@theAMJoe: "I don't believe it's Number One, actually. I'm fairly certain the Douchebag Song is Number Two, but we can check on that."
@SidekickSally: [*Sighs*] "Do you have to say that word?"
@theAMJoe: "What word is that, Sally?"
@SidekickSally: "You know exactly what word I'm talking about."
@BillyHeist: "According to *Billboard*, the Number One song is the Laughing Kittens video. It's called '*Laugh!*,' with an exclamation point, whatever that's about. Artists."

@theAMJoe: "I have a question, if I may. How did they do that? How did they get those Kittens to laugh like that?"

@GCobbleson: "I've been wondering that my damn self."

[*Laughter*]

@SidekickSally: [*Sighs*] "Could we please bring it back to the other song . . . because no one has a problem with '*Laugh!*'"

@theAMJoe: "I'm sorry. What song is it that you want to talk about now, Sally?"

@SidekickSally: "You're just trying to get me to say it."

@theAMJoe: "The Douchebag Song?"

@SidekickSally: "You really just like to say that word."

@theAMJoe: "It's a great word! Love that word! *Douchebag*. We can even say it on TV."

@BillyHeist: "I have to admit, there is something pleasing about saying the word *Douchebag*."

@SidekickSally: "Oh, stop it! Both of you!"

@theAMJoe: "I don't understand the problem, Sally. A Douchebag is merely a hygienic device."

@SidekickSally: "The Song on its own is rude enough. But now I have those cute little . . . little—"

@theAMJoe: "Pussies."

@SidekickSally: "—in my head, and I just think that is so disrespectful to women. Are one of you men going to back me up here, please?"

@GCobbleson: "Well, I can understand why, you know, some in our population might find the term *Douchebag* set to—"

@theAMJoe: "Pussies."

@GeneCobbleson: "—offensive, but does that really surprise any of us? Isn't that what people in the Music Business do? Attempt to generate controversy so that we start talking about it? You're just doing exactly what they want!"

@theAMJoe: "You know, it's possible, I mean, it occurs to me that maybe there's a message under the surface of this video that has nothing to do with women. But why would we talk about that? Let's just run a little of the clip, shall we?"

#cutelittlekittensvideo

@SidekickSally: "Look at that! Would you stop laughing, you three? Right there! That Kitten is twerking!"

#interjection

@mixerman: "So sorry to interrupt the commentary that would be news, but I feel I should interject here. I'd never noticed it before, but one of the cute little Kittens in our video seemed to be bouncing its little Kitten ass up and down in the air. It all seemed rather innocent at the time. But now that we were objectifying Kittens, I must admit, one of them was indeed twerking."

@theAMJoe: "Oh, I don't know, Sally. Does that look like twerking to you guys?"

@BillyHeist: "Not to me."

@GeneCobbleson: "Ummmmm . . ."

@theAMJoe: "I think you're making more out of this than you need to."

@SidekickSally: "And how do you know that? Do we know anything about this Artist—DJ Produsah Mixerman?—I mean, who is he? According to Google, he's either a small-time DJ from Europe, or he's a mixer. Does someone want to tell me what a mixer is?"

@BillyHeist: "I think the mixer is like . . . the sound guy. Is that right, Jim? . . . What's that? Oh, it's more complicated than that? But it's pretty much the same thing right? No?"

@SidekickSally: "And I've heard of a DJ, of course, but what is a Produsah?"

@BillyHeist: "A Produsah is like a guy who makes beats, I think."

@SidekickSally: "So he's a DJ and a guy who makes beats? Is there a difference?"

@theAMJoe: "We have a picture of him, Sally. We got this from *Billboard* magazine."

@SidekickSally: "Oh my god! They're pimps! Do you see that?"

@BillyHeist: "So I guess the Indian pimp is Knish Knosh Too. What's that? Ah, okay, according to the caption, let's see the middle pimp is Willy Show. And so the tall pimp there must be DJ Produsah Mixerman."

@SidekickSally: "It's disgusting. They dress like pimps!"

@BillyHeist: "According to his website, Mixerman is available for interviews. Let's see if we can get him in here for an interview tomorrow."

@SidekickSally: "Well, I for one would like to talk to this jerk."

@theAMJoe: "All right, we need to move on from this. In other news . . ."

[*Click*]

Cable channel 611: July 2, 3:10 a.m. PST

@SDouchey: "—his name is Mixerman, and from what we can tell from his website, he's a recording engineer who also writes some how-to books on the subject. You know what they say—those who can't do teach, right? Let's put up the picture we have of him."

@LChattlebreth: "No offense, but he is well past his best-before date. What's wrong with his face?"

@SDouchey: "It looks like it's being distorted. Oh! This is a hate site."

@LChattlebreth: "You really can't believe some lunatic with a hate site. I know. There are a number of them dedicated to me."

@SDouchey: "Oh, I've got tons of them myself. Let's get off his hate site and find another picture, if we could. Maybe from his Facebook feed? Do we have that? Great. Let's put it up on the screen."

@LChattlebreth: "Huh. Well, he's not horrible. He's a little old to be an Artist though, don't you think?"

@SDouchey: "He's certainly not what you'd expect from the Number Two Artist in the country."

@LChattlebreth: "Look at this! He's a liberal! Gross!"

@SDouchey: "It's just so typical of Artists. They're brainwashed by their parents into fantastical thinking, you know."

@Shillsleez: "And he went to public school!"

@LChattlebreth: "Oh! He's been fully indoctrinated, then. There's not doubt in my mind. He probably doesn't even believe in a white Jesus!"

#breakfast

[*Click*]

Cable channel 622: July 2, 6:00 a.m. PST

@Talkinghead: "The world wants to know, what is going on with all of these Kitten Videos? And what exactly is a DJ Produsah? *Produsah* isn't a new term, but according to our own Producers here on the show, it's often used as a derogatory designation for wannabes in the Music Business."

@Talkinghead 2.0: "That's right. Most legitimate Producers would not use the term *Produsah*. Nor would they refer to themselves as DJs, yet every one of these Kitten Videos lists the Artist as a DJ Produsah and MC duo. The first was DJ Produsah Mixerman and MC Knish Knosh Too. You may remember their video of twerking Kittens. But since that video was released, there have been others. There's DJ Produsah GQ, DJ Produsah Rev, DJ Produsah Empress, DJ Produsah the El Capitan, and that's just the top five! And the most mysterious part of all of this is that all of these Produsahs were successful Producers. Why would anyone give up a lucrative career as a Producer to become a Produsah? Isn't that a big step backwards? Let's take it to our favorite generic talking head standing by next to our brand-new custom-made Slate Jumbo Raven."

@Talkinghead 3.0: "Hey, guys! I'm on my own personal Facebook right now, and yes, as you can see, I only have five hundred Friends, but also, I too Shared the Laughing Kittens video. Let's go to my newsfeed right now. . . . As I scroll down on the Slate Jumbo Raven, you can see that Share after Share after Share . . . I mean, look at this. They're all Kitten Videos! And every one of these Kitten Videos has a Sitar in the arrangement. So I took a moment to count the number of Kitten Videos with Sitars, and so far, I'm at twenty. That's twenty videos, all of which have absolutely exploded with Shares and Views in a matter of just twenty-four hours. Of course, from what we can tell, all of this started with one Produsah. His name is Mixerman. Back to you, @Talkinghead 2.0."

@Talkinghead 2.0: "Thanks, @Talkinghead. Here's what we know so far: Mixerman is the owner of a recent start-up record Label called C@taclysmic Group Inc., and according to the California Secretary of State, he's not the only one involved here. His partner is listed as Kanish Kanish."

@Talkinghead: "I love Knishes."

@Talkinghead 2.0: "There is also one other player—Aardvark—but we have yet to determine his role in the Label."

#groupinterjection

@kanishkanish: "Ut oh."

@mixerman: "It's getting real now, huh?"

@aardvark: "How am I getting called out here?"

[*Click*]

Cable channel 604: July 2, 9:00 a.m. PST

@AnniePuntsman: ". . . and for every Produsah with a Sitar and a Kitten, there seems to be a Billionaire attached at the hip. Just look at this staggering statistic. There are currently twenty Kitten Videos performed by Sitar-happy DJ Produsahs, each of whom is mysteriously paired up with an MC Billionaire. I don't know, guys. Something is going on here. Weigh in for me."

@EssCup: "Where do I begin? I mean, this whole thing started because the women's groups were all riled up over Mixerman's disrespectful, borderline misogynist video. When you consider that the Kittens are just a metaphor for Pussies, while he's rapping about Douchebags, you have to wonder: What was this guy thinking?"

@ArbyKelper: "All due respect, EssCup, I think that you've mixed up the metaphors in this work, and it just seems to be a distraction. I realize this all started with a Produsah's questionable attitude toward women, but ladies, that's nothing new. Might I remind you that the Music Business doesn't have a good track record on women in general. There are very few women on the business side, and male Artists often depict women in a promiscuous manner. Clearly, what is news here is this influx of Billionaires into the Music Business, and it opens up one big gaping question: Are Billionaires controlling music?"

[*Click*]

Cable channel 622: July 2, 9:07 a.m. PST

@Talkinghead: "This just in. *Billboard* magazine has announced that for the first time in their 120-year history, they are temporarily shutting down the Hot 100 Chart. Their statement:

"'Due to the overwhelming number of Views, Shares, Pinups, Tags, Hashtags, Favorites, Tweets, and Mentions for Sitar-driven songs set to

Kitten Videos, we have shut down the Hot 100 Charts until further notice. As of this statement, the top twenty spots are locked, with no room for movement. Further complicating matters, no other songs are being Streamed, and no other Videos are being Shared. We have put the final Chart online. As of this moment, the Douchebag Song by DJ Produsah Mixerman and Knish Knosh Too is the Number One record in the country. However, it is important to note that only a handful of Views separates the Number One song from the Number Twenty song. For the first time in our hundred-plus-year history, there is no point in trying to keep track any longer. Thank you for your understanding in this matter."

@Talkinghead: "Joining us now to discuss what this means is . . ."

#endlessspeculation

[*Click*]

Cable channel 604: July 2, 11:00 a.m. PST

@Fieldreporter: "We're here at the house of Mixerman, as some have called it. It's a pleasant house in what used to be a quiet neighborhood near the beach. Bear with me, it's a little loud out here due to all the helicopters."

@DandriaSchnitzel: "No worries, Field. Tell us, has anyone seen Mixerman yet?"

@Fieldreporter: "Funny thing, that. We knocked on Mixerman's door about an hour ago, and we were a bit surprised when a Muslim Pakistani man wearing an orange turban greeted us. Unfortunately, he spoke very little American, and all we could really get from him was that, and I quote: 'Mixerman not here.'"

@DandriaSchnitzel: "Muslims? You realize orange turbans would make them Sikhs, not Muslims."

@Fieldreporter: "Well, I wouldn't want to speculate, @Dandria, but just take a look at this. If you'll follow me under this arboretum, according to neighbors, there has been quite a bit of unusual activity at this house, and here in the driveway is a Stingray, which as you know is an expensive American car. Does that mean something? Perhaps they drive an American car to disguise their American-hating ways. And look at this—it appears as if a bomb went off in the interior. Which begs the question: Is there a terrorist plot to take over the Internet? Music would seem such an unlikely place to begin an Internet takeover, but when you look at this car, it seems plausible. Now, just off camera here—if you could join me right here, sir, thanks—this is Rob the Electrician. He lives across the street. Tell us some of the things that have been going on lately, Rob."

@robtheelectrician: "Yeah, well . . . there's been a number of incidents involving police and these Muslim guys living in this house. And there are three dudes that are always being driven around in their fancy Bentley."

@Fieldreporter: "So you don't know any of them personally, I take it?"

@robtheelectrician: "We don't talk to neighbors around here."

@Fieldreporter: "And what are your thoughts on all these Kitten Videos?"

@robtheelectrician: "I don't care for them. I don't. I liked them at first. I guess I still like them, but I'm kind of scared, you know? What are these guys up to? Like, what kind of subversive message are they sending with all these Kitten Videos and Sitars. Is this a Muslim plot to brainwash us into sharia law?"

@Fieldreporter: "There you have it. People in this neighborhood are scared, and just want everything back the way it was. Between the helicopters and news trucks, that's unlikely to happen anytime soon. The big question on everyone's mind: Where is Mixerman?"

@DandriaSchnitzel: "Indeed. Where is Mixerman?"

[*Click*]

Cable channel 622: July 2, 1:00 p.m. PST

@BoltSpritzer: "We have with us a highly respected Music Producer to answer some of these questions for us. Joining us is the man they call the Rev. Do I have that right?"

@theRev: "That's right. Nobody beats the Rev."

@BoltSpritzer: "I see. First, perhaps you could define for us the term *Produsah*. We all know what a Producer is, but what is a Produsah, and what is a DJ Produsah?"

@theRev: "A DJ Produsah is just a fancy term for an Artist, you see."

@BoltSpritzer: "I'm sorry. So you're an Artist? No offense, but you don't think you're a little old for that?"

@theRev: "I'm not sure what age has to do with it?"

@BoltSpritzer: "And what about your relationship with Mixerman? Our research shows that you've worked with him in the past. Do you deny that you know Mixerman?"

@theRev: "Deny it? Of course not! I've known Mixerman for years."

@BoltSpritzer: "How about Kanish Kanish? The Indian Billionaire who has recently partnered with Mixerman? Do you know him too?"

@theRev: "Well, yes."

@BoltSpritzer: "How about a Billionaire who goes by the name Mukesh?"

@theRev: "That's my partner."

@BoltSpritzer: "Are you friends with DJ Produsah GQ?"

@theRev: "Yes!"

@BoltSpritzer: "How about a Billionaire named Kaisapaisa?"

@theRev: "I know them all, yes."

@BoltSpritzer: "You have to admit, sir, it's a little suspicious that you know so many Billionaires . . ."

@theRev: "I know lots of wealthy people!"

@BoltSpritzer: "Yes, I would imagine. But all of these Billionaires happen to have direct connections with seemingly washed-up Producers."

@theRev: "Washed up my ass! Have you seen my billboard on Sunset Boulevard?"

@BoltSpritzer: "How do you explain the fact that all of these songs sound and look like they were made by the same person?"

@theRev: "What planet are you living on? That's always how it's been."

@BoltSpritzer: "What about all the striking similarities between your videos and arrangements?"

@theRev: "What?"

@BoltSpritzer: "Mr. the Rev, are you in cahoots with Mixerman? Is there collusion going on here?"

@theRev: "What?! No! It's all Mixerman! He's the one that started this whole thing! He's the one that brought in Billionaires' Heirs from all over the world to manipulate the Views, and then the Shares! He's the one that's plotting and planning on how to get Spins and Streams! And then he couldn't leave well enough alone. He had to get people Talking, too! He's got this whole crazy formula to turn Billionheirs into Moguls. You've got the wrong guy here!"

@BoltSpritzer: "So Mixerman is the culprit?"
@theRev: "Mixerman is the Mastermind! Leave me out of this!"

#ouch

[*Click*]

Cable channel 604: July 2, 1:00 p.m. PST

#breakingnews

@Delandria: "This just in. The Internet can no longer keep up with all the Views and Shares. Most experts are blaming the sudden influx of Kitten Videos for the collapse. Pinterest, LinkedIn, Tumblr, Twitter, Reddit, and Instagram have all gone dark this hour. Just a moment ago, Facebook began the process of spinning down its servers. Currently, Google+ is the only social site standing. We don't expect that to last long."

[*Click*]

Cable Channel 622: July 2, 1:00 p.m. PST

#breakingnews

@BoltSpritzer: "This just in. Easter Island Records, which was report-edly on the verge of signing a very lucrative deal with start-up C@taclysmic Group Inc., owned by Mixerman and Kanish Kanish has just released a statement:

"'While it's true that Easter Island Records has been considering a relationship with C@taclysmic Group Inc., we have no intention of com-pleting that deal. We have nothing to do with this. We wish Mixerman all the best.'"

[*Click*]

Cable channel 604: July 2, 4:58 p.m. PST

@CCashews: "Let me finish tonight with this: I just think it's a real problem that our Musical System has been so corrupted by Billionaires' Heirs, as DJ Produsah the Rev so aptly put it. They've cornered the market with their Views, and they've diluted the people's Shares, and dammit, that's not what America is about.

"The Internet has been littered with their rather unoriginal and uninspired Kitten Videos. You can't put on the radio anymore without hearing a Sitar. All because some joker going by the name of Mixerman has brought it upon himself to import Billionaires from all over the world. That's how it appears, anyway. And to what end? Just to get ahead on the backs of all the other hardworking Produsahs out there?

"Well, guess what? The unthinkable happened today. The Billionaires are now in total control of the Music Business, and it's quite apparent that this whole dirty Kitten Cartel was hatched by a man who would be called Mixerman—a two-bit hack Producer and writer. I won't even give him the dignity of calling him a Produsah, because he's made such a mockery of the system, and tonight the chickens have come to roost. The Internet has gone dark. As of this moment, the people's ability to View and Share has been fundamentally muzzled, all because one modern-day Robber Baron had to have it all. I think that we as a Nation should make an example of Mixerman and his Billionaire Kitten Cartel. I say, throw them all in jail and lock away the key."

[*Click*]

Cable channel 604: July 2, 6:00 p.m. PST

RMeadows: "Good evening. Unless you're living under a rock, you're familiar with the scandal breaking all day over this man on your screen—he's known as Mixerman, and is now alleged to have organized Billionaires from all over the world to corrupt the Musical System. And it hasn't stopped there. Facebook, Pinterest, Tumblr, Twitter, you name it, they have all spun down their servers tonight because they can no longer keep up with the demand for Views, Shares, Pinups, and Posts—whatever your favorite social media site calls it. Not that it matters—they're all shut down. Nada. Nothing. There are no hashtags. There are no 'at' signs.

"Even Google—which has been desperately attempting to lure people to their clunky social media site lacking any kind of intuitive design or functionality—even Google got overrun today shortly after the other social media sites spun down.

"This story centered at first around the big question of whether it's in good taste to put a song about a device—that we don't often discuss here on the show—but it's about a device that women sometimes use for their own personal hygienic purposes. It's also a slur, or maybe not a slur so much as a slight, or an aspersion. I'll put it this way. You don't say it to someone that you're generally happy with, and I have to admit . . . it's a little awkward to even be saying the word on my show, but here it goes. Douchebag. There, I said it. And most of you have probably heard . . . the Douchebag Song . . . and you probably have seen the video of cuuuute little Kittens dancing, which had Feminist groups all up in arms this morning.

[*Dramatic pause*]

"The person on your screen right now is a Los Angeles Producer known as Mixerman. This is a picture of him in a recording studio. And he, according to his own website, is a mixer and Producer and a writer—maybe he's a banker and a conductor too! I don't know! But he says he's all of those things, which is kind of weird, right? How could someone do all of those and be good at any of them? But I have no reason to doubt him, I suppose. He seems like he's had a decent career in the Music Business. He's even worked on records that I know and like!

[*Sings*] "'She keeps on Passin' Me By . . .'

"Excuse me, I should never sing like that on TV. Love that song.

[*Awkward smiling*]

"Anyway, that was then and this is now, and while Mixerman may have worked on one of my favorite albums ever, there are a number of questions tonight as to who he is—exactly—and how he's come to be the most powerful man in music. Not because he owns the biggest Label. He doesn't. In fact, his Label is just a start-up. According to the Secretary of State in California, his Corporation C[a]taclysmic Group Inc.—there used to be an 'at' sign where the first *a* goes—cute, huh? Well, as it turns out, C[a]taclysmic Group is less than a month old. Yet somehow, from that position, he has managed to have a hand in the top five songs—very possibly the top twenty songs in America, and we believe that—through his shenanigans—he is at least partly responsible for the collapse of both the Billboard Hot 100 Music Chart and the Internet itself.

[*Dramatic pause*]

"We have just received some exclusive footage, literally—and I'm not exaggerating here—literally an hour before we went on the air. And in the footage, you will see the man known as Mixerman—and multiple sources have confirmed this—it's Mixerman in a secret meeting at the Redondo Beach Power Plant, with what appears to be a large number of very wealthy young men and women of various ethnicities, mostly Indian.

"I'm going to warn you. What you're about to see is disturbing. Some of you may want to . . . avert your eyes . . . Seriously. It's not pretty. Here it is . . ."

runtheclip

"I'm here at the Redondo Beach Power Plant, the perfect place for an Illuminati meeting. . . ."

"Take!
As much as you possibly can.
Waste!
What you do not need.
Laugh!
In the faces of those who have none, ha, ha, ha, ha—

Take! As much as you possibly can . . ."

"Holy shit! I can't take any more of this! It's the Illuminati!"

[*Screams and commotion*]

RMeadows: "Okay, now, it's kind of fast, so we're going to show it again, but before we do, on the left, you will see a very tall, perhaps even handsome man—if you're into that sort of thing, it just so happens I'm not—and that man there on the left of your screen, that man is Mixerman. And behind him you'll see all sorts of young people on yoga mats, and we have every reason to believe that most, if not all, of those fabulously dressed young people are ostensibly Billionaires. With a *B*. Or at the very least Heirs of Billionaires, or Billionaires' Heirs, as they were referred to by

DJ Produsah Rev in an interview with Bolt Spritzer. I can Share that with you now. This is amazing. Honestly, I didn't think Bolt had it in him."

runtheclip

BoltSpritzer: "Mr. Rev, are you in cahoots with Mixerman? Is there collusion going on here?"

TheRev: "What! No! It's all Mixerman! He's the one that started this whole thing! He's the one that brought in the Billionaires' Heirs to manipulate the Views, and then the Shares! . . . You've got the wrong guy here!"

RMeadows: "'You've got the wrong guy here,' he says. He also states that Mixerman is, quote, 'the one that brought in the Billionaires' Heirs to manipulate the Views and Shares.' And let's replay the Power Plant video again."

runitagain

"Take!
As much as you possibly can.
Waste!
What you do not need.
Laugh!
In the faces of those who have none, ha, ha, ha, ha—"

RMeadows: "Now, if you're saying to yourself, 'Hey! I've heard that chant before!' You sure have! In fact, it was the Number One song in the country on Saturday, but fell to the Number Two spot just before the entire Internet collapsed. The song is called "*Laugh!*" Italicized with an exclamation point. The title doesn't make any sense, because it's not a funny song at all. In fact, it's downright creepy.

"Honestly, we don't know who all these people are in this video. And I'm not going to start freaking out about the Illuminati right now, because I somehow managed to misplace my tinfoil hat! But according to a local Redondo Beach news reporter, there were as many as thirty chauffeur-driven luxury cars: Bentleys, Rolls-Royces, Mercedes, Hummers—you name it, if it was a high-end limo, it was lined up in front of the Redondo

Beach Power Plant in the bike lane, which was apparently a fiasco in its own right. But let's not get distracted by that! Because the idiocy of bikes in lanes that have to intermingle with cars coming out of parking lots isn't the big news here. No, it just so happens that Mixerman lives in Redondo Beach. And according to the reports we've been getting from outside his home, Mixerman has a Bentley and a driver too!

"I think it's clear that Mixerman has more than a casual association with this roomful of Billionaires' Heirs.

"Then there's Sunset Boulevard—you may know it as the Sunset Strip. Look at this footage. This is a reporter driving down Sunset today, and look at the billboards. One after another, billboards touting DJ Produsahs are lining the busy Los Angeles street. They go on for miles. The most perplexing thing is that they all say 'For Your Consideration.' Which is kinda weird. We are many months away from Grammy voting, which is what these kinds of ads are for. They're ads put out by Artists and managers and Labels begging for Grammy votes. It happens every year, but not on city billboards. Not like that. Sure, you'll see these sorts of ads in *Billboard* magazine, but according to our research, there has never been a street billboard ad campaign like this. It just seems like a big waste of money to try and reach Grammy voters on the Sunset Strip in the summer. Yet there they are. I suppose they have quite a bit of disposable cash.

"And so, everyone is kind of wondering, what's going on here? All day, the world has been looking for Mixerman, to no avail. His personal friend and peer threw him under a herd of Elephants on Bolt Spritzer's show this afternoon. News crews are staked out at his house, which is currently and mysteriously occupied by a group of Sikhs. If you don't know what a Sikh is, they are highly trained Indian martial arts experts—they are not Pakistani. Nor are they Muslim, as some news commentators have pronounced, embarrassingly, even on our own network.

[*Dramatic pause*]

"You have to wonder—how does someone like Mixerman take the top prize of the Number One song in the country without ever having put a record out as an Artist. I'm sorry. I mean DJ Produsah, whatever he is. He's never Published a song, not that anyone can find. He's never been on tour. Yet somehow, he is at the center of all of this. Some guy in Redondo who does too many things.

"What do you have to say for yourself, Mixerman? If it was you and your Billionaires' Heir cohorts who made the Internet go dark—and I think it's clear that it was—how are you going to fix this?

"Watch this space. You have to—with the Internet dark, TV is the only game in town."

[*Click*]

Cable channel 622: July 2, 6:10 p.m. PST

Scooper: "Joining us now is the man behind the now infamous video that no one can even Share since the Internet went dark—DJ Produsah GQ and his Billionaire Kaisapaisa, did I get that right?"

GQ: "That's right."

Kaisa: "Helllooooooo, Scooper!"

Scooper: "We've watched this clip a number of times now, and your claim—that this is an Illuminati meeting—is incredible. And you suggest that the Illuminati cleaned it from your phone?"

GQ: "Yeah, man. That's right."

Scooper: "Then how did you send it to us?"

GQ: "Because they missed a folder."

Scooper: "Don't you think if it was the Illuminati . . . I mean, do you think it makes sense that an organization as powerful as the Illuminati would make such a rookie mistake?"

GQ: "Uh . . . well . . . no . . . wha . . . huh?"

[*Click*]

Cable channel 107: July 2, 6:30 p.m. PST

NationNews: "This just in: There is widespread confusion in Suburbia tonight. Throughout the entire country—state after state, city after city, town after town—families have exited their dwellings and their cubicles, and have taken to the streets of America, and they're doing a most remarkable thing. They're Talking directly to one another—in person, without any distractions.

"The government is on high alert. Experts, think-tankers, and pundits agree that this could all turn ugly without warning. Given the vicious arguments that routinely occur on the Internet, officials are concerned as to how this may Manifest on the streets. There is growing fear for the security of the country. Will fights break out? For the moment, things are calm. We have correspondents all over the country Talking to residents outside of their homes. Here are just some of the comments from dissatisfied Middle Classaires."

Malefaction, NY

"You know, when I watched the Laughing Kittens to that song, I liked the message of it. But now that I listen to it in the context of Billionaires laughing at us, it's really disturbing."

Bridgegate, NJ

"I'm bored and it's all because of the Billionaires. All the music and the videos are the same, yet I can't stop Sharing or Viewing or even Talking about them. It's like I'm addicted. I just can't help myself. Those little Kittens are so cute! Now what am I supposed to do? I'm just out here on the street, aimless."

Methaven, FL

"I think that Mixerman needs to step up and fix this thing. Just look at the mess he's created. People are Talking to each other and Sharing their Views in person! What if people start Poking each other? Then what? This is downright dangerous."

Arid, CA

"Mixerman is the one that broke the Internet. He's the one that made it so that every song on the radio sounds the same. And he's the one that put the Billionaires in music. It's all his fault that I'm out here right now instead of Sharing videos."

Sludge Beach, MO

"This whole scandal makes me want to throw out all my CDs, but then I realized I did that years ago."

Walton Hills, AR

"I just think this all sends the wrong message to our children. We don't want them to grow up thinking like Billionaires. We're trying to bring them up as good people, and then we have to deal with this kind of corrupting influence? I don't think I can ever View another Kitten Video again."

Sketchy Fields, IL

"The Billionaires in music broke the Internet, and they're laughing at us."

Frackustown, TX

"If someone doesn't shine a light back on the Internet, I predict there's gonna be Second Amendment Remedies!"

Budford, CO

"Usually I put up a picture of my food for my Friends to see. But today, I Shared some sausage with my neighbor and he loved it! Who knew?"

Blackburn, KY

"Why should there be Billionaires in music anyway? Shouldn't they all be in the Tech Industry now?"

Muckhaven, ND

"When you let every Produsah have his own Billionaire, it makes a mockery of the system. This isn't how it was supposed to be. They took control of our Views and our Shares, and now they're deciding what's best for us rather than letting our voices be heard."

Blacksoot Bend, NC

"We need to get this Billionaire epidemic under control. This is the issue of our times."

BREAKING NEWS

"This just in: Senator Crou d'Etat is convening a Select Committee. The press conference is just getting under way.

[*Camera shutters chattering*]

"Good evening. I'm Senator Crou d'Etat. I'll make this brief. As you all know, the Internet has gone dark, and now there are people all over this country taking to the streets, and they're Talking to one another. This is a dangerous situation, and we in Congress must do all that we can to fix this as quickly as possible.

"In response to this dire emergency, I have convened a Senate Hearing to investigate how Billionaires managed to turn the whole Musical System into nothing more than a sham all so that they could concentrate the power in the hands of a few.

"I know that the press—the whole country, really—has been searching for the man they call Mixerman. We have found him."

[*Commotion*]
[*Camera shutters chattering*]

"We were able to reach the president of C[a]taclysmic Group Inc. this evening through the Indian Consulate in San Francisco. That led us directly to Mixerman, who has wisely accepted our invitation to the Hearing, along with his partner Kanish and his manager Aardvark. Mixerman in particular has expressed an interest in testifying. All the major players seem to be cooperating fully, and there will be no need for subpoenas at this time.

"My hope is that we can prevent the Billionaires in music from ever again corrupting the system that Americans hold so dear, and it is my promise to America that we will get the Internet turned back on. Soon.

"Whatever is going on here, we are about to get to the crux of the matter. Thank you, and may god bless the United States of America."

[*Commotion*]

Mixerman

CHAPTER TWENTY-FIVE

THE HEIR APPARENT

I have only a few recurring daydreams. Testifying before Congress? That's one of them. And now it was virtually a reality.

Of course, it doesn't take long before my fantasy devolves into *fuck-yous*, and then I immediately berate myself for allowing an imaginary politician to get my Goad. Losing one's cool is not how one wins an argument, especially in that forum. As a result of my overactive imagination, I've had a bit of practice, even if it doesn't amount to any experience.

Aardy made arrangements to hire a local DC Constitutional Lawyer who goes by the name of Jon Squirrly, but I for one don't intend to use him. Which is nuts, I understand. I'd be an idiot to speak in front of the Senate without actively engaging my counsel. But then, everything Kanish, Aardy, and I had done, we'd done under the umbrella of our Corporation—C[a]taclysmic Group Inc. And while it's true that our Corporation was not directly responsible for the collapse of the Internet, it could be reasonably argued that we were the catalyst. Regardless, no matter how I parsed it, I was being personally and publicly blamed for the misdeed.

The big problem with these kinds of select Committee Hearings is that they tend to serve as a platform for Senators to put on a show. I've watched enough of them to know. The Senators will interrupt those who convey inconvenient truths to them.

Of course, the Senators that are friendly to our position will surely give us the opportunity to say our piece. But let's face it. We had no allies in this fight. And as a startup Corporation, we had no ties to Washington. So, as excited as I was to testify, I didn't believe for a moment I'd get the opportunity to speak uninterrupted to power.

You'd think that the Senators would take it easy on us—after all, we could donate to their campaigns if they did. Three of the nine Senators on the Hearing panel were running for president, including the Chairman of the select Committee, Senator Crou d'Etat. Of all people! What with his starring role in my dreams lately. I almost felt as though I knew the guy.

You can be sure that Aardy, Kanish, and I spent yesterday's entire news spiral strategizing our moves. We were fortunate that the Feminists attacked us with a Molotov stink bomb. Were it not for that event, we'd have found ourselves under siege at the house rather than safely tucked away at the Crown Royale Hotel. As it was, the helicopters made it difficult to think, and they were a mile away from us. Imagine if they were directly overhead.

The Internet was still dark as of this morning. Radio stations were unable to use their automated Spin systems, and the DJs took to the airwaves to Talk to America. You would think that the collapse of the Internet would dominate the conversation, and while no doubt there was some of that, the coverage revealed something far more inspiring. The people made the best of it.

Parties broke out all over America, and people began to hang out and personally Talk and Share with one another. They rediscovered what it was like to Talk to someone who was fully engaged in a conversation, rather than distracted by their social media feed. It was the day before Independence Day, July 3, and so it should be of no surprise that the radio station DJs stopped Spinning Sitar songs and began to Spin patriotic songs. Let the celebration begin.

It was like an epidemic. The people Shared their experiences, and their stories, and their food, and their embarrassments, and their laughter with others in their proximity. Directly. Personally. They even Shared their political Views. And you know what they discovered? That everyone just wanted the same thing—a chance to get ahead.

How ironic is that? We had to go backwards to realize we all just wanted to get ahead.

Once the Internet went dark, and I was being publicly shamed for it, I was certain that I would be the most hated man in America. Possibly the world. And while there's no doubt that the people wanted their Internet back, it seems that most among us enjoyed the respite.

It reminds me of the time my childhood family vacation was so rudely interrupted by Hurricane Belle. It was the mid-'70s. We were in Cape May, a charming beach town at the very bottom of New Jersey. The family was holed up in my grandparents' bungalow as it was pelted by the seventy-mile-per-hour sustained gale-force winds. It was an experience I'd never recommend, despite the fact that I'm glad to have gone through it. I suppose that's just the writer in me.

The best part about that vacation was the time that we spent as a family. We Talked and we laughed, and we played board games and built jigsaw puzzles. Despite the less-than-ideal circumstances, we had fun. And you know what? I never once thought of it as a ruined vacation.

I'm not for a moment suggesting or rationalizing that we should go backwards to simpler times. I do, however, want to take my country back. Not from all the black and brown folks, mind you. That's what makes us great. I want to take it back from those who operate from a position of fear. Change is inevitable. Adapt or die. We should fear stagnation, not change. What the hell do you think keeps life interesting?

By morning, every radio station in the country was prepared to air today's Hearing. Every television station, big and small, was set to broadcast the press pool feed. Our Committee Hearing would face no competition from the Internet today. The whole country was watching and listening, and for this I was grateful.

Rajadut arranged everything for us. He handled all communications with the Senator and his staff. He got us out of the Crown Royale Hotel without incident. And then he put us on a private jet, where, thankfully, we all got some sleep. Rajadut determined that the Baltimore and Washington airports were infested with press, so he flew with us to Philadelphia and then personally drove us to the Indian Embassy in Washington, DC.

Our attorney, Jon Squirrly, stopped by the Embassy to go over the ground rules.

"Plead the fifth," Jon Squirrly advised.

"I'm Indian," Kanish pointed out.

"I'm Canadian," Aardy said.

"The Fifth Amendment begins with the words *no person*. So, you can plead the fifth even if you're not an American citizen. Here. This is what you say."

Jon Squirrly handed me a card, which I read aloud.

"'On counsel's advice, I invoke my right under the Fifth Amendment not to answer on the grounds I may incriminate myself.'"

"You're a natural. I'll see you at the Hearing."

On the orders of Senator Crou d'Etat, we were driven from the Embassy to the Capitol by the Secret Service, which, as it turns out, is even more efficient than being chauffeured in a Bentley.

We pushed our way through the sea of reporters to the Capitol building. They were pelting us with a cacophony of questions. Cameramen backpedaled in front of us. Still others chased from behind us. There were microphones and recorders and phones stuck into our faces. We had supporters on one side, detractors on the other. All of them screaming their beliefs at us. It was an American scene—charming in its aggressiveness.

Except for one thing.

The cameramen, the reporters, the protesters—every one of them—were Indian.

"What the fuck?" I said.

"What do you expect?" Kanish replied. "We're Billionheirs. We know how to purchase an audience."

"Then why are some of them protesting us?"

"It's all about the show. This is the way of the Billion-hair, don't you know?"

I swear I thought he said "Billion-hair."

"It's quite the show, indeed," Aardy mused.

"I wouldn't have it any other way," I agreed.

The Senate steward escorted us into the bustling Committee Room without fanfare and through a veritable sea of Indians wearing traditional Indian garb speaking in native Hindi tongue as they milled about in palpable anticipation. Senators and staff were locating their seats on the stage. Photographers were staking claim to impossibly small patches of floor. The broadcast cameras were well apparent.

Other than Rajadut, Sevaka, and Annapurna, there was only one other person that I recognized in the crowd. It was Paneer, and I swear he needed an extra chair just for his glare. Whatever. He'd wanted me to make his son famous.

We were escorted to our positions at the long conference table. The Rev, Mukesh, GQ, Kaisapaisa, the Empress, and Lakshmi were already seated, and in that order. There were three remaining spots front and center, each with a nameplate, a mic, and a glass of water. We took our seats in accordance with our assignments, which read from left to right: KANISH, MIXERMAN, AARDVARK.

"I don't suppose it was an accident that we're in the middle of the table," I said sarcastically to Aardy.

"There are no accidents," Aardy replied.

"This is no time for lessons," Kanish quietly admonished.

Senator Crou d'Etat made his way into the Committee room followed closely behind by staff. He had a seat and cracked some jokes with the other Senators. All of it seemed part of the show. I suppose he had a personal time limit on kibitzing, because without any warning, the Senator picked up his gavel and hammered it down two times. *Crack! Crack!*

It took a moment for everyone to settle down fully, but once the chamber was sufficiently still, the Senator commenced the proceedings.

"Good morning. Today we convene this select Committee to address the corruption of the Music Business by Billionaires. Senate Resolution 69 was adopted unanimously by the United States Senate on the evening of July 2 of 2015. Under its provisions the Senate has mandated the members of this Select Committee to investigate with god's speed the fraud that has been perpetrated upon this great country of ours.

"Under the terms of the authorizing resolution, this Committee is tasked with two goals, the first and most important being to return the Internet back to the people. The whole country is depending on this Committee for that, and we shall not fail in this momentous responsibility.

"Our second goal—an equally crucial assignment—is to determine whether it is in the interest of this country to allow Billionaires to corrupt our Musical System. Given the urgency of this matter, the Committee is tasked with completing its objectives in the measure of hours, not days. This is the issue of our times.

"It seems to this Senator, at least, that the American people can no longer trust the Musical System to address and protect their overall interests of diversification and choice. Our Constitution is the envy of the world, and it sets forth the principle that we are all granted the inalienable right to the preservation of life, liberty, and the pursuit of happiness. Today, there is a stain upon that most noble of sentiments."

The stain the Senator is referring to was most certainly on our education system, since that particular "right" isn't laid out in the Constitution. This Douchebag literally carries a miniature copy of the Constitution in his back pocket, which he is sure to wave anytime a camera is around, yet he doesn't even know that the phrase "pursuit of happiness" comes from the Declaration of Independence? The Senator continued.

"With the collapse of the Internet, the Views of Americans can no longer be counted. The idea that America's vote has been stolen from them by a cartel of Billionaires will not stand. It cannot stand. And we must do all that we can to root out the influence of this dangerous and powerful special interest group—the Illuminati."

"The Illuminati?" I blurted. This caused a commotion in the chamber.

Illuminati?   *Illuminati? Illuminati?*   *Illuminati?*   *Illuminati?*

   Illuminati?   *the Illuminati? Illuminati?   Illuminati?   The Illuminati?*

   Illuminati?   Illuminati?   Illuminati?   Illuminati?   *The*

Illuminati?   *Illuminati*   *Illuminati?*   *Illuminati*

"The congregation will remain quiet! The witness known as Mixerman will allow me to complete my opening statement without interruption."

"My apologies, Senator."

"Where was I? Ah, yes. May god bless this Committee. And may god bless the United States of America."

"Oh, right. I forgot," I dripped sarcastically. "You still had to bless yourself and this country. And how do you know that god doesn't bless the Illuminati, Senator?"

"Mixerman will maintain decorum."

"Excuse me, Senator, but have you no shame, sir? You're up there acting as if the Illuminati exists, and frankly, that's nothing more than a distraction."

"The witness will come to order or he will be found in contempt!"

"He is vehdy much in order, Senator," Kanish interjected. "You are up there on your high Elephant suggesting that there is a secret society of Heirs that rule the world, and you do it for only one reason—to stoke people's fears. It's reprehensible coming from someone in your position, and I would vehdy much suggest that you allow my friend to speak fully, and with minimal interruption. Otherwise, you will surely get nothing from us."

nothing from us   *nothing from us*   *speak freely*

   speak freely   *or you'll get*   *nothing from us*

     nothing from us   nothing from us

speak freely speak freely   *or nothing from us*

   speak freely   speak freely   or nothing from us

I really had no idea why Kanish thought he'd have any sway with the Committee, but the Senator waved me on, almost as if he were resigned to acquiesce.

"Fine." Senator Crou d'Etat sighed. "What do you have to say for yourself, Mixerman?"

"I'm not sure where to start," I replied.

"How about you start by shining a light back on the Internet, sir?"

"I would love to, Senator. But we didn't actually cause the Internet to go dark. Big Tech did that—a long time ago, as far as I'm concerned. No, sir. I'm here to help you answer your other question—the more pertinent question as far as I'm concerned—should we allow Billionaires to corrupt our Musical System?"

A hush came over the crowd in anticipation of the answer. Would I say yes? Or would I say no?

"And?" the Senator prodded.

"We shouldn't let the Billionaires corrupt any of our Systems."

Billionaires corrupt	they corrupt	they corrupt
Don't let the Billionaires		corrupt our Systems
Billionaires, Billionaires	the Billionaires corrupt	
Don't let the Billionaires	corrupt,	corrupt
Don't let the Billionaires		corrupt our Systems

I don't know any other way to explain it, but the murmurs coming from the peanut gallery were becoming progressively more organized in nature, and I wasn't the only one to notice. Kanish and Aardy leaned in for a brief sidebar.

"The crowd is really getting behind you," Kanish encouraged. "Try a rhyme."

"A rhyme?" I replied with a glance toward Aardy.

"He hasn't steered us wrong yet."

Frankly, I didn't need Aardy's counsel as much as I required a rhyme. Regardless, the Senator wasn't inclined to hold up the proceedings for a strategy session.

"I hope, we aren't interrupting you gentlemen with our Committee."

"Of course not." I chuckled uncomfortably.

While it's true that I come up with rhymes all the time, at that particular moment I wasn't feeling particularly rhymey. Between the glare of the lights, and the dozen or so Senators staring down on us in judgment, the scene was a bit intense.

"You were saying?" the Senator prodded.

"I was saying," I repeated.

"About the Billionaires corrupting our Musical System."

"Yes. I'm just having a difficult time coming up with a rhyme."

"You're what?"

"Kanish!" Aardy hissed. "You're the MC!"

Kanish nearly jumped out of his chair and *finally* belted out a rhyme.

"The Billionaires and their Corporations are a powerful lot. Their money distorts everything. How could it not?"

And then the most miraculous thing happened. A Chorus was born.

Billionaires. Billionaires.
A powerful lot.
Their money distorts everything. How could it not?

"What on earth is going on here!" Senator Crou d'Etat bellowed.

"I'm not exactly sure myself, Senator, but it seems to me that we have ourselves a Greco-Indian Chorus," I replied.

"A what?"

"A Greco-Indian Chorus. Excuse me for a moment. I just need to tell my MC something," I said to the Committee before returning to my sidebar with Kanish and Aardy.

"When I knock"—[*knock, knock*]—"that's your queue."

"Will do," Kanish replied with a thumbs-up and a smile.

"Mr. Mixerman! I don't know what's going on here—"

"Yes! My apologies. Let's talk about Billionaires. 'Cause I gotta say, Senator, my life was never so easy as the day I got me a Billionheir. In fact, I highly recommend the experience to all of you up there, and that includes Senators Glamram and Boobio. Oh, snap! Wait! What am I saying? The three of you already have your very own Billionaires! You're all running for president!"

[*Knock, knock*]

Kanish didn't miss a beat.

"Get yourself a Billionaire, and get one soon. 'Cause you can't become the Prez without a Billionaire's boon!"

Billionaire's boon, Billionaire's boon.
You can't become the Prez unless you get one soon!

Get one soon, get one soon.
No, you can't become the Prez without a Billionaire's boon!

As fascinating as I found the Greco-Indian Chorus behind us, I was more intrigued by the reaction of the Senators—or should I say, lack thereof. I just delivered some rather tough shots, and none of the Senators even flinched. They didn't protest. They didn't interrupt. They just sat there placidly. It was like the Cat had their tongues.

"You know, Senator," I continued. "Since the crash of 2008, the stock market has tripled in value. Meanwhile, two-thirds of us are living paycheck to paycheck. The Middle Class continues to shrink as the ranks of the Working Poor swell, as do the bank accounts of the Billionaires who fund your campaigns. In fact, the Billionaires are doing great. Why? Because our policies dictate it. And that's your domain, Senators. Congress has the power to change those policies, yet you do nothing."

"This is a Capitalist society sir! It is not the government's job to pick the winners and losers in a Capitalist society."

"I'm sorry, but that argument falls flat on the face of it, because anytime you do nothing, it's the status quo that gets the benefit. When you watch a person drowning and you choose to do nothing—not even to sound the alarm—then you have made a conscious choice, an immoral one. To do nothing, to allow a person to drown as you watch it happen, is a heinous act. It's an act of inaction. Inaction *is* action."

Kanish didn't even wait for me to knock on the table this time. He just jumped right in.

"You spend all your time just huffing and bluffing, and all you get done is a whole lot of nothing."

Nothing, nothing,
But huffing and bluffing.
Congress does nothing but bluffing and huffing.
Huffing and bluffing, bluffing and huffing.
The Congress sure does a whole lot of nothing.

"When you do nothing as Big Tech destroys industries because they can take advantage of loopholes to long-standing laws, regulations, and taxes that weigh upon their well-established brick-and-mortar competitors, not only are you choosing winners and losers, you're allowing entire industries to be destroyed in the process. Local taxi companies who bought medallions that come with mortgages are at a disadvantage against Uber. Local hotels that must adhere to strict codes and pay extensive taxes are at a disadvantage against Airbnb. Retailers who sell direct to consumer are virtually forced to undercut their own pricing and margins in order for their products to appear on Amazon, with little to no increase in overall sales. You know, you guys say it all the time—that Small Business is the engine that runs this country. By allowing Big Tech to operate unchecked, you are killing Small Business across the board. You're choosing the wishes of a handful of Billionaires and their Corporations over the needs of the People."

[*Knock, knock*]

"Big Billionaire business and their Big Billionaire ways, and the People don't benefit, we're here to say."

Big Billionaire business.
Big Billionaire ways.
People don't benefit, we're here to say.

"I might point out, sir!" Crou d'Etat exclaimed, "you are sitting among Billionaires. And Music is the very definition of Big Business!"

That got a big laugh from everyone at the table.

"Big Business, he says!" the Empress scoffed. "Music!"

"You gotta be kidding me!" the Rev exclaimed.

"Take it from me, Senator," Aardy joined in. "Music is most certainly not Big Business. Not anymore. As my good friend Bob Olhsson likes to say, the Music Business is really nothing but the Tech Industry's bitch. Music is a tiny little drop in the bucket when compared to Big Tech, which is one of the reasons why the Music Business is getting crushed right now. And just for the record, these aren't Billionaires next to us holding court."

Aardy knocked on the table two times. [*Knock, knock*]

"We ain't Billionaires holding court. We're Billionaires' Heirs. Call us Heirs for short," Kanish rhymed.

Billionaires' Heirs, Billionaires' Heirs.
The Billionaires' Heirs are holding court.

Billionaires' Heirs, they're holding court.
You can just call them Heirs for short.

"That's all rather interesting, I'm sure," Senator Crou d'Etat suggested. "But if it weren't for Big Tech, there would be no Internet."

"No, Senator," I replied. "You mean if it weren't for the Internet, there would be no Big Tech, but I'm not here to quibble over which came first. I think I speak for everyone at this table when I say the Internet is the greatest thing ever invented in any of our lifetimes. I can't believe I lived the first half of my life without it. And I personally wouldn't want you to change much about the Internet. Except for one thing. Stop letting Big Tech have their way at the expense of everyone else.

"If I create music, and millions of people are playing my song, whether I performed it, wrote it, or both—I should get paid fairly from my work. Capitalism requires a government willing to level the playing field; otherwise the Billionaires and the Corporations make out like Barons. We already learned this lesson around the time of the Great Depression—must we learn it again?

"Independent Artists and Songwriters should be able to make money when people Stream their songs, and they should all be paid on a per-Stream basis, an amount such that we create a robust Middle Class in Music. To do this, you should set Statutory payments to Artists and Songwriters when their work is Streamed and Viewed and Spun. It's time to address this issue, and to stop pretending like it's not a problem. You're allowing the Music Business to drown with your inaction.

"Meanwhile, the Big Tech companies are making billions because they barely have to pay anything for online content. That arrangement is all well and good for Aunt Mable's Cat video. It doesn't work for those of us who create art for commerce. If musicians can't make money, they can't make music, and I'm here to tell you that there are many amazingly talented people in this industry that can no longer make a viable living making music. Certainly not the kind of living that would allow them to retire one day. Which makes the System as it stands unsustainable. The only reason the Major Labels are still afloat is because they have lucrative backroom deals with Big Tech, cutting out everyone else in the process. The Internet was supposed to be the great equalizer, Senator. It's become anything but."

[*Knock, knock*]

"It's time for you to put Big Tech in check. We can't compete against a fully stacked deck."

Fully stacked deck, fully stacked deck,
Please do your job and put Big Tech in check
Big Tech in check. Big Tech in check.
We really can't compete against a fully stacked deck.

"Which brings us to Copyright protection. You allow Torrent sites in Russia and China to sell our Intellectual Property in the form of a subscription. Meanwhile, the Creators of that work get nothing. We really need to shut the Torrent sites down. They're breaking the law, they aren't from this country, and we Creators have no way to go after these entities for infringement. I realize the whole Internet had an epic freak over this a few years back, but creating a government agency that pulls the plug on foreign infringing sites is not going to ruin the Internet, nor is it a slippery slope. Foreign entities don't have inalienable rights in this country. If Russians are going to steal our work, so be it. But must we let the Russians sell illegal access to our work back to Americans who are breaking the law in the process? That's *Rrritarded*!"

"This is all fascinating, I'm sure," Senator Crou d'Etat interrupted. "But none of that addresses what you did."

"What we did?"

"Yes. What you did."

When in doubt, answer in rhyme.

"While I certainly hope you won't be disillusioned, I may as well tell you, we engaged in some collusion."

Collusion. Collusion. Don't be be disillusioned.
He really shouldn't tell you,
They engaged in some collusion.

Senator Crou d'Etat sat up a little straighter, and Kanish gave me a thumbs-up for my rhyme.

"So you admit to collusion, then!"

"Oh, stop your salivating, Senator. It's not like you're going to do anything to us. We're a Corporation!"

[*Knock knock*]

"We're a Corporation. We made an end run. Don't get high and mighty when we act like one."

They're a Corporation.
They made an end run.
Don't get high and mighty
When they act like one.

"There is no doubt, Senator. We skirted laws. We bent them, wrung them, twisted them, mangled them—we rationalized them to our advantage—we even spit on them. As a result, we caused the collapse of the Internet—a System that so many of us have come to rely upon. Our only real argument for the level of collusion that went on is that everybody else does it, and that includes all of you Senators sitting up there judging us. And in any just world, we should be held accountable for that. But we won't be, because the US doesn't punish Corporations for gaining advantage or reckless behavior. We bail them out and beg them to do it again.

"All that said, and despite my admission of collusion, I would argue, as would my attorneys, that we operated within the letter of the law, regardless of the spirit. At worst, my Corporation will ultimately have to settle for a plea deal including a fine that may as well be a slap on the wrist. There will be no admission of guilt. No time served. And I have half a mind to ask for a bailout.

"And since I'm on the subject of bailouts, the Big Banks nearly collapsed the entire financial system around the world, and you immediately bailed out the worst offenders and made them whole. Meanwhile, most Americans got to experience eight hellacious years of a sluggish recovery, while the bankers and the Billionaires continued to get fat. Super fat. Fatter than they've ever been in history. So fat that according to your colleague Senator Bernie Sanders, the top one tenth of one percent in our country now owns nearly as much wealth as the bottom ninety percent. That's outrageous.

"You bailed out our Financial Institutions under the premise that they were too big to fail. But if that's true, then why the hell didn't you break them up? You can't insist that you will never bail them out again, when they're even larger now than they were when you told us they were too big to fail. If they fail again, according to you, we would have no choice but to bail them out again. You are essentially allowing the Bankers to operate without risk. We hold all the risk, yet they make all the money. Is operating without any risk Capitalism? That sounds more like Corporate Socialism to me. And some of you call yourselves Conservative!

"You let the Financial Industry do what they want. You let the Oil Industry do what they want. You let Big Ag and Big Pharma and Big-Box Retail and Big Tech and Big Tort and the Billionaires who run those Big Industries dictate policy in this country, and all of it benefits them at our expense.

"So I don't believe, at the end of the day, that I will be in any personal legal jeopardy, Senator. And the only reason I'm here is because my Corporation can't speak for itself. Personhood has its limits, I suppose."

[*Knock, knock*]

"Here we sit before you, to offer full retort. We got Corporate personhood granted by the Court."

Full retort. Full retort.
We got Corporate personhood
Granted by the Court
The Court they gave us personhood
We are their retort.

"If the Senator would relinquish the floor."

"Senator Flaterther has the floor," Crou d'Etat announced.

"As enjoyable as your rhymes are, and as much as I can't understand how you're getting the congregation to Chorus like that, I would like to address this song titled '*Laugh!*' When I first saw the video with those adorable Laughing Kittens, I have to say, I loved the song. But then when I saw the chant video, the one from the Power Plant, frankly, I was disturbed. It's a downright subversive message, and I'd like someone to explain to me the meaning of it. Is this the motto of the Billionaires' Heirs? I suppose I'd like to hear from the person who wrote it, but I'm a little unclear as to who that is. According to my staffers, the credit goes to a . . . DJ Produsah Rev and MC Mukesh? Is that right?"

I seriously doubt the Rev had any intention of testifying beyond reciting the Fifth Amendment. But a call-and-response Chorus that kicks in anytime you rhyme, well that's something that any Produsah can understand. It should come as no surprise that he took the moment for himself.

"The song was performed by Mukesh and I, this much is clear. It was Lakshmi wrote the lyric you fear. She wrote the lyric in some other year."

This much is clear. This much is clear.
Lakshmi wrote the lyric you fear,
She wrote the lyric,
In some other year.

"I see. So you're Lakshmi? And you wrote the song?"

"That is correct, Senator," Lakshmi replied in her British accent.

"And who do you belong to?"

"She's with me, Senator," the Empress interjected. "And I would thank you to stop referring to her as if she were property."

"My apologies, Empress. So, Lakshmi . . . am I saying that correctly?"

"You are, Senator."

"Oh, good. So, you're the one in the video at the Power Plant leading the Illuminati chant, are you not?"

"That is not an Illuminati chant! That is a poem that I wrote at Oxford University while studying Karl Marx. As you surely know, he was a philosopher who argued that Capitalism was fatally flawed, and would eventually collapse into Socialism—a word that strikes the fear of god in so many of you Americans. He argued that the ruling class runs the Capitalist State in their own self-interests as they pretend to represent the common interests of the People. The Ditty, as my friend Kanish calls it, or the poem, or the chant, whatever you wish to call the bloody thing, ridicules Capitalism. It doesn't celebrate it. I am a Socialist."

Lakshmi pumped her fist into the air and announced in Hindi, "Shuru karana!" The Greco-Indian Chorus joined her in chant.

"Take as much as you possibly can."

"Order!" Senator Crou d'Etat screamed as he smacked his gavel with two more cracks.

"Waste what you do not need."

"You are out of order!" The Senator's gavel block was now bouncing in the air from the violence of his hammer strikes.

"Laugh! In the faces of those who have none, ha ha ha ha ha."

The entire congregation, including the Billionheirs next to us, craned their necks in unison as they performed their most disconcerting laugh.

"How dare you make a mockery of this Hearing!" Senator Crou d'Etat bellowed.

Defiance must be catchy or something. The entire table was starting to get a bit feisty.

"I do not understand," Lakshmi said. "Why does this chant upset you Senators. You do realize that the title of my poem is 'The American Way.'"

"I've never heard anything so preposterous!" Crou d'Etat cried out hysterically. "That's not the American Way!"

"No, sir," Kanish interrupted. "You are vehdy much correct. This is certainly not the way of Americans. It is, however, the way of the Douchebags, which sadly makes it the American Way."

"Must we use that disgusting term?" Senator Bayleen chimed in. "I think that this particular subject matter would be best addressed by a woman. Don't you, Senator Crou d'Etat?"

"Senator Bayleen has the floor," Crou d'Etat proclaimed.

"Correct me if I'm wrong," Senator Bayleen began, "but it's my understanding that you and Mixerman are the composers of the Douchebag Song?"

"That is correct," Kanish replied.

Kanish had the floor, but I felt this would be a good place for a rhyme, and I couldn't think of one, so I gave the table a [*knock knock*]. I suppose that was bad form, because Kanish gave me a Paneer-like glare. Still, he dropped a rhyme with great aplomb.

"Aardvark's Kittens were a vehdy nice touch. They made us so popular, perhaps a bit much."

Aardvarks and Kittens.
A vehdy nice touch.
They're so damned popular
Perhaps a bit much.

"I would even go so far as to say," Kanish continued, "that without Aardvark, none of this would have ever happened."

Aardy had a rather awkward smile plastered on his face at the mention. I really couldn't tell whether he was pleased or unnerved by the shout-out, but I suspect he was a little of both. Senator Bayleen picked up her interrogation where she'd left off.

"Perhaps Mr. Aardvark would like to explain to this Committee why he thinks it's appropriate to set a song about . . . Douchebags . . . to little Kittens, which some in the media speculate is merely a metaphor for . . . for . . ."

"Pussies, Senator?" Aardy asked.

"Correct."

"I am a small minority partner in all of this, Senator Bayleen. And I wasn't there when the Song was written, but I am the one who came up with Kittens."

The Song was written.
The Song was written.
It took a fucking Aardvark
To think up some Kittens.

The Empress, who clearly has a thing for Aardy, did not take kindly to this line of questioning.

"Cut me a frickin' break!" the Empress exclaimed. "How did you get elected Senator? I mean, I have nothing to do with that Song or video, but I can tell you woman to woman—it's not about Pussies."

"Yes," Aardvark continued, "I suggested we make a Kitten Video because they're so darn popular. It had nothing to do with Pussies."

"Well, I just find it so rude!" Senator Bayleen proclaimed. "There were so many other terms you could have chosen. Why such a disrespectful term as *Douchebag*?"

Since the Senator was discussing my lyric, I thought it only appropriate to answer the question personally.

"Well, Senator," I said, "I wanted to use *Fuckhead* . . ."

"Order! Order!" Crou d'Etat shouted as the hammer head from his gavel flew off and smacked him on the nose.

"Read my lips, Senator Putin," I shot. "I will speak freely in this chamber of the People or I will not speak at all. None of us will. Our attorney insists that we should take the Fifth, and if that's what you'd like, then go ahead and continue to dictate what words I can use."

"Trust me vehdy much," Kanish interjected. "You wouldn't want to police his words, Senator."

"As I was saying, Senator Bayleen, I would have preferred stronger language, but that wasn't an option given the puritanical, archaic, and unconstitutional banning of certain words from the airwaves. Frankly, Senator, that's *Rrritarded!*"

None of the Senators protested my use of the word *Rrritarded*, which I was quite pleased about. Crou d'Etat was rubbing the sting from his nose as his staffers frantically searched for the gavel head. I continued with my testimony.

"Not that I should have to discuss my artistic decisions with you, but given the absurd restrictions of radio and my aversion to hearing my words censored, I was pretty much left to choose between *Douchebag* and *Scumbag.*"

"*Scumbag?*" Senator Bayleen questioned. "Well, that would have been much better. Why not *Scumbag?*"

"I suppose that's why you didn't write the Song. Because you don't understand the difference between Scumbags and Douchebags. You see, Scumbags are dirty, Senator Bayleen. Douchebags, on the other hand, well, at least they're clean."

And . . . the Chorus.

Senator Bayleen.
Senator Bayleen.
The Scumbags are dirty.
The Douchebags are clean.

"Excuse me?" The Senator recoiled. "Whatever do you mean?"

Whatever do you mean?
Whatever do you mean?
The Scumbags are dirty.
The Douchebags are clean.

"I think the best way I can explain it is like this," I said. "When a Scumbag steals from you, that's a close-proximity transaction that involves fear and the possibility of death, and so we tend to throw the Scumbags in jail—give them hard time for years. Fuck 'em. We're certainly all for that.

"But when the Douchebags of this world steal from millions of us at a time, whether financially or environmentally, that's a remote transaction, one in which there is no direct contact between the perpetrator and the victims, and so we treat the Douchebags differently because, you know—at least the Douchebags are clean."

Aardy took a moment to clarify what I felt was a rather straightforward concept, but I was happy for the backup.

"What he's saying, Senator, if I might interrupt, is that we all surely have disdain for the Scumbags and the Douchebags in this world. But we treat the Douchebags differently, because at least Douchebags are clean."

"I've had enough of this!" the gavel-less Crou d'Etat exclaimed. "First, Ms. Lakshmi here tells us that this disturbing Illuminati chant is supposed to be the American Way, and then Mixerman and Aardvark tell us that this has something to do with Douchebags who are clean. Who are these Douchebags?"

"Ah, yes, yes, yes," Kanish said. "Now we are getting somewhere. The Douchebags are the Billionaires and their Corporations and, I dare say, the Politicians as well."

"Hold on just a moment, sir! How do you lump the Politicians in with Corporations and the Billionaires?" Crou d'Etat protested.

"How do we not? You are all in cahoots! Let us set aside the Politicians for a moment so that I might explain this without all the emotional fervor. The Billionaires and the Corporations create jobs and give away their money to charities. They sponsor nice events and do all sorts of vehdy good things for people, which they are sure to let everyone know about. They want credit for their good deeds. This is beneficial to their brand."

"Excuse me," Senator Bayleen interjected. "If you're doing good for the world, shouldn't you get the credit for it?"

"Most definitely. The problem is many of these same Corporations and Billionaires will crush anyone that gets in their way, will cut corners even if it puts tens of thousands of lives at risk, do not care if enslaved children in third-world countries make their products, will hide their money offshore to avoid paying taxes, will seek any and every loophole that the Corporations and Billionaires often put into the law themselves, all under the guise of having a seat at the table.

"The Corporations and the Billionaires who run them will stop at nothing to make as much money as humanly possible so as to benefit themselves at the expense of everyone else. The Corporations then promote their do-gooder nature by sponsoring charities in exchange for exposure. For a relatively small portion of their profits, they get credit for giving away millions. It's vehdy brilliant, when you consider it. The Big Corporations leave behind a wake of people in need because they can't earn a living wage, and then donate to the charities that help the people whose lives they ruin. In the meantime, the Corporations and Billionaires are treated like heroes."

"Well, this Senator feels that's a rather cynical view," Senator Crou d'Etat objected.

"May I remind you that I am the twenty-one-year-old Heir of a Billionaire. Cynicism is not a part of my makeup."

"I really don't think—"

"This much is evident, Senator."

Kanish took a moment to sip his water, and then returned to his most brilliant presentation.

"Which brings us to the Politicians. You see, the Billionaires and the Corporations also fund the campaigns of Politicians, such as yourselves. They donate a portion of their do-gooder money to you, and in exchange, you Politicians do their bidding, all the while staking claim to the do-gooder title yourselves."

I took a moment to turn and look at Paneer, who was three rows back. He was still scowling, but there was a little glint in his eye that said it all. Paneer was most certainly proud of his son. Of course, he flipped me the finger. Billionaires can be so testy sometimes.

"The Douchebag Song," Kanish continued, "is about the people and the Corporations who get in the way of progress under the pretense of doing good for society. Like the Billionaires who are touted as the job Creators as their employees are on food stamps. Or like the Politicians who insist they are sacrificing their valuable talents to become public servants, as if being a Senator isn't a well-paid job that can't be parleyed into a guaranteed payday as a lobbyist. Which leaves the people in this wonderful, beautiful country of yours to wonder: What it is that you do? Aside from threatening not to pay your bills, which downgrades the People's credit. Or threatening to drown the government, as if that wouldn't result in anarchy followed by takeover. Or repealing the law known as Obamacare dozens of times despite your predictions of death panels or job-killing proving untrue. Excuse me, but aside from inflicting damage upon your own country, what is it that you do?"

Don't ask me why, but for whatever reason, Kanish knocked two times on the table. He was passing the rhyme, but I was completely unprepared, and all I was thinking about at that moment was an article that compared the popularity of Congress with some rather undesirable health maladies. So I went with that.

"Chlamydia seems to have way more sway than the US Congress does today."

Chlamydia. Chlamydia.
It has way more sway.
Chlamydia has more sway
than the US Congress does today.

"That's enough!" Senator Crou d'Etat screamed. "I will have you know, we politicians sacrifice each and every day for the people of this country!"

"You see?" Kanish said. "You claim good as you interrupt me. Meanwhile, you are running a Super-PAC that is accepting millions of dollars, perhaps tens of millions of dollars, from Corporations that expect favors in return. Some of those Corporations may even be partially owned by foreign partners. Like my Corporation, for instance."

"And mine," Lakshmi said.

"And mine," Mukesh said.

"And mine," Kaisapaisa said.

"You'd best be careful where you're going with this," Crou d'Etat warned as he pointed his headless gavel threateningly toward each of the Billionheirs.

The crowd began to percolate at the threat issued by Senator Crou d'Etat. Senator Boobio on the far end was beginning to fidget, and Glamram nearly coughed up a fur ball, he was so upset. What the fuck just happened? Why were the three presidential contenders on the Committee so clearly unnerved?

Motherfucker.

"You gotta be kidding me," I whispered as I covered my mic. "You made donations to their Super-PACs!"

"Yes, yes. It seems tens of millions of dollars will buy you quite a bit of airtime in this city."

"Hey!" some Rando exclaimed from the back of the room. "I've got Internet again!"

The entire room instantly pulled out their phones to verify the claim, including all the Senators and the witnesses. My browser was still set to our

YouTube channel, of course, and while I did indeed have an Internet connection, the video itself was gone. It said so right on the screen: *This video no longer exists.*

Motherfucker! Google killed our Kittens.

"Well, look at that!" Crou d'Etat announced. "The Internet *is* back!"

The Senators were already on their phones, as were their Staff, and no one seemed to even be paying attention to the proceedings any longer.

"Senator?" I said.

"Senator?" I repeated.

"*Senator!*" I yelled.

"What? Oh, right."

The Senator leaned in to quietly powwow with the other Senators in his proximity. He looked to his left and made some gestures, then turned to his right to whisper to Senator Boobio.

"You wanted to say something?" Crou d'Etat muttered to Boobio. "Senator Boobio has the floor."

"Yes. I think we've heard all that we need. It's pretty clear to me these Billionheirs have made a mockery of the Musical System."

The congregation of Senators agreed enthusiastically with the assessment.

"Excellent, " Senator Crou d'Etat said. "Well, if there are no objections from any of the Senators, I would like to thank you all for your testimony. The Committee will now adjourn to a closed session so that we may make our recommendations to the full Senate. Have a nice Fourth of July, everyone. May god bless the Internet. And may god bless America."

The chamber exploded in commotion. Indians were screaming in Hindi. The Produsahs were yelling at the exiting Senators. Security were physically removing angry Indians from the room. Photographers shutterbugged. The Indian press bellowed questions, none of which would be answered.

Kaisapaisa, who still had a hot mic, put his hand on GQ's shoulder and made one last plea to the Senators as they made their exit.

"I should be able to marry this man that I love! Even if that means we both wear a glove!"

Poor Kaisa. The Chorus wasn't even paying attention anymore.

"Kaisa," I said, "same-sex marriage is legal across the country as of about a week ago. Don't you watch the news? You can marry whoever you want now. Justice Kennedy said so."

GQ began to weep, he was so overcome by emotion.

"What the fuck, dude?" GQ spluttered. "I didn't know you were the Bear type!"

"I am! I am!"

Well, that was surprising. Kaisa and GQ embraced and entered into full kiss as the pandemonium continued around us.

"You motherfucker!"

It was Paneer who was on the warpath, and who was most thankfully being held back by Rajadut, among others in the audience.

"You turned my son into a goddamned motherfucker Liberal. I will kill you!"

"Just like a Billionaire to confuse populism with liberalism!" I yelled back as Paneer was pulled from the building.

Once the rambunctious crowd had been systematically removed from the chamber, all that remained were us Produsahs and our Billionheirs. Now that the Internet was back, the country had already moved on to await the next self-inflicted disaster. Everything was back to normal.

The full Senate and House convened an emergency session that evening in an effort to pass the most important resolution of their political careers.

Resolved:

There shall be no Billionaires or Billionaires' Heirs corrupting the Musical System.

In the interest of moving forward, we hereby absolve the culprits in this matter.

The president signed it into law just past midnight. It was July 4th.

To remove the Billionaires from the Musical System was the most patriotic act Congress could have done. If only they'd done it for themselves.

It was evening. We were safely home after an immensely long day and hours of travel, and the three of us were well prepared to partake in some celebratory Medicine.

"I just spoke to Jon Squirrly," Aardy said as he handed each of us a Stella.

"What'd he have to say?" I asked.

"The Resolution is as we thought. We really are off the hook, gentlemen."

"I suppose the Senators didn't want people to realize there were foreign interests funding their campaigns."

"Certainly not. Then they'd have to give the money back," I replied.

"Cheers," we all chimed together.

The three of us clinked our glasses for what would surely be the last time—at least on this adventure.

"Such fantastic news!" Kanish said. "I'm going to miss my lessons vehdy, vehdy much. Please! Deliver to me my final lesson, my Guru."

"Of course, Kanish," I said.

To err is human. To be forgiven? Billionheir.

To err
To err
To be human is to err
It's human as human can be
But to be forgiven,
Why that's a luxury!
We give to the Billionaires
And we give to the Billionheirs
And we give to the Billion-hairs

Amen

Mixerman

CHAPTER TWENTY-SIX

THE WRAP

"What now, Kanish?"

"I suppose it's time for me to go to Wharton."

"The Wharton School can't teach you how to build and lose a billion-dollar business in a matter of weeks," I said.

"Yes. Only you can teach me that," Kanish replied.

That got more than a chuckle from Aardy, who was sorting through his things in preparation for his next adventure. He had once again joined the ranks of the unemployed, and it was time for him to be moving on. Asia was on his mind, a place that he visits with some regularity. Malaysia, Vietnam, Thailand, Laos. The warmer parts of Asia, that is. It was a little late in the year to even consider an Eight-Thousander climb.

"So what's next for you, Zerman?" Aardy asked.

"I'm not sure. But I've been thinking about moving to Asheville, North Carolina."

"Yes. I know that you like that place."

"I do. And now that my son is grown up, I'm feeling like it might be time to do some traveling."

"You should come to Asia for a spell, Zerman. There's a ton of opportunity there," Aardy advised.

"That's what Ambassador Caroline Kennedy said in an interview," I replied.

"Who do you think told her?" Aardy joked. "Anyway, whether you go to Asheville or Asia, I'm sure you'll get a ton of new stories."

"Nothing wrong with new stories," I replied.

Sevaka and Annapurna were packing up the Bentley for their return to India. Kanish made arrangements to have the Stingray towed back to the Exotic Car Rentals lot. Between the rental fees and the destruction of the interior, the bill came to just over $50K. He could have bought it for that. I suppose, in a way, he did.

Kanish, Aardy, and I sat around the table in the driveway for what would be our last C@taclysmic meeting. Kanish had donated the entire ten million to the three presidential Super-PACs. Not that it mattered. That money would have been confiscated anyway. I know this, because the whole deal, including the resolution that exonerated us, was all negotiated by Rajadut and Paneer. Really, the only reason we got off the hook in this whole affair is because Paneer, along with the parents of the other Billionheirs, donated the maximum to the campaign funds of every Representative and every Senator in Congress. This included Super-PACs, too.

Even if we'd somehow been able to keep the good-faith $10 million, it would have been sucked up by lawyers, as Google would have surely sued us out of existence. Paneer prevented that from happening as well. Don't ask me how. Billionaires work in mysterious ways.

All in all, Kanish puts the total bill in political donations at around $90 million, the irony of which wasn't lost on me. That was essentially the size of our deal with Willy Show. And if that number shocks you, worry not. By my calculations, Paneer has made that money several times over in interest since the day he first contacted me.

Aardy and I sold our shares of C@taclysmic Group Inc. to Kanish for $1. That was far more than the business was worth at this point, given the tax liability. Paneer would cover that as well. All in all, in terms of cold hard cash, it had to be the most expensive mentorship in the history of the position. Such is the risk of going big, I suppose. Of course, ultimately, it wasn't my risk.

Kaisapaisa and GQ Skyped us to announce their pending marriage. Apparently, Kaisapaisa's father wasn't all that surprised to learn that his son was gay, and in the ultimate gesture of acceptance, offered him a $250 million dowry upon marrying GQ. Of course, there was no reason to stay in music with that kind of money. Last I heard, they were in Northern California looking to purchase a vineyard. The Bear and his Queen would be wine Producers.

The Rev was now so famous from his Sunset Boulevard billboards that he was offered a role in a movie. He would play a record Executive, no doubt. Whether the Rev can act or not, I don't know, but at least there's still money in movies. For the now, anyway.

Mukesh and Lakshmi put in a bid to purchase the AES Power Plant so that they could develop the property into an open-air amphitheater, an idea they got from Kanish, who got it from Aardy. The likelihood of success in that venture was low. Surely they could buy off the Politicians. But no one has figured out how to buy off the residents of Redondo Beach yet. As sucky as it is to keep that ugly-ass Power Plant there, it's better than what will happen to the city once it's gone. There's nothing quite as efficient as greed to fuck everything up.

It was the afternoon, and Kanish was packed up and ready to go. I sparked up what would be our last Fatty together.

"What about Music, Kanish?"

"What about it?"

"That's it? You're done with it?"

"You think that I should ignore my most valuable lesson?"

"And what's that? I chuckled.

"There is no money in Music anymore."

"Ain't that the truth," I said. "But you know, Kanish, that could change if the Douchebags in Congress start doing their jobs. Besides, I think you learned a far more valuable lesson than that," I said.

"This is fantastic! I'm going to get one last lesson before I leave. Tell me it, my Guru."

"If you can't beat 'em, join 'em."

"Ah, an oldie but a goody! That is a wonderful lesson! I will have to say it to myself repeatedly as I drive to Philadelphia with my aunt and uncle and see the rest of this beautiful country of yours."

"I think that's a good idea, Kanish. When do your aunt and uncle arrive?"

"They have been here the entire time."

"They have? Where?"

"Who do you think drives us and cooks for us?"

"Sevaka and Annapurna are your aunt and uncle?"

The moment I'd said it, Sevaka appeared under the arboretum carrying Kanish's suitcase, which he put down momentarily to offer a hug.

"I would vehdy much like to thank you," Sevaka said. "We were certain that if anyone could kill Kanish's ridiculous dream to get into Music, it would be you. As it turns out, we were right. Again, on behalf of the entire family, we thank you."

"It was the least that I could do," I replied.

"We all look vehdy forward to reading your book on this adventure. You will stay precise as to how it all happened I presume?"

Before I could answer, the Empress pulled up in a Mercedes, her radio blasting. Surely it was satellite radio, because the song was "Nights Interlude," by Nightmares on Wax. That particular track always brings back memories for me, as it features the same Quincy Jones "Summer in the City" organ sample as is featured in the Pharcyde's "Passin' Me By."

The Empress got out of her car and walked up the driveway to join us.

"You ready, Aardy?" the Empress asked.

"I am," Aardy replied. "The Empress and I are going to go climb Thunderbolt Mountain in the Sierra Mountains before I take my trip to Asia."

"What about the BMW?" I asked.

"The Sikhs have agreed to drive it to Ottawa for me. They'll be by to pick it up later today."

"No worries," I said. "You got everything?"

"I believe I do."

The Empress took the remainder of the Fatty from the ashtray and sparked it up.

"Don't forget your darts, Aardy," the Empress said with a wink.

"This reminds me!" Kanish exclaimed. "We must blow up your Beaver!"

"Hopefully, he'll be blowing up my Beaver by tonight!" the Empress announced unabashedly.

"Next summer," Aardy said. "This will give us some time to develop the app so that everyone can enjoy a good game of California Beaver."

"This is fantastic! I'll tell you what we shall do. You start a Kickstarter campaign to fund the app. And then next summer we shall take to the Internet to blow it all up!" Kanish said excitedly.

Uh-oh.

*   *   *

It was a Sunday; the summer had nearly drawn to a close. Donald Trump was on the television explaining to his audience how he routinely gained favor from politicians by donating to their campaigns. He, on the other hand, couldn't be bought. It was a compelling argument.

The Goddess was beside me, reading her iPad, which she suddenly dropped to her lap with a sigh and a smile.

"Testifying before Congress, huh? I must have missed that while I was sailing around the Antarctic."

"Eh. So I got a little carried away."

"You think?"

"You know, real life isn't all that interesting."

The Donald declared the American Dream dead. Then he held up a balance sheet for the cameras. It was a simple balance sheet. A statement. Perhaps a dubious statement, but a statement just the same. It said:

I'M WORTH

10,000,000,000

TEN BILLION DOLLARS!!!!!

"Do you think that Kanish is going to like the story?" the Goddess asked.

"He lived it."

"Seriously."

"I hope so."

"Is Paneer going to pay you the money he owes you for completing the book?"

"He'd better. I held up my end of the bargain. Or I will have in just a bit."

"Why just a bit?"

"Because I have a few more words to go."

"A few more words to go for what?"

One hundred thousand vehdy, vehdy entertaining words, that's what!

Pay up, Paneer, you fucking Douchebag!

Mixerman

The Complete Zen and the Art Of Series
Mixerman
Print and Multimedia E-Book Editions

Print Editions

Zen and the Art of Recording

Written with the musician or recordist in mind, Mixerman walks readers through the recording process, elaborating on various micing techniques and revealing many studio secrets. This guide also features instructional videos with full audio fidelity to provide both visual and audible demonstrations to the reader.

9781480387430...............................$24.99

Zen and the Art of Producing

Mixerman lays out the many organizational and creative roles of an effective producer as budget manager, time manager, personnel manager, product manager, arranger, visionary, and leader, and without ever foregoing the politics involved in the process.

9781458402882 ....$24.99

Zen and the Art of Mixing: REV 2

Mixerman turns his razor-sharp gaze to the art of mixing and gives followers and the uninitiated reason to hope – if not for logic and civility in the recording studio then at least for a good sounding record.

9781480366572 ....$24.99

Multimedia E-Book Editions
With over an hour of bonus video content in each

Zen and the Art of Recording, Multimedia Edition
(epub)
9781495004513

Zen and the Art of Recording, Multimedia Edition
(Kindle)
9781495004520

Zen and the Art of Producing: Multimedia Edition
(epub)
9781495004483

Zen and the Art of Producing: Multimedia Edition
(Kindle)
9781495004490

Zen and the Art of Mixing, Rev 2: Multimedia Edition (epub)
9781495004452

Zen and the Art of Mixing, Rev 2: Multimedia Edition
(Kindle)
9781495004469

Also Available:
The Daily Adventures of Mixerman
9780879309459 .... $24.99

HAL•LEONARD®
www.halleonardbooks.com